EDINBURGH
EDUCATION AND SOCIETY
SERIES

General Editor: Colin Bell

Out of Bounds: Women in Scottish Society 1800–1945

edited by
Esther Breitenbach
and
Eleanor Gordon

EDINBURGH UNIVERSITY PRESS

© Edinburgh University Press 1992

Edinburgh University Press
22 George Square, Edinburgh

Set in Linotron Palatino
by Koinonia Ltd, Bury, and
printed in Great Britain by
Hartnolls Ltd

A CIP record for this book is available
from the British Library

ISBN 0 7486 0372 7

CONTENTS

NOTES ON CONTRIBUTORS

Esther Breitenbach
Esther Breitenbach is the author of *Women Workers in Scotland* (Pressgang 1982), and has contributed articles on women in Scotland to *Feminist Review, Cencrastus, Radical Scotland* and the *Scottish Government Yearbook*. She is currently a Research Fellow in the Department of Social Policy and Social Work of Glasgow University.

Callum G. Brown
Callum G. Brown is a graduate of the universities of St Andrews and Glasgow, and is a lecturer in Urban History in the Department of History at the University of Strathclyde. He is author of numerous articles, and of *The Social History of Religion in Scotland since 1730*. (London, Methuen, 1987).

Catriona Burness
Catriona Burness is a tutorial assistant in the Department of Modern History in the University of Dundee, and is a tutor for the Workers' Educational Association. Since completing her Ph.D. on *Conservatism and Liberal Unionism in Glasgow*, she has held research posts at Glasgow and Edinburgh Universities. Her interest in women and Scottish politics was developed and encouraged over 1987–1991, while she worked as a research assistant for Maria Fyffe, MP for Glasgow Maryhill.

Russell P. Dobash
Russell P. Dobash is Senior Lecturer in the School of Social and Administrative Studies, University of Wales College of Cardiff. His research interests include violence against women, violent men, child sexual abuse, and imprisonment. He is the co-author of *The Imprisonment of Women* and the recently published *Women, Violence and Social Change*.

Eleanor Gordon
Eleanor Gordon is a graduate of the universities of Edinburgh and Glas-

gow. She has taught in higher education in Scotland for some years and is a lecturer in the Department of Economic and Social History at the University of Glasgow. She is the author of a number of articles on women and work, and of *Women and the Labour Movement in Scotland* (Oxford University Press, 1991). She is a member of the committee and Chair of the editorial collective of the Scottish Labour History Society.

Elspeth King
Elspeth King is a graduate of St Andrews University. She was for many years keeper of social history at the People's Palace, Glasgow, and is now Director of the Dunfermline Heritage Trust. She is author of *The Scottish Women's Suffrage Movement* (People's Palace Museum, Glasgow 1978) and *Scotland Sober and Free: the Temperance Movement 1829-1979* (People's Palace Museum, Glasgow 1979). She is also author of *The Thenew Factor* (forthcoming), a book on the hidden history of women in Glasgow.

Linda Mahood
Linda Mahood was born in western Canada and is a graduate of the universities of Saskatchewan and Glasgow. She has done research on the sociology of the family, and is author of a book on women and prostitution in Scotland, *The Magdalenes: Prostitution in the Nineteenth Century*, (Routledge and Kegan Paul, 1990).

Ann McGuckin
Ann McGuckin is a graduate of Edinburgh University, and has worked as a researcher at the Centre for Housing Research, at the University of Glasgow.

Pat McLaughlin
Pat McLaughlin teaches in the Department of Sociology and Social Policy at the University of Stirling. His research has focused on historical and contemporary responses to alcohol problems, fear of crime and the experiences of victims of crime.

Lindy Moore
Lindy Moore graduated in sociology at the University of Durham in 1969 and in 1986 obtained a postgraduate diploma in librarianship and information studies at RGIT in Aberdeen. She is at present school librarian at St David's High School, Saltney, Chester. She has written on the domestic and classical education given to Scottish girls, and on women's suffrage in Scotland.

James J. Smyth
James J. Smyth is a graduate of the University of Glasgow, and was awarded a Ph.D. by the University of Edinburgh in 1987. He is currently a

Research Fellow in the Centre for Business History at the University of Glasgow. He is currently working on a book on *Labour and Democracy*, which will be published by Edinburgh University Press.

Jayne D. Stephenson
Jayne D. Stephenson is a graduate of Lancashire Polytechnic in Preston, and is the Local History Officer for Stirling District Council and the Smith Museum, Stirling.

1

INTRODUCTION

ESTHER BREITENBACH AND ELEANOR GORDON

It is a commonplace to say that Victorian society created a definition of femininity that idealised woman's domestic role as wife and mother, and that this definition was emphasised to the virtual exclusion of all others, no matter how much women's experience actually differed from this. The ideological force of this definition was extremely powerful, and it often worked to control and restrain women from full participation in public life. It has also been forceful enough to gain a perhaps too ready acceptance by many historians writing about Scottish society in the nineteenth and early twentieth centuries. As a consequence women's experience and women's participation in social and public life, and their participation in movements for social change, have often been overlooked. Until very recently, as far as Scotland is concerned this has even been true of the Women's Suffrage Movement, a movement which endured for a period of sixty years, and involved thousands of women in activities which were often very public and highly visible, from public meetings to mass demonstrations, from waylaying prime ministers to arson attacks. The present volume shows that the experience of Scottish women reached well beyond the confines of the home, and that whilst the prevailing ideology of womanhood was undoubtedly a restricting influence, it was one that was subverted, challenged, fought over, and often contradicted by the reality of women's lives.

In the introduction to *The World is Ill Divided*, the companion volume to this one, we noted the paucity of publications on the history of women in Scotland. It is therefore heartening to record that recently a number of books in this field have been published,[1] several of them complementary to the work presented here. This welcome development serves to underline not only the breadth of women's experience and their contribution to Scottish society, but also the potential richness of this historical seam. The chapters published here shed light only on some aspects of the history of Scottish women, and the scope for further research remains very wide. As such work progresses it must inevitably lead to a reconsideration of current orthodoxies about Scottish social and political history, as these have been derived from a concentration on the experience of men. In recent years there has been a growth in output of Scottish social history, much of which is valuable, and much of which seeks to challenge received wisdom, and to refine our understanding of various aspects of Scottish society. Despite its value, much of this work has remained either oblivious to the role of women, or content to sum up this role in broad generalisations. For example, Christopher Harvie, writing of the drinking habits of Scottish men, 'If the result was a certain social inadequacy, then it would have been much worse but for the women. They created a home-life and a sort of community-politics, even if only through policing by gossip. They stayed away from drink and crime, saved, organised their families, read. They were a coiled spring.'[2] This generalisation succeeds in being both complimentary to and contemptuous of women at the same time, regarding them as having a moral power and a hidden strength, but also exercising power in the community through a social interaction derogatorily referred to as 'gossip'. Harvie relies on myth, stereotype and idealisation to describe women's role in society, rather than genuine historical investigation. As Dobash and McLaughlin's chapter illustrates, the complexities of women's lives and the variety of their experiences are testimony to the inadequacy of simplistic characterisation.

Whilst the neglect of women in Scottish history is at last beginning to be remedied (often by those outside the academic historical establishment in Scotland), a particularly neglected area is the private and family lives of women. This is acknowledged by T. C. Smout, one of the leading contemporary social historians of Scotland. He comments that 'The history of the family, and of child upbringing and the place of women within and without the home, is so neglected in Scotland as to verge on becoming a historiographical disgrace.'[3] Nonetheless Professor Smout makes this comment in a footnote rather than in the body of the text, and as Elspeth King points out in her contribution, he himself makes few references to women, discussing the suffrage question in the context of a discussion on horse and dog racing. The present volume does give some indication of the existence of the problems of domestic violence, and of child abuse, and illustrates some of the devastating effects of poverty on family life, although this is an area which is still seriously under-researched.

Scottish society has often been characterised as 'exceptionally male dominated'. Whilst we would not dissent from this characterisation, it is not unproblematic, in that it seems to give rise too easily to the assumption that women were silenced, suppressed and passive. But the lack of visibility of women in Scottish history up till now is not a result of their absence from political, social or public life. It is a result of the blindness of historians to the significance of women's experience, not to say on occasion to the fact of women's existence. Even historians who are apparently sympathetic to the problem of women's lack of visibility betray the

assumption that women's natural status was one of anonymity. R. J.
Morris, in the introduction to *People in Society in Scotland 1830–1914*
writes, 'Women like Flora Stevenson emerged from anonymity because
they were determined to exploit to the full the limited niche which
Scottish society allotted to them.'[4] The assumption of male dominance
leads here to an assumption of female anonymity. But the women regarded as anonymous were not so in their own time. Many women spent
years in active struggle to break down limits imposed on their lives,
participated in important areas of public life, and were well known to
their contemporaries.

If women in Scotland have on the whole been poorly served by social
historians through neglect of women's position, this has not been remedied by some male historians who have claimed to take up their cause.
For example, Leah Leneman has rightly criticised J. D. Young for his ill-
informed remarks on the Victorian women's movement in Scotland[5] and
Elspeth King cites evidence about the concern of the Scottish women's
suffrage movement over domestic violence which flatly contradicts his
statements.[6] It is to be hoped that the neglect and ill treatment of women
by historians is a thing of the past. Now that women's history in Scotland
has begun to develop, it can be expected that both neglect and errors will
be remedied, and that debate will be informed by thorough research and
a feminist perspective.

This second volume on the history of women in Scotland brings
together material that throws light on significant areas of social, public
and institutional life in Scotland, covering a period from the mid-nineteenth to the mid-twentieth century.[7] It contains contributions that cover
a range of aspects of Scottish society, from religion to education to women's political activity within the suffrage movement and political parties. This is necessarily complex and varied, and no single theme runs
clearly through all the contributions. Nonetheless there are major themes
that emerge from several contributions, and these often overlap with one
another. Most significantly, if the previous volume showed that in the
world of work the sexual division of labour was no respecter of class, the
present volume shows that class was a significant factor in differentiating
the experience of women in other aspects of their lives, and that middle-
class notions of femininity were often espoused even by those women in
the forefront of the struggle to widen the scope of women's social role.
Furthermore these notions of femininity contributed to the development
of social institutions which controlled and restricted the lives of working-
class women, and middle-class women played an active part in this process.

The chapters examining women's and girls' experiences within education, industrial and residential schools, and in prisons and reformatories,
demonstrate that these institutions were the site of struggle around the
definition of gender roles, which were class differentiated, and that in this
process of struggle middle-class women were frequently engaged in

promulgating a feminine role for working-class women that was both restricting and patronising, while at the same time they were challenging restrictive definitions imposed upon them through entering employment and public life. This process is most obvious in the field of education and in industrial and residential schools. Middle- and upper-class women took an active part in the debate surrounding the development of these institutions, and many found paid employment within them. Within education there was a protracted campaign to introduce sewing lessons and domestic economy for working-class girls, in order to fit them for their roles as domestic servants, and wives and mothers. As Lindy Moore shows, the success of this campaign coincided with the introduction of school boards in Scotland, and as a consequence of this many more female teachers were recruited to the profession. Thus womens' entry to the profession was gained through a greater differentiation of the curriculum for boys and girls, and the creation of an education for working-class girls that was deemed appropriate to their gender and their station.

A similar pattern can be observed in the development of industrial and residential schools, precursors of the modern systems of institutional care for girls thought to be in moral danger. Middle-class women were active in philanthropic and voluntary activities which contributed to the development of these institutions, and many also worked in them as supervisors. The emphasis in the regimes of these institutions was on labour of a domestic type, such as sewing and laundering. Nonetheless, as Linda Mahood makes clear, despite an ideology of reform and rehabilitation, the regimes of industrial and residential schools were fundamentally penal, and served to exercise control over working-class girls' morals and sexuality.

Control and coercion were to be seen in their most extreme form within the prison system, though the forms that this took were subject to change over time. Russell Dobash and Pat McLaughlin trace the evolution of the Scottish prison system's treatment of women prisoners from benevolent paternalism to a more distanced controlling and punitive system, as the nature of class relationships changed with the development of industrial society in the nineteenth century. Scotland notably had a far higher proportion of women in its prison population than England and Wales, a fact that is ascribed primarily to poverty, which led women to prostitution and petty theft. The introduction of professional women staff into Scottish prisons in the mid-nineteenth century was seen as important in the development of the capacity of the prison regime to effect a moral transformation in women prisoners, through moral influence and the provision of morally and socially superior role models. As the century drew to a close the rise of the eugenics movement and a belief in the hereditary character of moral degeneracy led to an ideology of therapeutic treatment and to the development of inebriate reformatories. But, like industrial and residential schools, despite discourses of care and therapy, these institutions remained punitive in their treatments, and only served to widen the scope of mechanisms of social control over certain sections of the female population.

Despite the social and political changes affecting women in the early decades of the twentieth century, middle-class ideals of housewifery and domestic economy were still being used to police working-class women in the 1930s, as Ann McGuckin relates of Blackhill. This control was exercised through a network of services and agencies of the local state – factors, housing visitors, nurses and doctors.

From the evidence cited in the chapters in this collection the idea of woman as domestic, nurturing and morally superior retained enormous power throughout the nineteenth century, and its influence has continued well into the twentieth, even when it contradicted the reality of women's lives. It continued to have great force as the nineteenth century progressed and more and more middle-class women were engaged in public life and paid employment. Indeed, it was often this view that informed their endeavours on behalf of working-class women and girls. Though there was clearly a general tendency for middle-class women to be active agents in the social control of working-class women and girls, it was not universally the case that this role was accepted uncritically, and there were countervailing influences at work. Linda Mahood recounts the criticism that some women supervisors had of the effects on girls of the industrial and residential school regimes, and indicates that many were aware, notwithstanding the emphasis on the virtues of family life, that the family was not always a safe place for girls. Thus some women saw the institutions as having a function of child protection, though they were reluctant to acknowledge publicly the extent, or even the existence, of incest and abuse. Similarly in the case of education, though the lobby for domestic education finally gained the upper hand, there was resistance to the imposition of sewing lessons from girls, their mothers and from women teachers. It is perhaps surprising to modern feminists that the feminists of the 1870s supported sewing lessons and domestic economy for girls. They further argued that these subjects should also be taught to boys. This demonstrated an important strand of early feminist thought: that women's work should be equally valued and recognised.

As might be expected, within the sphere of religious activity the ideal of woman as moral guardian of the family reigned supreme. At times the influence of middle-class women can be detected in the leadership of the religious organisations described by the testimonies of women from the Stirling area, but on the whole the activities in which they took part appear to have been working class in character. This does not seem to have lessened the power of the ideology of the feminine however, and women were explicitly appealed to as moral guardians, especially by temperance organisations, which exhorted them to exert their moral influence on their drinking and gambling menfolk.

Temperance organisations frequently portrayed domestic violence as a problem caused by drinking. This, not surprisingly, often evoked a heartfelt response, but, despite denunications of men's violent behaviour, women were not encouraged to challenge their subordination to men. Callum Brown and Jayne Stephenson suggest that for Stirling women at least religious activities played a positive role in that they were a major source of leisure and social activity, since many women had little access to other forms of activity outside the home. Whilst this is clearly true for the working-class women who gave their testimonies, there were considerable variations in the pattern of social and recreational life throughout Scotland, according to locality and class. For example, there is evidence that in Scotland in the early twentieth century the socialist movement provided a network of social and cultural organisations which played an important role in attracting substantial numbers of working-class women to the struggle for a wide range of social and political reforms as well as meeting social and recreational needs.[8]

For middle-class women a major focus of activity was the struggle for the vote. As a number of commentators have noted, accounts of the women's suffrage movement have been dominated by the Pankhursts and what was happening in London and little has been written of events in other parts of England.[9] The Scottish movement was extensive, and while its organisations were affiliated to British organisations, its networks had an indigenous strength and a considerable degree of autonomy. The women's suffrage movement has often been characterised dismissively as a middle-class movement, but it had both working-class precedents and working-class adherents. Another misplaced criticism of the women's suffrage movement was that it was only concerned with the issue of the vote. The issue of the enfranchisement of women was in itself of the utmost political importance, but Scottish suffragettes held a wider view of sexual politics, and they debated and campaigned around issues such as the conditions under which women worked in factories, the evils of sweated labour, and domestic violence.

Following the winning of the vote there was widespread debate about the best ways to organise and recruit women party members, and how to win women's votes. While it was not easy for women to be adopted as candidates and even less easy for them to win seats, both Unionists and the Labour Party showed great concern over how women would vote. But this concern betrayed fundamentally patronising and paternalistic assumptions about women – since it is clear from the evidence that Catriona Burness advances in her chapter that both parties felt women would be easily duped by their rivals, and that they were not capable of rational thought on political issues. At the same period changes in party organisation took place, though in conflicting directions – in some cases women's sections and organisations were abolished, and in others they were created. None of the changes in party organisation had a noticeable effect in promoting women candidates, and only eight women were returned as MPs from Scotland between 1918 and 1945. Though this number is very small, Scotland's record in sending women to Parliament was similar to other European countries in which women were enfranchised at approximately the same time. It is an irony of history that the first Scottish woman MP, the Duchess of Atholl, was an anti-suffragist, just as it is an irony that the first British woman Prime Minister had no time for equal opportunities. Most of Scotland's women MPs in this period were married, though all but one were childless. Jean Mann – the exception proving the rule – was, however, a mother of five and was given active support with childcare, in order that she could follow a political career. This demonstrates that the right to vote, whilst a prerequisite for women's entry into parliamentary politics, is not in itself a sufficient condition for equal participation.

It is a truism that it is easier to uncover evidence about the powerful than the powerless, and by extension, the middle class rather than the working class. To some extent the chapters substantiate this. In the description of the development of institutions – penal, educational, reformatory – working-class women are seen as acted upon rather than as self-conscious agents. In formal politics again it is the women of the middle-class who appear to be more actively involved. However because middle-class women had a higher profile this does not mean that working-class women were absent from the political arena. James Smyth's chapter argues that the lineage of working-class women's political activity stretched back further than the housing struggles of the First World War, and that it was broad in scope, encompassing the vote, peace campaigns, and the cooperative movement.

Women's capacity to organise was not restricted to the formal political sphere. The testimonies of the women from Blackhill show how women fought against the odds to retain their dignity. Of particular importance to them was their solidarity in resisting the control mechanisms of the local state. This resistance took the form not only of mutual assistance, emotional at times of distress such as bereavement, and financial, through the organisation of menages, or savings clubs, but it also took the form of rejection of state services, such as medical inspections. Too often such services and the manner of their delivery tended to stigmatise and to humiliate, and through rejecting this outside help, the women of Blackhill maintained their self-respect.

The ideology of domesticity and the family was a powerful force controlling the lives of women throughout the nineteenth century though its force has diminished in the twentieth century. Middle-class women, who themselves challenged this view in practice by extending their roles outside the home through gaining access to employment and public life, often continued to subscribe to the view as appropriate for working-class women. Social institutions such as education, religion, institutions of care and reform, and the penal system, powerfully enforced this view and engaged middle-class women as active agents in this process. This was despite the paradox that the habits and morality of domesticity and family life were often being promoted to those to whose lives it had least relevance.

The view of women as confined to the domestic sphere was not only inappropriate to the reality of working-class women's lives, but as the nineteenth century progressed it became less and less appropriate to the reality of middle-class women's lives. Women's access to public life, through employment, philanthropy, public service, religious organisations, and political activity was extensive, and many women fought to extend this further throughout their lives. Women who fought for entry into higher education also sat on school boards and campaigned on issues concerning girls' education; women medical graduates were prominent in the women's suffrage campaign; leading suffragettes stood as candidates for Parliament. The overlaps and interconnections are many and fascinating, and show that a broad perspective on women's position in society was common, and that the need to tackle many issues simultaneously was well understood.

Two major themes emerge from the chapters collected here – that of the conflict of interest between middle- and working-class women, and that of the extensive involvement of women in public life. The institutional life of Scotland has acted as a force to control and confine women within the domestic sphere, and to punish women if they strayed too far from this. However, the need for the elaboration of these systems of social control, and the constant effort that was put into promulgating the ideal view of womanhood, suggest that it was a view that never gained the widespread acceptance amongst women that has often been assumed.

Women have struggled against this confinement, and if they did not reject the ideology of the feminine outright, they nevertheless subverted it in action, to the extent of creating what can justifiably be called a women's movement in the latter decades of the nineteenth century, a movement whose support and influence was considerable, and which was certainly visible to contemporaries. Middle-class women were implicated in the social control of working-class women by the very processes through which they extended their role in social and public life, though some were able to transcend barriers of class, and work politically alongside working-class women. While there still remains a great deal to be discovered about the history of women's lives in Scotland, the evidence brought together in this volume is sufficient to show that women's involvement in activities outside the home was widespread and varied, taking many different forms – political, religious, philanthropic, educational and social; and that women played an active part in the shaping of Scottish society, and in the transformation of their own role within that society.

NOTES

1 For example, Leah Leneman, *A Guid Cause*, (Aberdeen University Press, 1991); Linda Mahood, *The Magdalenes: Prostitution in the Nineteenth Century*, (Routledge, 1990); Eleanor Gordon, *Women and the Labour Movement in Scotland 1850–1914*, (Clarendon Press, Oxford, 1991); Judith Fewell and Fiona M. S. Paterson, *Girls in Their Prime: Scottish Education Revisited*, (Scottish Academic Press, Edinburgh, 1990).

2 Christopher Harvie, *No Gods and Precious Few Heroes*, (Edward Arnold, 1981, reprinted 1987) p. 118.

3 T. C. Smout, *A Century of the Scottish People*, (Collins, London, 1986) p. 292.

4 R. J. Morris and W. Hamish Fraser, (eds) *People and Society in Scotland 1830–1914. Vol. II* (John Donald, Edinburgh, 1990) p. 2.

5 Leah Leneman, *A Guid Cause*, (Aberdeen University Press, 1991) p. 11.

6 Chapter by Elspeth King in this volume. James D. Young. *Women and Popular Struggles*, (Mainstream, Edinburgh, 1985) p. 107.

7 The first volume is Eleanor Gordon and Esther Breitenbach, (eds) *The World is Ill Divided – Women's Work in Scotland in the Nineteenth and Early Twentieth Centuries*, (Edinburgh University Press, 1990).

8 See Eleanor Gordon, *Women in the Labour Movement in Scotland 1850–1914*, (Clarendon Press, Oxford, 1991).

9 Chapter by Elspeth King in this volume; Leah Leneman, *A Guid Cause*, (Aberdeen University Press, 1991); Jill Liddington and Jill Norris, *One Hand Tied Behind Us*, (Virago, London, 1978).

2

EDUCATING FOR THE 'WOMAN'S SPHERE': DOMESTIC TRAINING VERSUS INTELLECTUAL DISCIPLINE

LINDY MOORE

THE UTILITY OF AN ACADEMIC EDUCATION FOR WOMEN

In eighteenth-century Presbyterian Scotland an academic schooling which might encourage women to think independently was generally considered irrelevant to or even irreconcilable with women's subordinate role. Elizabeth Mure commented that:

> the women's knowledge was gained only by conversing with the men, not by reading themselves . . . The men thought justly on this point, that what knowledge the women had out of their own sphere should be given by themselves and not picked up at their own hand in ill-chosen books of amusement.[1]

Nevertheless, at an academic level a gradual change in attitudes became discernible under the influence of Enlightenment perspectives.[2] As a strategy for the maintenance of communal cohesion within a society eighteenth-century Scottish literati saw as becoming increasingly individualistic, fragmented and unethical, they propagated a 'new view of women as the catalysts and managers of sensibility within the protected haven of the domestic and private sphere'.[3] While conservatives believed the discipline of book-learning would endanger women's natural and valuable sensibility[4] and make them discontented with domestic duties, liberals suggested that women should be educated in a manner which would make them rational as well as sensitive and virtuous companions for men.[5]

Though the nineteenth century produced a growing number of individuals who argued for women's absolute right to education, views on what constituted woman's sphere and what education this necessitated, continued to be more influential. Early nineteenth-century Scottish writers on education were influenced by Enlightenment theories about the development of the individual. If the earliest intellectual, moral and physical experiences of a child had as powerful and lasting effects as was claimed, then it was the mother who wielded the greatest influence on a child's future character. The issue of 'education for motherhood' was taken up by liberal Scots who looked to an intellectual education which would provide women with both the knowledge and the logic necessary to make rational and therefore moral decisions and train their children to do likewise.[6]

Educationalists also became concerned about mothers' factual knowledge. Surveys revealed the high level of infant mortality and more importantly, its variation by social class, which indicated that it was largely the result of social rather than inherent physiological causes and was therefore preventable, while scientific discoveries were permitting a greater and more widespread understanding about the causes of disease and ill health:[7]

> The Creator has taught the inferior creatures to rear their young successfully by instinct, but he has not conferred this guide on the human mother. One of two conclusions, therefore, appears to follow. He has intended either that she should use her faculties of observation and reflection, in acquiring all the knowledge requisite for the proper treatment of offspring, or that she should recklessly allow a large proportion of them to perish.[8]

Evangelical Elizabeth Hamilton, who was sufficiently concerned to write *The Cottagers of Glenburnie* in 1808, parodying the lack of working-class housewifery in the Scottish Highlands, believed that gender-related preconceptions internalised by girls before school age were responsible for working-class women's inability to retain and therefore teach their own children what they themselves learnt at school. She viewed needlework as a form of laziness since it could be performed mechanically; the solution lay in an intellectual education which incorporated a thoughtful religion:[9]

> In proportion as the female mind has been emancipated from the fetters of ignorance, the female character has risen in respectability. Whenever religious principle has been made the basis, it has been seen that a liberal system of education, instead of producing a dislike to, or dereliction of peculiar and appropriate duties, has enabled women, without infringing on any duty, to enlarge their sphere of usefulness, and to extend, beyond the narrow precincts of the domestic roof, the beneficial influence of maternal solicitude and maternal tenderness.[10]

In the utopian 1830s, when education was seen as the panacea for all social ills, several of the Scottish educational reformers emphasised the value of an intellectual education for future working-class wives and mothers.[11] George Combe's views were widely publicised in lectures, journals and publications and put into practice at the William's Secular School in Edinburgh, where subjects such as physiology were taught to both sexes.[12] James Simpson proposed a national system of education for children from 5 to 14, including subjects such as civil history, physiology and civil rights, for both working-class and middle-class children, boys and girls; while David Stow believed a syllabus which included geography, civil and biblical history, geometry, drawing and natural history for boys and girls aged 11 to 15, would produce 'good fathers, good mothers, and respectable citizens, – in one word, real Christians'.[13]

More compatible with the Presbyterian temperament and beliefs than the 'intellectual system' of teaching (which involved pupils actually understanding what they were taught) was the idea that exposure to the process of an academic education was as important as the content learnt. Intellectual study developed a mental discipline which could be used to control 'the passions' and regulate behaviour.[14] As the human faculties existed for the service of God it was also positively virtuous for the individual to develop them as fully as possible, and since learning required hard work and discipline, educational success proved the individual's moral worth. In the pre-Disruption years both moderates and evangelicals in the church supported the English Bible and catechism as the basis of elementary education but 'it was universally acknowledged that "secular" subjects like history, literature, and elementary science benefited religious education wherever they could be taught.'[15] To insist that no good could come from secular knowledge was to confuse religious instruction with dogma: 'We have long believed that intelligence and religion are near of kin' said the Reverend John Robertson in 1860.[16]

More extreme evangelicals considered literacy and elementary education merely the tools for knowledge, which could be for good or ill depending on the content. They argued for a specifically religious education incorporating moral and occupationally orientated instruction which would teach the working class their place in the divine order. But men such as James Begg and William Hetherington believed that education should consist of both teaching and training; while the latter might be aimed at girls' presumed domestic future, the former involved the capacities of an immortal being and, although there was no necessary connection between intellect and morality, education, *per se*, 'was a blessing'.[17]

Thus while English ladies were supported by churchmen, the nobility, and many of the school inspectors, when they criticised too much academic education for working-class girls because it gave them ideas above their station, and recommended training in domestic economy as an antidote to intellectual vanity, similar views expressed by their Scottish counterparts gained much less support.[18] The idea that girls were being educated for the 'woman's sphere' was no less prevalent in Scotland but academic instruction was deemed a necessary part of the process. Even institutions such as the Glasgow Magdalene Institution, or the Haddo House Club formed by Lady Aberdeen for north-east servant girls in 1881, used intellectual education as a means of moral training.[19]

SOCIALISATION THROUGH DOMESTIC TRAINING

Nineteenth-century social problems created by industrialisation, trade depression and crop failure combined with political unrest and Chartist agitation did cause many of the upper and middle classes to look for alternative educational approaches, however. Throughout the 1840s and early 1850s the problem of social order was discussed by the Scottish press and the General Assemblies of the Church of Scotland and the Free Church. The home mission approach adopted reflected the churches' tendency to see self-improvement and personal responsibility, rather than state intervention, as the solution. Belief in the importance of the family as the basic socialising unit led to the concept of social control of the working class through the domestic training of future working-class wives and mothers. Female 'schools of industry'[20] would provide training in domestic skills (needlework and where possible cookery, laundry work and cleaning) and religious instruction under a trained and selected female teacher. The proposed curriculum was similar to that of the numerous dame schools which had sprung up as the educational control of the presbyteries slipped in the eighteenth century, but the schools of industry would be under upper-class rather than working-class control. The rules for the Female Subscription School at Athelstaneford, drawn up by two men in the 1850s, neatly summarised the juxtaposition of moral, religious and domestic objectives. Needlework, sewing, knitting and shaping of garments should be taught:

> It would also be desirable if the teacher could give occasional addresses or instructions in the general management of a household and in such branches of female domestic duties as are suited to the rank in life of the children and can be practically taught in the school. . . . Particular attention is to be paid to the Religion, and the moral training of the children. Also to their general behaviour and deportment – the teacher enforcing cleanliness and urging upon them the necessity of becoming acquainted with, and paying the greatest attention to their house duties – also of always conducting themselves with courtesy, civility and propriety.[21]

Girls often had religious works read to them, or sang hymns and psalms whilst sewing – 'to beguile the tedium and monotony of their manual employments' as one minister expressed it, without conscious irony.[22] Domestic training was thus seen as providing both practical training and a moral element. It would improve working-class living standards and also inculcate middle-class virtues such as cleanliness, tidiness, thrift, industry, perseverance and steadiness of character.[23] Enforced by religious teaching it would spell out for working-class women that their role was domestic; housewifery and providing for husbands and children were their responsibility. As wives, the provision of tidy, welcoming houses and well-cooked meals would encourage their menfolk to stay at home away from the temptations of the public house and the brothel.[24] As mothers their job was to cater for their children's health, their religious, moral and intellectual education and provide a role model for them (especially daughters), to follow. And more pragmatically, if women did have to do paid work, they would be ready-trained as seamstresses and domestic servants.[25]

Ladies' committees were considered essential for the success of girls' schools or female industrial schools:

> The nobility and gentry have been great public benefactors in the cause of female education. The money expended is only part of the benefit. It is most gratifying to see the increasing number of ladies of rank and wealth who take quite a personal interest in the education of the daughters of the poor. This *personal* interest on the part of the upper classes . . . is life and soul to a girls' school.[26]

As Schools Inspector Middleton's remark indicates, the committees were required not so much for technical reasons as to provide models of middle-class femininity and to ensure that the requisite morals and habits were being inculcated by the girls. Such committees were necessary if the schools were to survive, or at least to survive in the approved form, since in many areas they needed support in the form of funding, provision of materials and selling outlets, and everywhere the schools were inclined to lapse into ordinary day elementary schools, which were probably both more interesting and more lucrative for the female teachers, if they were not prodded in the right direction. The influence of the committees or the proprietors' wives was also necessary to encourage girls' attendance through personal persuasion, rewards (usually in the form of prizes) and even compulsion. As the difficulty in raising funds was to indicate however, not all 'ladies' were as concerned about the subject as could be wished and the lack of supporting committees, even for sewing classes, was a frequent complaint.[27] Ladies' committees continued to be encouraged by the school boards established throughout Scotland following the 1872 Education (Scotland) Act, though some women considered the presence of women on the boards themselves was even more beneficial:[28]

> As regards School Boards, surely it is a definite loss to the children attending them to be deprived of the influence of cultured ladies who would take an interest in their manners and morals in a way no man can do. These lady members, again, could charge themselves with the appointment of recognised lady managers, who would regularly visit the girls' schools, become the friends and trusted advisers of the women teachers and of the children, and take special supervision of the teaching of such subjects as sewing and domestic economy.

THE DEBATE

The attempt to impose middle-class morality on working-class people through the practical training of women in femininity was not new in

Scotland. In the eighteenth century the upper classes had introduced spinning schools for working-class women, to train them in a domestic economic industry which would prevent them doing unsuitable outdoor work and to keep them busy; at that period a high premium was placed on being actively occupied at all times.[29] In the early nineteenth century there were many examples of schools largely or wholly concentrating on domestic subjects supported by upper and middle-class women. Ministers writing in the *New Statistical Account* noted the moral benefits of such institutions.[30] Moreover, those with a strict Calvinist outlook uninfluenced by Enlightenment ideas had always considered an intellectual education incompatible with any woman's domestic duties.[31] In the mid-nineteenth century there was, however, concern about disrupting the existing educational system. There were also doubts about the suitability of teaching practical work in schools. And given the widespread belief amongst the educated middle class that an intellectual education performed a cultural, moral and religious function, the idea of concentrating on practical training in domestic subjects was not accepted by everyone as being the best method of educating girls for domesticity. It was no coincidence that when the Aberdeen and Banffshire Mutual Instruction Union offered a prize for the best essay on 'female education in relation to the wants of the age, with special reference to the rural districts' in 1851, the winner, emphasising women's maternal influence, strongly advocated an intellectual education which would enable women to set a moral and rational example, care for their children's health and encourage their intellectual development.[32] Although there was an increasing emphasis on moral discipline rather than intellectual freedom, academic teaching was still regarded as the main purpose of the school, even by advocates of domestic training. Ideally, parents should provide moral training and the church religious instruction; any non-academic support provided by the school was seen as a purely temporary measure.[33]

The conflict between demands for a better intellectual education for girls and demands for more specifically domestic training for them resulted in ambiguities and inconsistencies on the part of both individuals and institutions. Simon Laurie, secretary of the Church of Scotland Education Committee and later Professor of Education at Edinburgh University, believed, for example, that education should consist of a balance between instruction and mental discipline, but above all he believed education should be ethical. Although he considered that language was the only subject to incorporate both intellectual discipline and knowledge and that the vernacular language was the key to all other education, he was prepared to sacrifice even this to ensure the ethical training he considered specially necessary for girls: 'the deficiencies of "mistress's grammar" are far more than counterbalanced by the prominence given to industrial skill, – itself both a womanly accomplishment, and exercising a feminine influence.'[34] At a later date arithmetic was often mentioned as the subject most suitably sacrificed to domestic subjects.[35] The impact of the intellectual yet patriarchal tradition of Scottish education on academic opportunities for girls has been examined elsewhere.[36] The remainder of this chapter examines the campaign initiated by the Scottish upper classes and the English education authorities to make practical training in sewing and domestic economy an integral part of the education of elementary schoolgirls in Scotland and the reaction this provoked.

THE CAMPAIGN FOR THE INTRODUCTION OF SEWING

In 1824 the General Assembly of the Church of Scotland established a committee to examine religious and educational provision in Scotland. Four years later the committee referred to the importance of educating girls:

> in those peculiar branches of education which are proper to their sex, and suited to the stations in life for which they are destined, and of the means of acquiring which, in the Highlands and Islands, there is a grievous deficiency, – it may be almost said, an entire want.[37]

The committee had been influenced by the action of several eminent Church of Scotland women who had formed an association to promote female industrial education in the schools, and had obtained the support of the Duchess of Clarence. The church's attempt to attach 'industrial schools' (part-time sewing teachers) to its existing schools was unsuccessful, but the purpose, the method, the tepid enthusiasm of the church and the more energetic support of upper-class Scottish ladies presaged attempts to come.

The first Scottish school inspectors, appointed in the 1840s, promoted sewing both as a practical means of raising the living standards of working-class homes (though the potential impact was much exaggerated) and for the inherent moral and cultural values it was seen as developing in the pupils themselves. The second point was especially promoted by Her Majesty's Inspector John Gordon, previously the first secretary of the Church of Scotland Education Committee. He observed approvingly that at one school the girls were taught to sew and shape clothes 'to habituate to thrift and reliance on their own industry quite as much as to give the lesson in handicraft'.[38] HMI John Gibson suggested there was a general need for industrial education taught by well-qualified women; as no such education was given in the parochial schools (women being legally prohibited from teaching in them), sewing was left to private enterprise and therefore often unavailable and even less often well taught.[39] Many of the establishments were nothing more than dame schools and although it was supposedly the practice for girls to 'go on' to sewing schools after 'completing' their elementary education, this was more often a counsel of perfection.

However, in the mid–1840s Gordon detected an increase in the number of schools of industry being established and supported by ladies, 'who are no strangers to the cottages of the poor, and who would endeavour by instruction of this sort to improve their domestic condition'. Gordon ascribed this to the fact that elementary education was becoming more practical and as girls did not need such a high literary standard as boys, there was time for them to study domestic economy.[40] The new attitude was reflected in an increasing number of personal endowments for female schools, and by the case of the Fife Philip bequest. Philip, who died in 1828, had left money for the academic education of the poor, without any reference to domestic training; but in 1846, by a Deed of Incorporation, a clause was included permitting the managers to use part of the funds to provide for the instruction of girls in sewing and knitting.[41]

The 1845 House of Lords Select Committee asked several witnesses leading questions about the value of either separate schools for girls or of sewing schools. The convenor of the education committee, William Muir, confirmed that the Church of Scotland wished to encourage 'female' schools, not as a substitute for the ordinary public school, but as an additional department for needlework and domestic economy.[42] Little was done however, until 1849 when Muir had the opportunity to inspect several sewing departments during a visit to the Highlands. Impressed both by the 'endless disorder and filth' in which the Highlanders lived and by the appearance and behaviour of the girls attending the sewing schools, he was converted to a belief in the importance of such schools as a means of inculcating 'order and cleanliness' in the home. That year the General Assembly made a special request for what it called 'a new class of schools' which were:

> calculated to impart to a most influential class of the rising generation habits of industry, order, and domestic economy, and to promote in a high degree not only domestic happiness, but social prosperity and religious principles among many thousands of future generations.[43]

A women's association was established to raise funds for the Church of Scotland's scheme, but grass-roots support was weak; the active campaigners were based in Edinburgh and Glasgow and despite their efforts fund raising proved difficult.[44] The educational census returns for 1851 illustrated the lack of importance attached to the subject by most Scots, despite the increasing interest amongst the upper classes; only 17 per cent of all Scottish schoolgirls were learning sewing compared with 39 per cent of English and Welsh girls and the difference was even greater when the elementary public schools alone were compared.[45]

In 1852 a more powerful and influential society, the Scottish Ladies' Association in Support of Female Industrial Schools (SLA), was formed. Its object was:

> so to educate the female children of the labouring classes as both to fit them for discharging aright the appropriate duties of their

station, and to animate them with a spirit which shall oblige them to these duties by the binding sanctions of religion.[46]

This was to be achieved by adding a suitable training in sewing, knitting, spinning, laundry work, kitchen work and household economy to girls' usual curriculum and:

> through the agency of properly educated and Christian teachers, to cultivate in the pupils the various qualities which constitute true character; and, above all, a deep sense of personal responsibility for the use which they make of every talent which God bestows upon them.

In order to ensure a source of 'properly educated and Christian teachers' an informal committee was formed to supervise female teachers attending the Church of Scotland Edinburgh training college. For several years about a dozen female students were recruited and given additional training in domestic economy. In 1853 the arrangement was formally taken over by the SLA and a boarding house was established, initially accommodating eighteen of the female Normal School students, at which they could learn cooking, laundry work and household management as well as sewing (which was also formally taught at the training college).[47]

In 1858 Louisa Hope, the leading figure in the SLA, organised a petition signed by 130 of 'the principal ladies of Scotland' to complain 'in the strongest possible language' about the deficient teaching of needlework.[48] The petition argued that female teachers were currently being trained 'too fine', with insufficient emphasis on domestic economy and needlework and that in schools taught by certificated teachers needlework was subordinated to 'mere head lessons'. Not surprisingly, since the sentiments echoed those of the English Privy Council, the petition presented by 'a deputation of noblemen and commoners' was courteously received 'and not quite uninfluential'. The same year government regulations were introduced requiring needlework and domestic economy for female Queen's Scholars training to be teachers.

In view of the new regulations and the success of the unofficial boarding house, the Church of Scotland decided to take over the house and extend it, with the assistance of a sub-committee of ladies. But supportive as the Church of Scotland had been of attempts to encourage domestic economy in the schools – both as a corporate body and via its individual members – it nevertheless felt it was being unduly pressured by the Privy Council. A major difference of opinion on the relative value of intellectual and domestic training became evident when Lingen, secretary of the Committee of Council on Education Board, implied that the marks for domestic economy alone would be sufficient to judge the standard of the female candidates for teacher training:

> The Committee – while of opinion that *practical* instruction in cooking and sewing is essential to every young woman, and is to female teachers especially most important, as enabling them more

efficiently, through book instruction or otherwise, to influence the
habits of the district in which they labour – have thought it necessary to urge the necessity of maintaining in due prominence the
literary education of female teachers. The fact is, that the
acquirements expected both in male and female teachers in
England are much below what have been always found necessary
in this country, where the labouring and middle classes of our rural
parishes are taught together. Their Lordships' term of 'schools for
the poor', however applicable in England, both as a description of
the elementary school, and as suggesting the principle on which
instruction given in them is to be regulated, and the status of the
teacher is to be fixed, has never been recognised among us . . .[49]

However it was the Privy Council which held the purse strings and could
have the last word. Regulations were introduced requiring the provision
of sewing lessons as a condition of the government grants to schools. The
General Assembly Committee insisted that it supported the aim of this
regulation, but that as it was impossible for more remote or poorer mixed
schools under masters to comply with the regulation, the teachers would
lose the existing augmentation of their salary and therefore move to
schools where facilities for sewing could be provided, leaving the most
needy regions both without sewing provision and in the hands of un-
trained teachers.[50] Lingen's response indicated the priority the English
authorities attached to sewing:

Their Lordships consider that a temporary reduction in Scotland of
the number of mixed schools able to claim augmentation for
masters . . . would be fully compensated by increased attention to
the industrial education of girls.[51]

As a concession the Privy Council agreed that mixed schools where no
sewing was provided could be counted as boys-only schools for capita-
tion purposes: 'Their Lordships think this will be allowed to be a very
moderate method of marking the importance which they attach to the
industrial instructions of girls in schools for the poor.' Lingen concluded
with a threat directed at the existing arrangements for female teacher
training:

Unless the present system can be shewn to be practically consistent
with the industrial training of girls, there will be a successful reaction against the intellectual instruction which female students in
Normal Colleges now usefully receive.

Meanwhile upper-class women continued to press for more domestic
training for girls and teachers. The Social Science Association, which met
in Scotland in 1860 and 1863, was used to press the point further with
papers by Mrs Gordon, daughter of the principal of Edinburgh University, Louisa Hope, daughter of an ex-president of the association and Mrs
Hamilton. The veteran educational reformer, Lord Brougham, supported
them in his opening address to the Glasgow meeting, arguing that

training the working class for their future occupations (which for girls meant domesticity), should have priority over other education, and if necessary rewards and pressure should be applied by school patrons to ensure this.[52]

INSTITUTIONAL RESPONSE

Forced to act from the need to obtain the government grant if many of its schools were to survive, the Church of Scotland Education Committee took over the SLA's female and sewing schools. A special three-yearly national church collection was approved but the first was a total failure, reflecting the lack of widespread Scottish support. Individuals – in the form of such representative Scottish figures as Miss Burdett Coutts, the Duke of Sutherland and the Bell Trustees – helped to offset the disappointing public response, and by 1864 the Church of Scotland was supporting fifty sewing departments in connection with its 170 mixed schools under masters while another twenty-three sewing schools were supported from other sources.[53] One consequence of the campaign to introduce sewing into Scottish schools was an amendment of the law restricting parochial schools to male teachers, but two years later Gordon estimated that only one in eight of the parochial schools in his district had taken advantage of the 1861 Act to establish sewing departments.[54] Meanwhile the Free Church encountered even greater difficulties organising classes as more of its members were in the poorer Highland areas and it had smaller financial resources. Frequent references to the value of sewing schools in the remotest areas were balanced by other references to the lack of funds to establish more; often a class could only be established if one elsewhere was closed.

As a long-term solution, it was suggested that where mixed schools were the norm, expense would be saved and greater efficiency introduced if an 'infant and industrial room' under the supervision of a female teacher was added to existing buildings rather than a separate school being erected, a recommendation which had already been made by the school inspectors.[55] The question was investigated by the Argyle Commission, but as it was ambiguous on this, as on many other occasions, whether the term 'industrial school' included sewing classes or referred only to departments providing practical training in all forms of housewifery, the answers were of doubtful value. The Assistant Commissioners did note that there was unnecessary duplication in many areas since schools were compelled to provide at least sewing classes to obtain the grant, even though there might also be a satisfactory (and grant-aided) separate school of industry serving the locality.[56]

It also became evident that in areas where schools were too poor to support more than one teacher the appointment of a trained woman would enable schools supported by voluntary organisations not only to obtain a sewing teacher but obtain a certificated teacher more than competent to teach other subjects.[57] These co-educational female schools should be distinguished from those deliberately established for girls only. The latter were part of a more extreme movement which saw total separation of girls from the contaminating influence of boys and the permanent presence of a female teacher for both academic as well as practical domestic training, as the means of feminising working-class girls and in particular, as a specific solution to the issue of immorality which was highlighted by the publication of the illegitimacy figures in the 1850s.[58]

The school inspectors reported on some of the desperate stratagems employed to meet the Privy Council's regulations. Often sewing lessons were provided by a female relative of the master. If none was suitable local seamstresses or dressmakers or even the schoolmaster's domestic servant might be pressed into service.[59] In many cases the arrangements were left to the master who was seldom enthusiastic, and finding suitable accommodation proved more problematic than had been anticipated,[60] but finance remained the chief difficulty. Sometimes fees were charged to cover the cost (though this could be self-defeating when the pupils were unenthusiastic anyway) and in some cases it was worthwhile for the master to pay for the lessons himself, while in the parochial schools some sewing teachers' salaries were paid for by the heritors.[61] Funds were also needed for materials; one inspector attributed a decline in sewing classes to the increased price of cotton during the American Civil War.[62]

THE CLASSROOM RESPONSE

Even where some form of sewing provision was organised, it did not prove easy to persuade the potential pupils of its value. Throughout the 1850s and 1860s philanthropic upper- and middle-class associations, school managers and school inspectors reported that the purpose of teaching girls plain needlework was not 'duly appreciated by those whom it is intended to serve.'[63] Many parents felt it was a waste of precious school time which should be spent on the book-learning which would enable their children to get on in the world;[64] others wanted to know if the pupils would be paid for their work.[65] Many of those who did intend their girls to learn sewing expected to follow the old tradition of successional learning of subjects and send them to classes after their elementary 'academic' education was completed.[66]

Teachers were faced with the need to enforce attendance and no means of doing so. 'What is to be done in such cases?' asked a master, when a parent refused to permit his daughter to go to sewing lessons.[67] An Aberdeenshire teacher reminded his pupils that all girls over the age of 7 were expected to attend the sewing lessons. They promised to do so and for a few weeks there was a better attendance before numbers again dropped off.[68] The first Edinburgh School Board found that several of its schools had not introduced sewing on the grounds that it would not be popular with parents and noted that even where it had been introduced, holding the lesson at the end of the day evaded the issue as it was then outside the four hours which counted for school attendance.[69]

The content of the lessons was also disputed. The upper classes wanted only plain sewing to be taught to emphasise the utilitarian objective.[70] Inspectors criticised the lack of mending and darning and were keen to encourage more practice in cutting out, without which they felt girls would be unable to make clothes for the family.[71] Understandably, the girls and teachers preferred knitting and fancy work[72] and possibly skills such as embroidery offered the prospect of some economic return in the future; several writers testified that plain sewing did not;[73] and sometimes parents refused to permit their daughters to learn it.[74] A school manager commented that:

> parents grudge every hour spent at school in plain sewing, and very rarely allow their girls to remain long enough to acquire anything but the rudiments. When their services are required at home any part of the day, it is the general custom to request the teachers to send them home at the sewing hour, as the least important.[75]

Rural and town schools suffered a similar experience of at best erratic and often very poor attendance for sewing lessons. Sometimes quite half the class arrived without any 'work' [garments in need of mending or darning], an excuse one teacher blamed firmly on the parents, though it was accepted as genuine in poverty-stricken areas.[76] Excuses for non-attendance at sewing classes received by the Aberdeen School Board included ill health, bad eyesight, home duties and want of work. The Board dealt with the last problem by arranging to provide sewing materials for the poorer pupils.[77]

The *Scotsman* sympathised with parents who objected to their daughters being forced to learn sewing at school:

> In England it is assumed that without a sewing class no girls' school can be complete. . . . In Scotland, however, there has been considerable difficulty in getting the sewing class generally introduced. Dr Woodford says there is a great prejudice in some places against them: 'parents object to needlework at the common school and in early years as a waste of time which they wish to be otherwise employed.' Mr Gordon naively says that 'there is less difficulty in "establishing the sewing mistress" than in procuring the attendance of the children to take her lessons, even when given without charge.' We confess to a considerable sympathy with the good old Scotch pride of those disobedient parents who 'maintain, *with a livelier feeling than might have been expected*, that the family can educate to the needle quite as well as the school.' This lively feeling was carried so far that an attempt to enforce attendance at a sewing class resulted in the withdrawal of the girls from school altogether![78]

The secretary of a small voluntary school summarised the attitude of many sections of Scottish society when he commented that the school taught 'what is in my opinion even more important – namely, reading and writing, with Religion and the other ordinary branches of elementary education'.[79] When a male member of the Edinburgh School Board recommended that sewing should form a 'prominent' part of the girls' curriculum, Flora Stevenson objected that the girls' intellectual education should take priority:

> While she regarded sewing a very important thing, she was not of the opinion that it was the main object of their education. If there was a proper system of instruction, very much less time would do to teach girls all that was required in this branch.[80]

Fewer mixed Scottish day schools seem to have adopted the more common English practice of taking girls apart all afternoon for sewing. It occurred most often in Episcopalian schools, the Roman Catholic schools in Glasgow,[81] and in single-sex girls' schools where the sewing was often superior to that in mixed schools, but academic standards poorer and subject options fewer, due in part to the influence of the ladies' committees.[82] It was significant too, that whereas the sewing teachers attached to the Church of Scotland's mixed schools were not expected to provide more than an hour's lesson a day, the General Assembly wanted teachers at its girls-only schools to spend 'a large portion of each day' on 'industrial' subjects.[83] Not all schools provided daily sewing lessons, but in the majority where girls spent one hour a day on sewing, this constituted a fifth of their total school time.

Opposition to the introduction of sewing, and of domestic economy, can be over emphasised. Local differences in educational traditions, provisions and personalities resulted in enormous variations in the educational expectations of different Scottish communities. Parents had fixed ideas about the subjects to be learnt at the local school and at some schools objected as strongly to their daughters being taught grammar or geography as to their learning sewing in others.[84] Often the objection was to the change in procedure or to learning the subject in a different school, rather than to the subject itself. There were references to pupils' keenness and in some cases girls attended school only, or primarily, *for* the sewing lessons. Stow had to restrict girls under the age of 10 to one hour a day in his female industrial school, to ensure they also attended the ordinary school.[85] Teachers in Gaelic-speaking areas, where girls seldom stayed long enough to gain more than a smattering of English before they left to learn sewing elsewhere, asked for funds for sewing departments so as to persuade the children to stay longer at their academic subjects.[86] And one of the most successful female teachers, whose pupils subsequently passed the university local examinations and on one occasion the Aberdeen University Higher Certificate for Women, started in the 1880s by persuading girls to stay on at school for sewing lessons.[87] She did, however, entice them with the fancy work and embroidery so criticised because of its middle-class connotations rather than with plain sewing. It was female teachers who most often recorded pupils attending school for sewing only, which may have been because they were now seen as the equivalent of the old sewing school to be attended after reading and writing classes at the parochial school taught by the master.[88]

Undoubtedly, sewing lessons were introduced against the wishes of a large number of girls, parents and teachers but the exact balance of support for, or opposition to, needlework is difficult to estimate since most of the information was provided by middle-class witnesses. For example, the widespread 'indifference' which was reported may have been precisely that, or it may have been a form of passive resistance. By the 1880s the campaign had theoretically succeeded and there were few later references to any opposition. In 1872 68 per cent of the girls in all government inspected schools were reportedly being taught sewing, although school log books and inspectors' comments throughout the 1870s indicated that the reality seldom matched the theory and there was still widespread absenteeism and evasion.[89] Attempts by the Scotch Education Department (SED; it became the Scottish Education Department in 1918) to standardise and reorganise the sewing syllabus in 1876 led to complaints from teachers about the excessive demands, especially for girls under 7 who had previously been exempt.[90] Indeed, until sewing was made a class subject in 1886 and the instructor actually watched classes in action, there was little incentive for teachers since the grant did not depend on the standard reached and the subject was consequently often taught very superficially, simply 'going through the motions'. In 1866 Sellar and Maxwell had described it more roundly as 'a farce' which had been in large measure forced upon the schoolmaster and sometimes even involved inspectors being shown the same 'completed' garment on successive visits.[91]

The school inspectors all made gestures of approval about sewing and undoubtedly most of them felt very strongly on the subject; but at the same time they constantly reinforced the message of the higher status of academic subjects. There was continuous calculation of the numbers studying secondary subjects, especially the traditional university subjects, and comparisons of 'best' schools excluded sewing – implicitly, and sometimes explicitly, – seeing it as a handicap and outside the strictly 'educational' curriculum.[92] Schoolmasters, and some mistresses, were markedly less enthusiastic, one referring to sewing as 'a great bugbear in the way of the girls'.[93] The pressure of the Revised Code examinations meant teachers frequently used the sewing time to drill girls in examinable subjects they were weak in, especially when inspections were looming, while the higher status of other subjects meant the sewing lesson was often 'pushed out'.[94] Parochial schoolmasters and more academically orientated teachers who disliked any detraction from their pupils' school lessons often arranged for the sewing lesson to be outside school hours, perhaps coinciding with an extra-curricular Latin class or lessons for the pupil-teachers.[95] In small schools were the master was keen and a female pupil bright, there was little doubt which subject she would be encouraged to pursue; there were four girls in the Latin class at Dyce parochial school in 1875 where the sewing was held at the same time, and girls at Fordyce public school dropped sewing as soon as they moved onto secondary subjects.[96] But this required the overriding of gender-related expectations by both teachers and pupils and where the teachers were less committed, or in the larger schools where pupils were often divided by sex, this was less likely to occur. Nevertheless, it was relevant that the larger school boards, where the economies of scale would have permitted the establishment of separate boys' and girls' schools, deliberately chose to set up co-educational schools on academic and moral grounds, although a minority rightly argued that sewing and other gender-specific teaching would be easier to organise in single-sex schools.[97]

THE CAMPAIGN FOR DOMESTIC ECONOMY

The reports of the English school inspectors placed considerable emphasis on the education and training of girls for domestic service, with references to the views of English ladies on the matter. But although upper-class Scottish women held similar views, expressed most publicly and forcefully by Louisa Hope at the 1860 Social Science Association meeting, and although the Glasgow members of the Elders' Daughters' Association formed a separate branch to concentrate on training 'orphans and destitute daughters of the honest poor as domestic servants',[98] training for domestic service in the elementary public schools was only discussed once by a Scottish inspector and then unfavourably:

> The common school cannot be made to serve the purpose of an apprenticeship to a trade . . . it cannot be expected to turn out skilful cooks or accomplished housemaids. I am far from discouraging or making light of elementary instruction in domestic economy . . . but it is one thing to train a girl to lay out limited means to the best advantage on the food and clothing of her own home. It is a very different thing to prepare her for the duties of a servant in a mansion. These duties must be learned by active service, and there is little reason to fear that they will be ill-discharged, because her mind has been informed and her intellect and her morals cultivated at school.[99]

Practical domestic training was sometimes found in schools supported by subscription or where the original endowment was insufficient, as these schools were often dependent on the sale of work from the institution for financial support. In the 1850s an inspector reported that spelling at a Glasgow school was poor because the committee of ladies required that a large portion of the children's time be given to sewing which contributed to funds for the school; at another school it was reported that girls had to clean, wash, knit and sew for funds, leaving little time for 'education'.[100]

It was, however, primarily at ragged schools,[101] established as reformatories or to provide for potential vagrants, and at endowed institutions, often residential, established to aid minority categories, such as orphans, destitute, or deaf and dumb children, that girls were to be found specifically being prepared for domestic service. The school inspector reported of one that it was 'not strictly an educational establishment; it is more for the purpose of turning out a decent respectable class of house servant'.[102] Girls in these establishments spent much of their time in housework and sewing. At the Boys' and Girls' Hospital at Aberdeen the boys cleaned while the girls washed and cooked and then the girls spent the whole afternoon sewing while the boys had lessons in arithmetic, natural philosophy or grammar.[103] In 1861 a Madeira gentleman left an endowment for an institution for fatherless or orphan girls in the north of Scotland:

> The girls shall be taught reading, writing, and some knowledge of accounts for a short period per day; but the chief routine shall be to teach them tidy habits, to sew, cook, wash, and other requisites to make them good working men's wives or efficient domestic servants.[104]

The Wick trustees could expect little other financial support and so planned for the girls to do sufficient paid washing and sewing for the establishment to be self-sufficient. Even where more enlightened trustees wished to liberalise the education provided in endowed hospital or day schools, it could be difficult to do so without tedious and expensive legal proceedings. In many cases the differentiation to be provided in the education and training of boys and girls had been written into the original settlement and so the trustees were restricted by the over-specific terms of an endowment which no longer reflected contemporary attitudes.[105]

Despite the efforts of the Scottish Ladies' Association and individual proprietors to establish and support separate day 'industrial' schools for training girls in practical domestic economy, few of these survived long and in 1866 a survey of seventeen counties found only six active schools.[106] Facilities for practical training in laundry work, cleaning or cooking were not only expensive to establish but then required a continuous supply of provisions for cookery lessons and clothing for laundry work as well as mending for sewing lessons. Nor was expense the only consideration; practical work was too closely related to that of the charitable institutions and of domestic service to be popular.[107] Consequently separate industrial schools seldom showed sufficient reward for the cost and effort entailed and it was generally agreed that private provision alone would never be able to ensure adequate domestic training facilities.[108] Attempts to introduce such lessons to the existing schools faced even greater difficulties of organisation[109] and greater opposition. There was:

a very foolish prejudice among mothers against allowing their children to take a share in scrubbing the school floor in the way of a lesson. They hold that they do not send their girls to be servants to the schoolmistress, but to learn their lessons.[110]

Parents and pupils seldom differentiated between courses intended to train girls as servants and those intended to train them as housewives and were hostile to both. A Free Church inspector considered there was little possibility of anything but theoretical study of such subjects in Scottish mixed schools, and even this seldom consisted of more than a few lessons using a class-book such as Tegetmeier's *Manual of Domestic Economy* and perhaps one or two essays.[111]

Nevertheless, there were many who did favour the idea of training girls in domestic economy as a means of improving working-class living standards. Whereas in the 1850s and 1860s the campaign for practical 'industrial work' concentrated on the introduction of needlework to the curriculum, in the 1870s and 1880s it extended to other domestic subjects, especially cookery and hygiene. One Scot, writing about pauperism, wanted compulsory schooling in social and domestic economy introduced for female factory workers – to be held in the women's 'leisure' time, not in working hours of course. But failing such compulsory measures, Buckminster, from the Department of Science and Art, concluded that efforts to teach domestic economy to working-class women through lecturers were doomed to failure and that it was necessary instead to get at the captive audience of female pupils.[112] This was borne out at the voluntary domestic science schools which were established in Edinburgh and Glasgow in the 1870s by upper middle-class women who moved in élite circles but were involved with the women's movement for higher education, suffrage and wider occupational opportunities. These women wanted to raise the standard of working-class housewifery, but they also wanted to raise the status of the domestic role ('home rule for women'), partly by emphasising its scientific aspects. After their efforts to provide demonstrations and classes for working-class women failed, they turned their attention to getting domestic economy accepted as an academic school subject.[113]

The establishment of school boards throughout Scotland under the 1872 Education Act had introduced new possibilities; while the Scottish Society for the Propagation of Christian Knowledge (SSPCK) wanted to hand over its ordinary schools to the school boards and concentrate on extending its 'industrial' operations and developing housewifery courses,[114] both feminists and conservatives campaigned for domestic economy to be introduced to the curriculum of the board schools themselves. Miss Guthrie Wright was the leading campaigner in Edinburgh, while Professor Milligan was amongst those who pressed the subject on the Aberdeen School Board.[115] HMI Hall argued that the cost of practical classes in cooking, washing and dressing:

> would be trifling in comparison with the advantages which would accrue to the masses of our population from the adoption of the suggestion now made. Our school boards have the matter in their own hands, and if they can accomplish it for us they will earn the approbation of all who think that the secret to the amelioration of the working man's condition in life lies in no small measure in cheerful homes, clean and neatly mended clothes, and palatable food.[116]

Feminists felt the subject was equally relevant to boys. Flora Stevenson suggested on a number of occasions that boys should have industrial training, especially in cookery – a suggestion always rejected by the male members of the Edinburgh Board.[117] She was not alone, however, in considering the subject important for all children; several inspectors raised the issue: 'Much of the "Domestic Economy" is admittedly of more importance than any other subject in the Fourth Schedule. But changing perhaps the name. . . would the subject not be every whit as suitable and important for boys?'[118]

The Privy Council's response to pressure for teaching in domestic economy mirrored its reaction to the issue of needlework. Regulations were introduced but no funding for training or facilities was provided. Courses in specific subjects had been established in 1873 as a means of enabling some form of post-elementary education in the grant-aided elementary schools to be continued. In 1876 regulations were issued by the London-based SED prohibiting girls from being examined in even one specific subject unless they were also taking domestic economy. In 1879 there were further amendments to ensure that girls studied both sections of the syllabus – clothing and washing as well as food and its preparation.[119] It was expected that most work would be from books, though two hours of cookery a week were permitted to count towards school hours. Teachers objected strongly, the Dundee Educational Institute of Scotland passing a motion against compulsory domestic economy; while the Aberdeen School Board disliked the priority given to domestic economy over other academic subjects, and was even more indignant that the school managers were expected to cover the expenditure of providing 'the only instruction in the department of Domestic Economy above-mentioned that is likely to be of permanent value to girls'. Aberdeen appealed to the other school boards to support its complaint and sent a memorandum to the SED, requesting a grant towards the provision of cooking facilities.[120] In the meantime, an Instructress in Cookery and Superintendent in Needlework was appointed at Aberdeen, a special sub-committee set up and a centre established, after consultation with Buckmaster, at which cookery lessons could be provided – but only out of school hours.[121] Most of the work continued to be from books which fitted the academic ethos but could be very dull. For example, for the specific subjects course, girls were expected to know about the composition and nutritive value of foods, which in practice consisted of rote learning of terms such as 'albuminous' or 'nitrogenous'.[122] It was not until 1882 that a special grant was introduced for girls over 12 years of age taking cooking; even then needlework still received more emphasis. In 1893 regulations for the training of specialist teachers, including cookery, were introduced, but again no funding was provided. Nevertheless, as grants were attached to the teaching of specific subjects and about 20 per cent of the pupils in average attendance at board schools studied them, the regulations resulted in the desired increase in the number of girls studying domestic economy. Only 783 pupils were voluntarily examined in the subject in 1875–6, but two years later the number had increased twentyfold, though the total number of pupils examined in all specific subjects only quadrupled.[123]

The system of specific subjects was ended in 1898, and higher grade schools were established for pupils studying at least three years post-elementary. Intended initially as science schools, they could also provide a 'commercial' education and special courses, including a curriculum designed for girls which had to include practical training in household economy.[124] Despite official intentions most of the higher grade schools instead became embryonic secondary schools and the clash of their academic pretensions and their original socio-cultural objectives was most obvious in the case of girls. An inspector criticised the schools' tendency to start several foreign languages in the first year which effectively excluded practical courses from the curriculum:

> This is of prime importance in connection with the work of the girls where Cookery, Housewifery, and even Needlework have been neglected in favour of a study of languages which, in many cases, has been carried no further than the most elementary and, therefore, the most useless stage.[125]

In 1903 the SED introduced two-year supplementary courses for the majority of pupils who would remain at elementary schools, leaving at 14 rather than going on to secondary schools. These lasted until 1923 and consisted of core courses in English and civic responsibilities and a choice of one of four special courses – commercial, industrial, rural and inevitably, 'household management' for girls. The inspectors' reports for 1904–5 described the typical supplementary course taken for seven months by 'a clever girl in a good school'. During fifteen hours of morning work per week she studied seven English literature books and wrote precis, memorised a number of poems, read ten library books and wrote a fortnightly essay. Arithmetic included decimals and the metric system and there were courses on citizenship, colonial history and hygiene. The ten afternoon hours a week were devoted to practical housewifery, cookery, laundry work, needlework and dressmaking, plus music and physical exercises.[126] Thus in the twentieth century the English tradition of a girls' curriculum in which almost all of every afternoon was devoted to practical domestic training finally prevailed in the elementary schools of Scotland.

Nevertheless, as Corr has noted, the institutionalisation of domestic instruction for girls into the school curriculum throughout Britain was only beginning. In the early twentieth century government reports and the eugenics movement led to anxiety about the health of the nation and child-rearing became a national rather than a moral duty. In Scotland a Glasgow councillor called for 'the training of older schoolgirls in household duties so as to stop the supply of ignorant motherhood' and there were demands that cookery should be made compulsory. The voluntary Glasgow, Edinburgh and Aberdeen cookery schools were placed under the control of the SED; grants were provided for training teachers in 'household management' subjects; and there was an 'unprecedented expansion' in the number of schoolgirls studying domestic subjects in the years before the First World War.[127]

Scottish feminists were ambivalent about girls studying the theory of domestic economy. It was advocated by the founders of the voluntary cookery schools, women members of school boards and the inspectresses, appointed from 1902, as a means of motivating girls to widen their intellectual horizons, as well as providing them with a scientific understanding of matters relating to their future household duties.[128] Others, like Maria Ogilvie Gordon, deliberately emphasised the domestic relevance in order to get girls admitted to subjects, such as chemistry and physics, generally closed to them.[129] But more radical feminists saw the emphasis on domestic science for girls as a retrograde step, which not only emphasised that woman's 'proper' sphere was domestic, but restricted their education to a portion of each academic subject in a way that did not occur for boys.[130]

As the development of the higher grade schools illustrated, the earlier tension as to whether girls' education should consist primarily of academic learning or practical training still existed. Continuing problems with staffing, accommodation and public opinion meant that even in 1909 the level of provision varied considerably between regions; more than half the schools in Renfrew offered cookery classes but only ten schools out of 166 did so in Argyle. Although some inspectors asserted that the value of cookery classes was appreciated by 'everyone', others complained that it was still 'taken for granted in some quarters that book-learning is the only means of intellectual and moral discipline that should be open to the future citizen.'[131] Despite the imposition of domestic subjects and an increasingly sharp demarcation between primary and secondary schooling resulting from government legislation and reflected in the prohibition of academic subjects in the supplementary courses, in 1900 working-class women constituted 21 per cent of the women students at Aberdeen University and 28 per cent of those at Glasgow, while 19 per cent of the women at Edinburgh University in 1900 and more than half of those matriculating at Aberdeen in 1902 had been educated solely at elementary public schools.[132]

SUMMARY

Scottish Enlightenment theories gave a new importance to domesticity. The consequent need to improve women's reasoning abilities, scientific knowledge and morality, so that they would be able to fulfil this role, led to the promotion of an academic education for both middle-class and working-class girls.

Subsequent concern about maintaining order at a time of social and political unrest resulted in schemes to utilise the feminine influence to direct and contain working-class aspirations. Emphasis was placed on training working-class girls in domestic skills, as a means both of raising working-class living standards and of providing the opportunity for inculcating appropriate moral, cultural and religious precepts which would be passed on in the family environment.

The appointment of female teachers was part of the feminisation of the girls' curriculum, rather than a perception of mistresses as equal academic and professional colleagues; the 1861 Education Act spelt this out when it permitted heritors to appoint women to give instruction in female industrial and household training and 'elementary' education only, in the parochial schools. The response of the Church of Scotland reflected the contradictions resulting from an emphasis on the value of intellectual discipline combined with a belief in the subordinate and domestic role of women. As a result female teacher training students were encouraged to study academic subjects such as French as well as history and geography, but not the traditional secondary subjects, maths and Latin, even though some of them had learnt these while at school. Before 1872 they were seldom appointed to anything but 'industrial' or infant school posts, despite the repeated admission of their academic superiority in those subjects studied by both sexes. This left a legacy of gender-differentiated occupation and status in the teaching profession which was continued by the SED, and survived even the introduction of graduate female teachers.[133]

Opposition to the introduction of sewing and domestic economy in Scotland was largely due to the belief that intellectual discipline was the best means of developing an intelligent, moral and cultured individual; but it also resulted from the inertia of custom, the opposition of teachers and lack of funds. The tradition of mixed elementary schools, the teaching of higher subjects in those schools, the attendance of a proportion of middle-class girls, and the initial lack of female teachers, all reinforced opposition. Early attempts to introduce comprehensive training in all aspects of domestic economy failed and even attempts to introduce sewing were unsuccessful until it became a condition of the government grant and hence too expensive to ignore. Widespread practical education in other domestic subjects was not feasible in most areas until the establishment of school boards.

The education of girls was a subject many women felt prepared to speak out about. Conservative women criticised the male educational establishment for its opposition to domestic training. The support of Scottish feminists from the 1870s may seem more surprising but reflected an attempt to raise the status of domesticity. Pressure from the English authorities was ultimately responsible for the introduction of domestic subjects into the Scottish curriculum, and as in England,[134] the state continued thereafter to promote an increasingly formalised gender-differentiation.

Since neither the ethos nor the content of domestic subjects fitted the Scottish ideal of education they have been ignored by historians of Scottish education. Those familiar with the history of educational provision for working-class girls in England may be impressed by the extent of Scottish opposition, both from within the educational establishment and in the classroom, and by the widespread belief in the value of an academic education for girls.[135] Those more familiar with the tradition of a democratic, classless, co-educational Scottish education may be struck by the evidence that many Scots actually supported a class- and sex-specific education intended to restrain, rather than provide opportunities for, the 'lass o' pairts'.

NOTES

1 E. Mure, *Some Observations of the Change of Manners in my Own Time, 1700–1790* quoted in J. G. Fyfe (ed.), *Scottish Diaries and Memoirs 1746–1846* (Eneas Mackay, Stirling, 1942) p. 66.

2 J. Rendall, *The Origins of Modern Feminism: Women in Britain, France and the United States, 1780–1860* (Macmillan, London, 1985).

3 J. Dwyer, *Virtuous Discourse: Sensibility and Community in Late Eighteenth Century Scotland* (John Donald, Edinburgh, 1987) quotation p. 6.

4 'Noctes Ambrosianae', *Blackwoods Edinburgh Magazine*, XII, October 1823, p. 493; 'The sketcher', ibid., XXXV, February 1834, p. 180.

5 'On the influence women have upon society', *Scots Magazine*, September 1804, pp. 673–5; 'Strictures on the present plan of female education', ibid., November 1804, pp. 835–7.

6 'Female schools for cleanliness, morals, and decorum', *Scots Magazine* March 1804, pp. 198–202; April 1804, pp. 249–53; May 1804, pp. 329–333; B. Grant, *Sketches of Intellectual Education, and Hints on Domestic Economy, Addressed to Inexperienced Mothers*, 2 vols., (J. Young, Inverness, 1812); E. Hamilton, *Letters on the Elementary Principles of Education*, 2 vols., (Bath, 3rd edition, 1803), *A series of Popular Essays, Illustrative of Principles Essentially Connected with the Improvement of the Understanding, the Imagination, and the Heart*, 2 vols., (Glasgow, 1812) and *Hints Addressed to Patrons and Directors of Schools* (Longman, London, 1815); Profes-

sor Leslie (quoted *Scotsman,* 10 February 1827); Cunningham (quoted *Scotsman,* 1 May 1833); J. Simpson (quoted *Scotsman,* 12 November 1842).

7 B. Grant, *Sketches of Intellectual Education;* 'Female schools for cleanliness', *Scots Magazine* pp. 250–1 fn; A. Combe, *The Management of Infancy, Physical and Moral,* revised and edited by Sir James Clark, Bt., (Maclachlan and Stewart, Edinburgh and London; 10th edition, 1881) vii–x. (The first edition was published in 1840); 'Column for mothers', *Chambers' Edinburgh Journal* [CEJ], IV, 25 July 1835, p. 208.

8 G. Combe, 'On female education' in *Lectures on Popular Education; Delivered to the Edinburgh Philosophical Association in April and November 1833* (Maclachlan, Stewart, Edinburgh; 3rd edition, 1848) pp. 50–60 (quotation p. 53).

9 E. Hamilton, 1815, pp. 20–1, 127 and 1812, I, pp. 65–74.

10 Ibid., p. 42.

11 Individual writers' definition of 'intellectual' was relative to contemporary practice; in early years it might only mean that all girls should be taught the 3Rs.

12 G. Combe, 'On female education'. Versions of this were published as 'Education', *CEJ* 3 (118), 3 May 1834, pp. 106–8 and 'Woman in her social and domestic character by Mrs John Sandford', *Phrenological Journal,* VII, (XXXI) 1831–2, pp. 410–27. See also 'Education', *CEJ,* 3 (107), 15 February 1834, p. 20; letter to *Scotsman* from William Bell, 6 August 1851.

13 *Necessity of Popular Education as a National Object* (Adam and Charles Black, Edinburgh, 1834) esp. pp. 183–4 and see his evidence in *Report from the Select Committee on Education in England and Wales, Together with the Minutes of Evidence: Appendix, and Index* (PP., 1835), Appendix no. 3; D. Stow, *The Training System Adapted in the Model Schools of the Glasgow Educational Society* (W. R. McPhun, Glasgow, 1836) p. 174.

14 E. Hamilton, 1803, I., p. 202; G. E. Davie, *The Democratic Intellect: Scotland and the Universities in the Nineteenth Century* (Edinburgh University Press, Edinburgh, 1961) p. 189. For specific examples see *Minutes of the Committee of Council on Education* [MCCE]. PP., 1841–2, p. 99, and 1846, II, p. 472; Education Commission (Scotland), *Report on the State of Education in the Country Districts of Scotland* by A. C. Sellar and C. F. Maxwell [hereafter Sellar and Maxwell] (PP., 1867, xxv) p. 159; *Report of the Committee of Council on Education; with Appendix* [RCCE] PP., 1861–2, p. 216 and 1870–1, p. 312; Education Commission (Scotland), *First Report by Her Majesty's Commissioners Appointed to Inquire into the Schools in Scotland* (PP., 1865, xvii) p. 186; 'The importance of the school in connection with the Church', *The Home and Foreign Missionary Record of the Church of Scotland* [HFMR], October 1859, p. 243; Isa M. Croal, 'The higher education of women', *Educational News,* 25 April 1885, p. 271.

15 D. Chambers, 'The Church of Scotland Highlands and Islands Education Scheme', *Journal of Educational Administration and History,* VII (1), January 1975, p. 16.

16 'The sermon', *Transactions of the National Association for the Promotion of Social Science, 1860* [TNAPSS] p. 2; see also J. Tulloch 'The parish school in relation to plans of national education for Scotland, to the universities, and the Church', ibid., pp. 343–4.

17 J. Begg, *National Education for Scotland Practically Considered; with Notices of Certain Proposals on that Subject* (Johnstone and Hunter, Edinburgh; 2nd edition, 1850); W. M. Hetherington, *National Education in Scotland, Viewed in its Present Condition, its Principles, and its Possibilities* (Johnstone and Hunter, Edinburgh; 2nd edition, 1850).

18 Louisa Hope, 'Girls' schools', *TNAPSS, 1860*, pp. 397–404; Mrs Story, *Later Reminiscences* (Maclehose, Glasgow, 1913) p. 12; *MCCE*, 1853–4, p. 943.

19 L. Mahood, 'The domestication of 'fallen' women: the Glasgow Magdalene Institution, 1860–1890' in D. McCrone, S. Kendrick and P. Straw (eds.), *The Making of Scotland: Nation, Culture and Social Change* (Edinburgh University Press, Edinburgh) p. 151; J. Drummond (ed)., *Onward and Upward: Extracts (1891–96) from the Magazine of the Onward and Upward Association Founded by Lady Aberdeen for the Material, Mental and Moral Elevation of Women* (Aberdeen University Press, Aberdeen, 1983).

20 Not to be confused with 'industrial schools' established for vagrant or criminal children. The term 'female' school simply signified a school taught by a woman; the pupils might be all girls or boys and girls and the subjects taught might be solely domestic, or include the 3Rs or include all subjects. The term caused confusion for contemporaries as well as for historical researchers. Practical courses for boys were also attempted in the 1840s and 1850s, but were unsuccessful. They were reintroduced as specific subjects in 1883 and as supplementary courses in 1903.

21 MS. Scottish Record Office, HR 476/1, 'Rules of the Athelstaneford Female Subscription School' in Minute Book of the Athelstaneford Heritors 1857, pp. 44–6.

22 Association for the Religious Improvement of the Remote Highlands and Islands in connexion with the Free Church of Scotland, *Ninth Annual Report* (1859) p. 7.

23 *MCCE* 1851-2, p. 1009–10; *MCCE* 1852–3, p. 1198; J. Gordon, 'On the state of education among the mining population of Lanarkshire', *TNAPSS, 1860*, pp. 374–5.

24 *Report of the Committee of the General Assembly for Increasing the Means of Education in Scotland, Particularly in the Highlands and Islands [RCGA]* (Edinburgh, 1849) p. 8; *MCCE* 1851–52, p. 1009–10; Education Commission (Scotland), *First Report*, para. 150–1.; editorial, *Scotsman*, 28 April 1855.

25 'Elders' Daughters' Association', *HFMR*, XI (1856), p. 153.

26 *MCCE* 1846, II, p. 477; *MCCE* 1848–49–50, II, p. 574; *MCCE* 1853–4, pp. 672 and 1052; *MCCE* 1856–7, p. 675; *RCCE* 1860–1, pp. 237 (quotation), 225; *RCCE* 1861–2, p. 230; *RCCE* 1862–3, p. 142; E. Lipp, *Scottish Aspects of Child Education a Century Ago* (Rainbow Enterprises, Aberdeen, 1979) p. 84.

27 *MCCE* 1846, II, p. 458; *RCCE* 1860–1, p. 225; *RCCE* 1862–3, p. 171; *RCCE* 1863–4, p. 251; *RCCE* 1865–6, p. 326; *RCCE* 1871–2, p. 90.

28 MS. Aberdeen District Archives [ADA], Aberdeen School Board, Minutes of the Board 1873–1876, 9 March 1876; *Report of Women's Conference on Women's Work* (D. Wyllie, Aberdeen, 1888) p. 41 (quotation).

29 A. F. Tytler, *Memoirs of the Life and Writings of the Honourable Henry Home of Kames. . .* 2 vols., (Creech, Edinburgh, 1807) II, pp. 13, 64; M. Plant, *The Domestic Life of Scotland in the Eighteenth*

Century (Edinburgh University Press, Edinburgh, 1952) pp. 153–5; I. F. M. Dean, *Scottish Spinning Schools* (University of London Press, 1930) pp. 62, 70–1, 82–7.

30 R. Marshall, *Virgins and Viragos; a History of Women in Scotland from 1080–1980* (Collins, London, 1983) pp. 252–3; *MCCE*, 1846, II, p. 459; MS. Scottish Record Office, GD 46/17/68, Heads of a plan for establishing a female school at Stornoway, under the patronage of the Honourable Mrs Stewart Mackenzie of Seaforth for the purpose of teaching the female youth of Stornoway reading, writing and needle work and spinning. (22 August 1825); *Presbyterial and Parochial Reports on the State of Education in Scotland, 1842* (Edinburgh, 1843) pp. 31, 51, 56, 123.

31 L. Moore, 'Invisible scholars: girls learning Latin and mathematics in the elementary public schools of Scotland before 1872', *History of Education*, 13 (2), 1984, pp. 121–4.

32 W. Anderson, *Female Education in Relation to the Wants of the Age* (Smith, King, Aberdeen, 1851).

33 *MCCE 1842–3*, p. 323; *MCCE 1846*, I, p. 489; *RCGA*, 1850, p. 38. The persistence of this attitude is indicated in Scotch Education Department [SED], *Reports, &c. issued in 1909–10* (PP., 1910), section B, p. 40.

34 H. M. Knox, 'Simon Somerville Laurie, 1829–1909', *British Journal of Education Studies*, X, (1961–2), pp. 138–52; [S. S. Laurie], *Report on Education in the Parochial Schools of the Counties of Aberdeen, Banff and Moray Addressed to the Trustees of the Dick Bequest* (Constable, Edinburgh, 1865) p. 189. Compare also Gordon's criticism of the introduction of industrial training for male pupils (*MCCE* 1846, II, p. 476) with his support for female industrial schools.

35 G. W. Alexander, 'Primary and secondary education in Scotland' in C. S. Bremner, *Education of Girls and Women in Great Britain* (Swann Sonnenschein, 1897), p. 245; D. MacGillivray, 'Fifty years of Scottish education' in J. Clarke (ed.), *Problems of National Education* (Macmillan, London, 1919) p. 19.

36 L. Moore, 'Invisible Scholars', pp. 121–37.

37 *Abstract of the Report of the General Assembly for Increasing the Means of Education and Religious Instruction in Scotland, Particularly in the Highlands and Islands* (Edinburgh, 1828) p. 8.

38 *MCCE 1848–49–50*, II, p. 560 (quotation); *RCCE 1862–3*, p. 169.

39 *MCCE 1841–2*, p. 102.

40 *MCCE 1846*, II, p. 511; see also *Presbyterial and Parochial Reports... 1842*, esp. pp. 16, 20, 24, 31–2, 56 and 123 (on Dundee).

41 Eg. E. Lipp, *Scottish Aspects of Child Education a Century Ago*, pp. 79–85; MS. Scottish Record Office, HR 476/1. 'Rules of the Athelstaneford Female Subscription School' in Minute Book of Athelstaneford Heritors 1857, pp. 44–6; Endowed Schools and Hospitals (Scotland) Commission, *Appendix to Third Report*, 2 vols., (PP. 1875, xxix), I, pp. 128, 130, 136, II, pp. 1 ff.

42 *Report from the Select Committee of the House of Lords Appointed to Inquire into the Duties, Emoluments, and Present Condition of the Parochial Schoolmasters in Scotland...* (PP, 1845, xix.) para. 639, 989, 1147.

43 *RCGA 1849*, pp. 8–9; *RCGA 1850*, p. 12 (quotation).

44 'Elders' Daughters' Association for Female Education in Scotland', *HFMR*, VII, March 1852, p. 52; *Scotsman* 23 May 1868.

45 Census of Great Britain, 1851, *Religious Worship and Education, Scotland, Report and Tables* (PP., 1854, lix); Census of Great Britain, 1851, *Education, England and Wales, Reports and Tables.*, (PP, 1854). See also comparative statistics for sewing in *MCCE*, 1852–3. The term 'public' school is used throughout this chapter in the Scottish sense of a school open to all; after 1872 it technically meant a school controlled by a local authority, such as a school board.

46 'Second Annual Report of the Scottish Ladies' Association for Promoting Female Industrial Education in Scotland, for 1854', *HFMR*, X, May 1855, pp. 95–6.

47 Ibid.; 'Report to the General Assembly by the Committee on Education', *HFMR*, IX, 1854, p. 146. (The annual reports were also published separately.)

48 L. O. Hope, letter in the *Scotsman*, 18 February 1865 and 'Girls' schools', op. cit., p. 401. Louisa Hope had already published her views in *The Female Teacher: Ideas Suggestive of her Qualifications and Duties* (Paton and Ritchie, Edinburgh, 1853).

49 Quoted in 'Annual Report to the General Assembly by the Committee. May 1859', *HFMR*, XIV, July 1859, p. 149.

50 'Education scheme. Annual report to the General Assembly by the Committee. May 1860', *HFMR*, XV, 2 July 1860, p. 150; see also 'Needlework versus popular education', letter, *Scotsman*, 15 March 1864; Education Commission (Scotland), *First Report*, p. 193. In 1860 Woodford reported visiting fifty-three mixed schools which were too poor to organise sewing classes and so could not obtain the grant (*RCCE* 1860–61, p. 217).

51 Letter dated 11 May 1860 quoted in 'Education scheme. Annual report to the General Assembly by the Committee. May 1860', op. cit.; *RCCE* 1859–60, xxi.

52 L. O. Hope, 'Girls' schools', *TNAPSS, 1860*, pp. 397–404; 'Opening address by the Right Hon. Lord Brougham and Vaux', ibid, p. 19; Mrs Gordon, 'On the training of primary schoolmistresses', *TNAPSS 1863*, p. 382; Mrs Hamilton, 'On the industrial training of girls in the humbler classes', ibid.

53 'Female schools and the education scheme', *The Church of Scotland Home and Foreign Missionary Record* [*CSHFMR*], New Series, I, November 1862, pp. 195–6; *Scotsman* 29 May 1862; 'Education Scheme', *CSHFMR*, III, December 1864, p. 217–8.

54 *RCCE* 1863–4, p. 238.

55 'Remarks on the General Report by Presbyteries on School Examinations 1853', *HFMR*, IX, January 1854, pp. 1–3; 'Education scheme', *HFMR*, XV, 2 July 1860, p. 151; *MCCE*, 1841–2, 114, 122 and 125; *MCCE* 1851–2, p. 1084.

56 Sellar and Maxwell, *Report on the State of Education*, Appendix I, and p. 125.

57 *Scotsman*, 24 May 1864; Education Commission (Scotland), *Second Report by Her Majesty's Commissioners Appointed to Inquire into the Schools in Scotland. With an Appendix. Elementary Schools* (PP, 1867, xxv), p. cl.

58 D. F. Sandford, 'On female education and industrial training' in *Two Short Lectures* (Grant, Edinburgh, 1855) pp. 11–21; Sellar and Maxwell, *Report on the State of Education*, p. 66–7; S. S. Laurie, *Report on Education in the Parochial Schools*, pp. 188–9; 'Female school scheme', *CSHFMR*, V, 1 May 1866 pp. 25–6.

59 *RCCE* 1867–8, p. 391; *RCCE* 1859–60, pp. 235, 248; *RCCE* 1864–5, p. 258.
60 *RCCE* 1859–60, p. 273; *RCCE* 1861–2, 205.
61 *RCCE* 1859–60, p. 273; *RCCE* 1863–4, p. 238; MS Grampian Regional Archives [GRA], Log Book of Cairnbanno Madras [Free Church] School 1863–79, 29 May 1866; MS GRA GR6S/A12/1/1 Bucksburn Public School (formerly Newhills Free Church Congregational School) Log Book 1864–1907, 11 January 1870.
62 *RCCE* 1864–5, p. 258. See also Association for the Religious Improvement . . . Free Church of Scotland, *Thirteenth Annual Report* (1863), p. 20.
63 *RCCE* 1858–59, p. 215; *RCCE* 1863–64, p. 238; MS. GRA, AC5/ 115/1A, Log Book of Cairnbanno Madras School 1863–79; MS GRA Log Book of Garvock School 1866–1888; MS. GRA, GR6S/ B1/1/2, Log Book of the General Assembly School Aberchirder 1864–78, 13 May 1867.
64 *RCCE* 1859–60, p. 273; *RCCE* 1860–1, p. 217; *RCCE* 1863–4, pp. 240, 257, 261; Sellar and Maxwell, *Report on the State of Education*, p. 87 fn.
65 *RCCE* 1859–60, p. 235; *RCCE* 1860–1, p. 217.
66 *RCCE* 1858–9, p. 273; *RCCE*, 1863–4, pp. 257, 261; MS. GRA, Garvoch School Log Book 1866–88, 6 June 1873.
67 MS. GRA, Log Book of Macduff Free Church School 1863–1877, 29 August 1864.
68 MS. GRA, GR6S/A12/1/1, Bucksburn Public School (formerly Newhills Free Church Congregational School) Log Book 1864–1907, 4 and 9 January, 18 February and 24 March 1869.
69 *Scotsman* 5 March 1874.
70 *MCCE* 1850–1, p. 890; *MCCE*, 1851–2, p. 1009; *RCCE* 1860–61, p. 237; *RCCE*, 1864–65, p. 258; letter, *Scotsman*, 22 August 1867.
71 *RCCE* 1867–8, p. 430; MS. GRA 5/68/1 Linhead School Log Book 1866–89, 31 January 1873.
72 Sellar and Maxwell, *Report on the State of Education*, p. 111; letters, *Scotsman*, 11 February 1865, 22 August 1867; *RCCE*, 1870–1, p. 318; MS. GRA GR6S/B54/1/1. Peterhead Female Parochial School Log Book 1864–74, 7 July 1869.
73 Letters, *Scotsman*, 9 and 11 February 1865. Attempts to teach learning skills such as embroidery (*RCCE* 1858–9, p. 215) came under heavy criticism (e.g. 'Report of the Ladies' Association in Support of Gaelic Schools in Connexion with the Church of Scotland', *Sixth Report*, quoted in *HFMR*, VIII, 1853, pp. 38–9).
74 *MCCE* 1853–4, pp. 949, 951.
75 Letter, *Scotsman* 9 February 1865.
76 MS. GRA, AC5/115/1A, Log Book of Cairnbanno Madras School 1863–1879, 19 July 1866, 31 March 1871, 5 March 1872 and problem noted six more times in 1872; MS GRA Log Book of Garvock School 1866–88, 9 June 1869 and 3 December 1869; Association for the Religious Improvement . . . Free Church of Scotland, *Ninth Annual Report*, (1859) p. 17, *Fourteenth Annual Report*, (1864), pp. 5, 23; *Fifteenth Annual Report* (1865) pp. 14, 23.
77 MS., ADA, Aberdeen School Board, Minutes of the Board 1873–76, 9 March 1876.
78 Editorial, *Scotsman*, 23 August 1864.
79 'Needlework versus popular education', letter, *Scotsman*, 15 March 1864.
80 *Scotsman*, 2 April 1874.

81 *RCCE* 1862–3, p. 179; *RCCE* 1863–4, p. 218.

82 *MCCE* 1853–4, p. 943; *RCCE* 1864–5, p. 265; *RCCE* 1869–70, p. 401.

83 'Female school scheme', *CSHFMR*, V, May 1866, pp. 25–6.

84 *MCCE* 1853–4, p. 958, 963, 978; *RCCE* 1863–4, p. 261; MS. GRA, AC5/148/1, Overton (Overtown) School Log Book 1869–1915, 3 December 1869, 23 November 1871 (but on the earlier date the teacher noted this was the first such case he had experienced); Sellar and Maxwell, *Report on the State of Education*, p. 87 fn.; MS GRA, AC5/134/1, Glenbuchat School Log Book, 7 May 1872.

85 MS. GRA, AC5/115/1A Log Book of Cairnbanno Madras School, 11 December 1866, 30 May 1870; Association for the Religious Improvement. . .Free Church of Scotland, *Fifth Annual Report* (1855), p. 2 and *Seventh Annual Report* (1857) p. 13; D. Stow, *Moral training and the training system* (Blackie, Glasgow; 5th edition, 1841) p. 367.

86 Association for the Religious Improvement. . .Free Church of Scotland, *Fourteenth Annual Report* (1864), p. 5. A similar reason was given for the establishment of an industrial school at Bridge of Earn (*MCCE* 1853–4, p. 1037) and see *MCCE* 1856–7, p. 641.

87 W. Barclay, *The Schools and Schoolmasters of Banffshire* (Banffshire Branch of the EIS, Banff, 1925) p. 251.

88 MS. GRA, AC5/134/1, Glenbuchat School Log Book 1865–74, 26, 27 December 1865, 30 January, 7 February 1866, 25 November 1867; MS GRA, 5/86/1, Linhead School Log Book 1866–89, 4 February 1867, 8 March 1867.

89 Letter, *Educational News*, I, 17 June 1876.

90 *Educational News*, II, 14 and 24 March 1877.

91 *RCCE* 1872–3, p. 254; Sellar and Maxwell, *Report on the State of Education*, p. 125.

92 *MCCE* 1855–6, p. 671. *RCCE* 1864–5, p. 265; *RCCE* 1871–2, p. 88; *Report of the Committee of Council on Education in Scotland* [*RCCES*] 1877–8, p. 211.

93 MS. GRA, GR6S/B42/1/1 Log Book of Macduff Free Church School 1863–1877, 16 February 1865; MS. GRA, AC5/115/1A, Log Book of Cairnbanno Madras School 1863–79, 11 December 1866; *Educational News*, I, 26 February 1876.

94 MS. GRA, GRA6S/A12/1/1, Bucksburn Public School (formerly Newhills Free Church Congregational School) Log Book 1864–1907, 15 and 26 September 1865; MS. GRA, GR6S/G11/1/1, Cluny School Log Book 1864–73, 11, 14, 15, 18, 21 and 22 January 1869; MS. GRA, AC5/148/1, Overton (Overtown) School Log Book 1869–1915, 13 June 1870, 31 May 1872; MS. GRA, AC5/115/1A, Log Book of Cairnbanno Madras School 1863–79, 10 November 1871, 12, 26 April, 7 June and 16 August 1872.

95 MS. GRA, GR6S/B40/1/1, Longhaven School (formerly Coldwells) Log Book 1869–1901, 19 January 1877; MS. GRA, AC5/115/1A, Log Book of Cairnbanno Madras School 1863–1879, 14 March 1871, 29 September 1872; MS. GRA, AC5/148/1, Overton (Overtown) School Log Book 1869–1915, 11 January 1871.

96 MS. GRA, AC5/148/1, Overton (Overtown) School Log Book 1869–1915, 24 February 1873, July 19 1875; D. G. McLean, *The History of Fordyce Academy; Life at a Banffshire School 1592–1935* (Banffshire Journal, Banff, 1936) p. 73.

97 *Scotsman*, 2 April 1874; *Aberdeen Journal*, 25 August 1874; G. W. Alexander, 'Primary and Secondary education in Scotland', p. 244.

98 'Glasgow Elders' Wives and Daughters' Association', *CSHRMR*, IV, April 1865, p. 14.

99 *RCCE* 1860–1, pp. 255–6. See also R. A. Bayliss, (ed.), *Aberdeen School of Domestic Science: an outline history* (Robert Gordon's Institute of Technology, Aberdeen, 1979) p. 12.

100 *MCCE* 1851–2, p. 1057; *RCCE* 1860–1, p. 219.

101 Confusingly, these were sometimes called industrial schools.

102 Endowed Schools and Hospitals (Scotland) Commission, *First Report* (PP., 1873, xxvii) 736.

103 Ibid., esp. p. 721; R. A. Bayliss, *Aberdeen School of Domestic Science*, pp. 7–11.

104 Endowed Schools and Hospitals (Scotland) Commission, *Appendix to Third Report*. 2 vols., PP., 1875, xxix) II, p. 277.

105 Cf. problems encountered by the trustees of the Edinburgh Merchant Maiden Hospital.

106 Sellar and Maxwell, *Report on the State of Education*, p. 166 and Appendix I, evidence of D. Middleton.

107 'Report of the Ladies' Association in Support of Gaelic Schools', *HFMR*, VIII, February 1853, p. 38–9; *RCCE* 1859–60, p. 249; C. L. Warr, *Principal Caird* (Clark, Edinburgh, 1926) p. 127; L. J. Saunders, *Scottish Democracy 1815–1840: the Social and Intellectual Background* (Edinburgh, 1950) p. 269.

108 *RCCE* 1862–3, p. 142.

109 *MCCE* 1855–6, p. 671.

110 *RCCE* 1859–60, p. 235.

111 *RCCE* 1861–2, p. 237; *RCCE* 1860–1 p. 226; *RCCE* 1863–4 p. 240.

112 G. King, *Modern Pauperism and the Scottish Poor Laws* (Murray, Aberdeen, 1871) p. 61; 'The practical teaching of cookery in board schools', *Educational News*, II, 27 October 1877, p. 531; H. Corr, 'The schoolgirls' curriculum and the ideology of the home, 1870–1914', in Glasgow Women's Studies Group, (ed.) *Uncharted Lives: Extracts from Scottish Women's Experiences, 1850–1982* (Pressgang, Glasgow, 1983) p. 81.

113 H. Corr, 'The schoolgirls' curriculum', pp. 74–97; E. T. M'Laren, *Recollections of the Public Work and Home Life of Louisa and Flora Stevenson* (Private publication Andrew Elliot, Edinburgh, 1914?); E. Miller, *Century of Change 1875–1975: One Hundred Years of Training Home Economics' Students in Glasgow* (Queen's College Glasgow, Glasgow, 1975); A. C. Geddes, *The Forging of a Family* (Faber and Faber, 1952) pp. 135–6. See also P. Blyth, 'An experiment in the practical training of domestic economy', *Life and Work*, I, September 1879, pp. 141–3. Flora Stevenson and Phoebe Blyth were members of the first Edinburgh School Board. The *Scotsman* had suggested training institutes for cookery should be established under a 'professor' in 1855.

114 Endowed Schools and Hospitals (Scotland) Commission, *Second Report* (PP., 1874, xvii) paras. 8473–5.

115 A. M. Milligan, *In Memoriam: William Milligan D. D.* (Aberdeen University Press, Aberdeen, 1894), pp. 25–6; MS., ADA, Aberdeen School Board Minutes 1873–6, 14 January and 13 May 1875.

116   *RCCE*, 1872–3, p. 255.
117   H. Corr, 'The schoolgirls' curriculum', p. 93; *Scotsman* 2 April 1874; M. Burton, 'Sewing in public schools', *TNAPSS 1880*, p. 495.
118   *RCCES* 1877–8, p. 211; Report by J. MacLeod, *RCCES* 1880–1.
119   SED, *Code of Regulations for the Day Schools of Scotland*, (PP., 1876) Article 21 (e); SED, *Education (Scotland) Reports*, (PP., 1878–9), p. 102.
120   *Educational News*, I, 14 October 1876 and 3, 26 October 1878; MS. ADA, Aberdeen School Board Minutes 1876–79, 9 November 1876, 8 February 1877, 14 December 1878. Greenock, Paisley, Govan, Perth and Dundee School Boards also petitioned the SED.
121   Ibid., 12 April 1877, 13 December 1877, 14 February 1878, 4 April 1879; 'The practical teaching of cookery in board schools', *Educational News*. For some of the subsequent developments at Aberdeen and Glasgow see R. A. Bayliss, op. cit., and E. Miller, op. cit., An account of the Glasgow School Board contains no reference to the subject, apart from one photograph (J. M. Roxburgh, *The School Board of Glasgow 1873–1919*) (University of London Press, 1971).
122   T. R. Bone, *School Inspection in Scotland 1840–1966* (University of London, 1968) p. 113.
123   Calculated from N. A. Wade, *Post-Primary Education in the Primary Schools of Scotland 1872–1936* (University of London Press, 1939) pp. 58, 60.
124   Ibid., p. 106.
125   SED, *Reports, &c., Issued in 1909–1910*, Section C, pp. 62–3 (quotation); section H, p. 17.
126   J. Scotland, *The History of Scottish Education*, 2 vols., (University of London Press, 1969) II, p. 57.
127   H. Corr, 'The schoolgirls' curriculum'; E. Miller, *Century of Change*, p. 27; A. Wright, *The History of Education and of the Old Parish Schools of Scotland* (Adams, Edinburgh, 1898) pp. 246–8.
128   SED, *Reports, &c., Issued in 1909–10*, Section B, pp. 49–50; Mrs Bannatyne, 'Teaching of Domestic Science: some practical aspects', *Educational News*, 12 July 1912; E. Fish, 'The interests of girls in elementary and continuation schools' in J. Clarke, *Problems of National Education*, pp. 76–100, esp. pp. 91–2.
129   M. Ogilvie Gordon, *On the Teaching of Girls* (Aberdeen University Press, Aberdeen, 1904) p. 12.
130   F. Melville, 'The education of women' in *The Position of Woman: Actual and Ideal* (J. Nisbet, 1911) pp. 118–34.
131   SED, *Reports, &c., Issued in 1909–10*, section C, pp. 60–1 (quotation), Section D, pp. 12–13.
132   R. D. Anderson, *Education and Opportunity in Victorian Scotland: Schools and Universities*, (Clarendon Press, Oxford, 1983) pp. 303–4, 312–5; University of Aberdeen, *Record of the Arts Class of 1902–1906* (Aberdeen, 1927). Of course allowance for the relative size of the different social classes shows the chance of such educational opportunities was heavily weighted against working-class girls.
133   H. Corr, 'The sexual division of labour in the Scottish teaching profession, 1872–1914' in W. M. Humes and H. Paterson (eds.), *Scottish Culture and Scottish Education 1800–1980* (John Donald,

Edinburgh, 1983) pp. 137–150. M. G. Clarke, *A Short Life of Ninety Years* (privately published, 1973) pp. 30–40.

134　Eg. C. Dyhouse, 'Good wives and little mothers: social anxieties and the schoolgirls' curriculum, 1890–1920', *Oxford Review of Education*, 3 (1), 1977, pp. 21–35; A. Turnbull, 'Learning her womanly work: the elementary school curriculum, 1870–1914' in F. Hunt (ed.), *Lessons for Life: the Schooling of Girls and Women 1850–1950* (Blackwell, Oxford, 1987) pp. 83–100; M. Gomersall, 'Ideals and realities: the education of working class girls, 1800–1870', *History of Education*, 17 (1), March 1988, pp. 37–53.

135　As the above works show, opposition did also occur in England.

SELECT BIBLIOGRAPHY

W. Anderson, *Female Education in Relation to the Wants of the Age* (Smith, King, Aberdeen, 1851).

'Annual Report to the General Assembly by the Committee – May 1859', *Home and Foreign Missionary Record of the Church of Scotland*, XIV, July 1859, pp. 147–54.

M. Bannatyne, 'Teaching of Domestic Science: some practical aspects', *Educational News*, 12 July 1912.

M. Burton, 'Sewing in public schools', *Transactions of the National Association for the Promotion of Social Science*, Edinburgh meeting, 1880, pp. 495–7.

G. Combe, 'On female education' in *Lectures on Popular Education; Delivered to the Edinburgh Philosophical Association in April and November 1833* (Machlachlan Stewart, Edinburgh; 3rd edition, 1848) pp. 50–60.

H. Corr, 'The schoolgirls' curriculum and the ideology of the home, 1870–1914' in Glasgow Women's Studies Group (ed.), *Uncharted Lives: Extracts from Scottish Women's Experiences, 1850–1982* (Pressgang, Glasgow, 1983) pp. 74–97.

'Education scheme. Annual Report to the General Assembly by the Committee. May 1860', *Home and Foreign Missionary Record of the Church of Scotland*, XV, July 1860, pp. 147–53.

E. Hamilton, *Hints Addressed to Patrons and Directors of Schools* (Longman, London, 1815).

L. Hope, 'Girls' schools', *Transaction of the National Association for the Promotion of Social Science*, Glasgow meeting, 1860, pp. 397–404.

F. Melville, 'The education of women' in *The Position of Woman; Actual and Ideal* (J. Nisbet, London, 1911), pp. 118–34.

E. Miller, *Century of Change 1875–1975; One Hundred Years of Training Home Economics Students in Glasgow* (Queen's College, Glasgow, 1875).

'The practical teaching of cookery in board schools', *Educational News*, II, 27 October 1877, p. 531.

D. F. Sandford, 'On female education and industrial training' in *Two Short Lectures* (R. Grant, Edinburgh; 1855), pp. 11–21.

'Second Annual Report of the Scottish Ladies' Association for Promoting Female Industrial Education in Scotland, for 1854', *Home and Foreign Missionary Record of the Church of Scotland*, X, May 1855, pp. 95–6.

3

FAMILY TIES: LADY CHILD-SAVERS AND GIRLS OF THE STREET 1850–1925

LINDA MAHOOD

By the late nineteenth century in Scottish industrial cities, as elsewhere in Britain, reform-minded men and women responded to the problem of juvenile criminality by establishing institutions for the control of the street children who were at risk of falling into crime. This period marks the earliest recognition of juvenile delinquency as a social rather than a penal problem; thus, young offenders were less likely to be seen simply as 'culpable criminals', than victims of bad families and parental neglect.

The language of class and gender was an integral part of this movement to save the street children. The idea that middle and upper-class 'ladies of culture'[2] had 'special qualifications' for the supervision of reformatory and industrial school children, especially girls, had wide public support among both feminists and anti-feminists.[3] Many women, influenced by evangelicalism saw their philanthropic work among delinquent girls as a sacred duty. 'Be we married or not, we women can influence the little children', a titled woman from Edinburgh wrote. 'If every woman in this country would take one family and look after them and bring them and themselves to Christ's feet, we should have a better and happier world'.[4] Women's child-saving activities were justified by the traditional 'women's sphere' argument and the belief that women's innate moral superiority could be put to social use.[5] It was simply assumed that these ladies would grace the 'homes of the underprivileged in the same way they graced their own homes'.[6]

In contrast to this rather stereotypical view of the Victorian 'Lady Bountiful', not all of these women were volunteers and their activities were not limited to Bible reading and fund raising. A great many earned their livelihood, as superintendents, teachers and social workers in those institutions which provided an outlet for the growing middle-class female labour force. Drawing inspiration from leading philanthropists like Elizabeth Fry, local branches of Fry's British Ladies' Society for Promoting the Reformation of Female Prisoners were formed in Edinburgh, Glasgow, Aberdeen, Greenock and Perth, and rescue homes for 'fallen' women and wayward girls were established. Many of these institutions joined Mary Carpenter's Reformatory and Refuge Union and some were certified as industrial schools and reformatories in the 1850s. Indeed, work within the child-saving agencies was a step out of women's traditional role and a way into the 'public' sphere for many middle-class women. Edinburgh's Mrs Duncan McLaren, who had marched with Fry through the gaols of Newgate, argued that it was the 'imperative duty of women to become informed of the state of society in order that they might stand on the defensive against the inroads of immorality'.[7]

THE RESIDENTIAL AND DAY SCHOOL SYSTEM

According to Michael Ignatieff, a new social history of the institution has begun to be written. This is a history about 'living battles of the confined against their suffering, and about the new professional classes [who] tied their social assent to the new institutions'. The challenge for this new history is to think of the institution as 'a social system of dominance and resistance, ordered by complex rituals of exchange and communication'.[8] Following Ignatieff, this chapter will examine the familialist ideology which was embedded in these institutions and working class reaction to middle-class women's child-saving initiatives. It will be argued that the regime of moral reform in residential and day schools was based on a bourgeois model of the 'ideal' proletarian family culture and class-specific ideologies of girlhood and femininity.

Three inter-related statutory institutions for children under 16 were established by the late nineteenth century and brought under the Children Act in 1904: industrial schools, reformatories and day industrial schools. These schools provided an 'alternative to the imprisonment of children, rather than ending it'.[9] Industrial schools were established under the Industrial Schools Act (1854). They gave magistrates the power to send children under 14 found begging, wandering, homeless or otherwise neglected by their parents to an industrial school until the age of 18. In 1866 detention was extended to first offenders under 12, and so kept them out of prison. Children between 12 and 16 convicted for offences punishable in the case of an adult by penal servitude or imprisonment, were sent to reformatories under the Youthful Offender Acts (1854) where they could be detained until the age of 19. Between 1854 and 1893 offenders first had to complete a fourteen-day prison term so links continued with the ordinary prison system. It was argued that the only difference between reformatory children and industrial school children was that the latter were 'caught younger'.[10] Inmates in these residential schools were required to undergo at least eighteen months' incarceration and be 14 years old and hopefully to have reached the third standard in school before they were eligible for the parole system called 'licensing'.

It was felt that the Education Act (1870), which made school attendance compulsory and authorised the creation of school boards, could be used for the 'saving of young children from parental neglect'. Officers were appointed to round up truants between 6 and 14 and bring them before the court. Non-residential day industrial schools were established in Glasgow by amending the 1866 Act and the Glasgow Juvenile Delinquency Act (1878). The power to establish such schools in the rest of Scotland was given under the Day Industrial Schools Act (1893). These schools were totally under the management of women and intended for children whose parents who could not ensure their children's attendance at school and for truants.[11] Attendance was compulsory and the students were confined to the school from 6 am to 6 pm. Many children were sent to these schools who in former days would have been sent to residential schools. Conversely, children could be sent to residential schools for misbehaving in day schools.

THE LADY BOUNTIFUL AND THE SUBVERSIVE FAMILY

Throughout the nineteenth century industrialisation brought increasing wealth and prosperity to middle-class homes. Bolstered up by strong kinship networks, the middle-class family emerged with a new self-confidence. Aspiring to inclusion in the governing strata they were eager to insert themselves into the 'public gaze' through a myriad of religious, philanthropic and scientific societies.[12] This climate gave rise to the familialist ideology (the autonomous nuclear family unit, headed by a male breadwinner, supported by his domesticated and nurturant wife), known in its Victorian form as the doctrine of 'separate spheres': the notion that 'women's role should be exclusively within the domestic sphere', became the normative ideal for many middle-class families.

In stark contrast, the working-class family did not weather the industrial revolution nearly so well. Middle-class familial ideology bore little, if any, relation to the realities of life for the urban poor. Waves of immigration had dislocated traditional kin networks and left poor families to struggle with new problems: slum living, disease, overcrowding and unsteady wages, with no external support. This made it extremely difficult for poor families to combine long hours of employment with the care and nurture of their younger members, and parental supervision for children over the age of 12 was unlikely.[13] The working-class family was still very much an economic unit and its continued survival depended on the financial contribution of all members. At very young ages girls were expected to work outside their homes and the pennies they earned babysitting, running messages and errands, street-selling, or doing small jobs in local businesses and factories contributed to the family coffers. Like boys, poor girls roamed the streets searching for combustible, edible or saleable booty.[14] This contradicted the ideology of familialism and aroused indignation and pity among middle-class observers. Reflecting their own beliefs and experience of childhood as a time of innocent pleasure, lady child-savers were united in the belief that children, particularly girls, belonged under the protective arm of their families.

For them, the 'purity of the home was understood in terms of its difference to the immorality and danger of the street'.[15] It was feared these girls would soon 'be "on the street", not just in it'.[16] As the editor of Edinburgh's *North Britain* wrote:

> These girls are the young recruits who are continually swelling the ranks of our Old Town prostitution. As the little boy ties his toy-sword to his side and sighs for the day on which he will be able to enlist as a soldier, so do these little girls study to imitate the prostitute, as they sigh for the day on which they will, like her, have money to spend. They look forward and upward to the time when they will enter their teens and walk the streets like those whom they envy.[17]

In their effort to determine the causes of female delinquency, lady child-savers focused on the conditions of family life among the very poor, which at best they regarded as overcrowded and dirty, and at worst notorious for the promiscuous mixing of the sexes, which was regarded as producing the next generation of drunkards, paupers, child-deserters, thieves and prostitutes. It was assumed that girls growing up under these conditions were in constant danger of falling into crime. According to a female parish inspector in Glasgow:

> If the girl lives in a squalid overcrowded slum dwelling, with its unwholesome conditioning where the common decencies of life can scarcely be carried out . . . where the children have been allowed to remain out to all hours in dark, ill-lit closes and stairs, where the father of the family bets and drinks, not to mention the mother doing the same, then I say, the girl would hardly be human if she did not fall prey to temptation.[18]

Girls 'at risk' were readily identifiable by their defiant and 'unfeminine' behaviours: going to the pictures, dancing, listening to gramophones, flirting with boys, staying out late, and associating with older girls of questionable reputation. The evil result of allowing girls to sell news-papers and other items in the streets was said 'often to lead directly to prostitution'.[19] They accepted that few street girls were actually criminals but just 'acting upon the only education they had received from vicious parents'.[20] Not guilty then, but not innocent either, the girls in this study (similar institutions existed for boys but they operated on a separate model of reform) required incarceration and rehabilitation in special schools rather than prisons. According to the superintendent of Chapelton Girls' Reformatory, a reformatory was 'a very good place for any girl criminal or not'.[21]

The statistics on the charges under which the 283 girls were incarcer-ated in Scottish residential schools in 1894, produced for the 1896 Select Committee, supports the view that these girls were not serious offenders. Only 2 per cent of the industrial school girls were committed for theft (7.3 per cent of boys) and 69 per cent of the reformatory girls had no previous record at all. This is of particular interest when compared to the reformatory boys' statistics. Only 18 per cent of the boys were first offenders and 66.6 per cent had already had two previous convictions. This suggests that girls were treated more harshly than boys – they were taken up more quickly and sent to reformatories for first offences.[22]

While reformatory girls were all over 12 years of age and the majority had been convicted of a criminal offence, industrial school girls were generally incarcerated for begging (12 per cent); wandering (58.7 per cent); as homeless or orphaned (14.5 per cent); uncontrollable at home (2.8 per cent); frequenting the company of thieves (3.2 per cent), residing in brothels or with prostitutes (4.8 per cent).[23] More girls than boys were taken up for wandering, destitution, and residing in brothels and as stated above for first offences. Furthermore 78 per cent of the industrial school girls were under 12, whereas only 68 per cent of the boys were, which suggests that industrial school girls were on average younger than the boys.[24] As Schlossman and Wallach point out, '[t]his so called chivalrous attitude leads to earlier intervention and longer periods of supervision' for girls who are seen as especially 'vulnerable to evil and temptations.'[25]

There is a darker side to the high proportion of girls committed for 'wandering' that cannot be ignored, which also explains why residential care was favoured over day industrial schools or evening curfews to keep children off the streets. Linda Gordon argues that the patriarchal authority structure of the nuclear family expects girls to be dependent, obedient and sexually pure until marriage. Girls were expected to stay home and obey their father, submitting to his will and protection.[26] This presented a double bind for girls who could not stay at home. Frances Hepburn of the Scottish National Society for the Prevention of Cruelty to Children (SNSPCC) explained that many girls who had been 'afraid to remain in the house alone with the father at home . . . contracted the habit of wandering.'[27] The society recommended that such girls be sent to industrial schools. An examination of the Maryhill Girls' Industrial School register in Glasgow between 1914–16 and 1920–25 indicates that 'wandering' was a convenient category for a variety of 'unspeakable' forms of physical and sexual abuse. These little girls were described in the admission books as 'shockingly neglected', 'verminous' and 'badly knocked about', which explains why 8, 9 and 10 year-old girls would prefer staying out all night, roaming cold dark streets and sleeping rough on stairs or in toilets, rather than return to their homes.

The Maryhill girls' register suggests that concern about incest was only alluded to by reference to the number of beds in the house and the SNSPCC did not record such cases in their widely circulated annual reports.[28] When Helen McDonald (13) was picked up for wandering it was recorded in the register that her house had only 'one bed in a single apartment for two grown up girls and a son (20) . . . the moral upbringing was very much against [Helen] getting a chance in life.' The case notes on other girls are fairly explicit about family violence. Nevertheless, the women continually committed these girls for wandering, which implicates them in the conspiracy of silence that other writers have argued has historically surrounded sexual abuse and family violence, thus keeping it 'the best kept secret'.[30]

> Jane Peterson (13) and Mary Brown (6) [step-sisters]. Father in Duke Street Prison charged with incest. The stepdaughter has not been to school since December owing to parents' behaviour. He was out of late drinking very heavily. The family lived in a one-room house, and the girls slept with their father.[31]

> Betty Scott (13). The mother is dead. The father is of drunken habits. An older sister was admitted to Stobhill recently. She is pregnant and her brother 18 years of age is responsible for her condition. He has been apprehended on a charge of incest. The girl is 16 years of age. The two girls with the brother and father occupied the one bed. The father says he did this because of the cold weather.[32]

> Mary Thompson (10). The girl was today discharged from hospital where she was under treatment for gonorrhoea. Allegations are made by her that the stepfather had assaulted her on different occasions.[33]

It must be emphasised that the inmates of girls' institutions were not primarily victims of physical or sexual abuse. The total population never amounted to more than a fraction at any given time, but these examples have been used to illustrate the contradiction of familialist ideology. The incest taboo was as strongly held in the nineteenth century as in any other period. It was punishable by the death penalty in Scotland until 1887.[34] Its violation 'suggested disease at the heart of what Victorians regarded as essential to the moral, religious, social harmony of their society: the virtuous Christian family.'[35] Gordon argues that historically society has dealt with the problem by shifting the locus of sexual abuse outside the home, thus letting the fathers and male relatives off the hook, but not mothers.[36] Evidence suggests that this was the case in late Victorian Scotland, both in public discussion and in the manner in which admissions to individual institutions were made in private. Between 1920 and 1925, 18 per cent of the girls in Maryhill had been found living in brothels. Although the school treated these girls as 'at risk' and was reticent about calling them 'prostitutes', it had no such reservations about their mothers. In fact, girls were frequently incarcerated because their mothers (and sometimes aunts and sisters) were said to be generally unfit prostitutes, brothel-keepers, drunkards, immoral, mentally deficient, cohabiting with men, having too many illegitimate children or illegal abortions, possessing criminal inclinations or carrying venereal disease. It was argued that whenever girls went 'wrong' the mother was to blame. According to a female parish inspector, 'mothers have a mistaken idea that ignorance is innocence and leave the matter at that'.

Very often when a mother is spoken to after her girl has gone wrong, the answer one gets is, 'but I did not know'. I feel I would like to punish every woman who says 'I do not know', when she is asked where her girl or boy goes in the evenings.[37]

According to Gordon, when family violence moves outside the home, victims of abuse are changed into delinquents and abusers became strangers and 'dirty old men'.[38] This logic is observable in Scotland in 1911 where public attention was focused on juvenile prostitution, a phenomenon that was safely outside the home. This climate supported conferences on 'Social Evil' in Glasgow and 'Public Morals' in Edinburgh. The publication of the Lock Hospital statistics by Mrs Maitland Ramsey, MD, the surgeon of the hospital, revealed that thirty-four girls under 16 had been admitted for venereal disease in Glasgow alone.[39] The shock resulted in the formation of the Glasgow branch of the National Vigilance Association (NVA). Mrs James T. Hunter, founding member and Lock Hospital director, predicted that, 'many of them, when assaulted as children, grow up to be dissolute women.'[40]

Exposés of casual sex, street-corner boys, parental neglect and female precocity produced by the Scottish Council for Women's Trades at their Glasgow conference revealed that the brassy and unremorseful 15-year-old laundress quoted below, was typical of many of the independent working-class girls who spent their evenings flirting with boys and listening to gramophones in the Italian ice-cream parlours.

> I am sure it was A.B. I got the trouble from, as he had connection with me on a Thursday night, and on the following night, he had connection with my chum . . . A week afterwards, we both felt something wrong. We both bathed ourselves with Condy's fluid. She got better, but I got worse, and was not able to walk. . . . [My grandmother] got the doctor to examine me, and he sent me to the Lock Hospital. I never importuned on the streets, and I did not get money from any of the lads.[41]

The council concluded that these ice-cream shops were the 'first pubs' for boys and girls:[42] 'they were the dens from which boys learned to gamble and steal and girls exchanged their "virtue" with soldiers for 'chocolate, trumpery scarves [and] cheap jewellery.'[43]

For the most part it was the sexual precocity that these independent working-class girls displayed that was the greatest source of anxiety and alarm. It was believed that early sexual experience (abuse or seduction) led to prostitution. Maryhill girl Lizzy Dunlop (13) was found going to 'picture houses and begging money from men.'[44] Hannah Montrose (age 11) let a man take her 'to the pictures and kept her out late at night.'[45] Sarah Walters (age 13), and her friend Joan McCall, (13, also) 'were found frequenting the banks of the Clyde where they were meeting men who gave them money for immoral purposes.'[46] These cases presented a problem because they were not passive victims; they had not been drugged or duped and seduced by strangers but willingly entered into relationships with men of their own choice. The challenge then was to catch girls 'at risk' early and to channel them into an appropriate regime of moral rehabilitation in reformatories or industrial schools, depending on their age.

MORAL REFORM: 'AS LITTLE MAIDS IN ANY MAN'S HOUSE'

Veronica Beechey argues that familialist ideology may be 'reproduced through social institutions either directly, through overt proclamations, or indirectly, through institutional ritual and practices'; consequently familialist ideology can be embedded in seemingly non-familial institutions,[47] such as residential and day schools for delinquent girls. According to the testimonies of the women to the parliamentary commissions, traditional feminine responsibilities and values could be taught to girls outside the structure of the nuclear family. It was assumed that girls would learn these roles by emulating the ladies who governed the schools. Therefore as much attention was paid to the character of the women who ruled the institutions as to the inmates' characters. It was stressed that they be women of 'a social class superior to [the inmates] own mothers',[48] as they would mould inmates in their own image and thus 'the wrong done in the home'[49] would be corrected. For example the servants' quarters in the Glasgow Girls' House of Refuge were placed far from the girls' dormitories, otherwise 'there is needless temptation to their mixing with the domestic servants.'[50] The Home Office criticised many schools where the 'instructors were really people of the domestic servant class and therefore of a very rough and ready character'.[51]

The state stood *in loco parentis* to these girls and was obligated to fulfil the duties and responsibilities which the law imposed on parents as to the education and employment of their children Moreover, new 'scientific' studies of criminology documented a connection between crime and illiteracy and it was hoped that a general education would raise a girl's intellectual faculties and increase her ability to judge between right and wrong and to resist temptation.[52] The Act of Parliament for industrial schools also stipulated that industrial training be provided. The Act relating to reformatories, however, did not, but the general model rules required industrial training for both schools and stipulated four to six hours a day for reformatories and no less than four hours a day for industrial schools.[53] With this much time devoted to the classroom and the rest of the day partitioned out to industrial work, there was little time for more than the 3Rs and housewifery.

Girls under 10 received full-time schooling under Section 5 of the Education Act (1878). This did not mean that they did no industrial work. Light occupations, such as polishing boots, were encouraged to 'keep them from idleness and weariness during the hours not devoted to school or to drill or play.'[54] Girls between 10 and 14 were educated on the 'half-time system' which ensured them four hours' secular instruction daily until they passed the third standard. The school day was divided between early morning and late afternoon, the middle of the day being devoted to industrial labour. Girls entering these institutions were described as extremely 'backward'. To the statement: 'bees make honey', a Chapelton girl responded: 'That's not true, mum. The bumble bee makes nae honey; it is John Buchanan that makes honey in his factory.' Her matron explained that 'some [girls] could neither read nor write', but added, 'they have a fine command of language of a certain kind.'[55] Nevertheless, after the age of 14 little attention was paid to education. The lady Home Office inspector recommended that girls, regardless of their education level 'concentrate on domestic matters because she was very likely to earn her living by housework.'[56]

Talk of motherhood and sisterly feelings aside, however, the lady child-savers seldom approached the girls as anything other than potential agents of domesticity: future maids or mothers.[57] The lady Home Office Inspector explained that it 'is the natural thing for the girls to care for the house.'[58] While it was hoped that inmates would shake off their 'low class' taint by restricted access to their families, no Eliza Doolittles would be found in these residential schools. It was not intended that inmates rise above their station. Cameron testified that 'there are certain limitations to our work and our powers. We cannot turn out a refined child.'[59] The matron at the Girls' House of Refuge refused to teach crocheting or fancy work: 'It unfits for more useful occupation, and has a dissipating tendency upon the mind.'[60] Hunter-Craster claimed that she would not dream of 'training [inmates] as clerks, typewriters, and that sort of thing . . . It would not be possible to make a highly-paid governess out of a reformatory girl.'[61] She mocked a male inspector's suggestion that she teach decimal fractions and geometry to Chapelton reformatory girls.

> I said I would be quite pleased to teach them how to boil a potato in the time they were teaching geometry; we had so much arrears to make up in training on domestic things and decent habits, and to lead them to a better way of living. [Many a] good wife had existed who did not know how to read very well. Many a good mother had admirably brought up a family without any great literary knowledge.[62]

Industrial training focused on housework, laundry and sewing. It was intended to 'drive home the fundamental importance of cleanliness and order.' According to Lady Griselda Cheape 'the first moral medicine is "discipline" . . . Washing is good, it gives regular work and teaches cleanliness of body and soul.'[63] Some schools ran large full service laundries, others did laundry for neighbouring boys' institutions, while others did only their own. Sheets, blankets and uniforms gave girls experience in 'rough work', and 'fine work' experience was gained doing personal laundry for the staff. It was recognised that this practice would not prepare inmates for high wage work in commercial laundries, but they could begin as 'little maids in any man's house.'[64] At the age of 12 girls were also introduced to the needle by mending their own clothing in order to prepare them for the important task of making an outfit for service. The younger girls knit hosiery for the institution. In some schools girls received small wages for their labour and this money was kept in a bank account for them so that they would learn the value of honest labour, thrift and financial management skills.

The plan of the day industrial schools was not compatible with much industrial training. Nevertheless the time not devoted to elementary school, drill, recreation and meals was filled by girls cleaning, washing, cooking and other work of the house.[65] Critics of this system complained that it subjected girls to excessive drudgery, scrubbing and rough work. In mixed-sex schools the girls were often made to do the work for the boys which encroached on their education time.[66] As a former student of Rose Street Day School recalls:

> When you got to be 12 the girls were taught how to keep house . . . Taught to clean, taught to work, to scrub . . . During the afternoon after you came 12, we had a place down underneath the kitchen . . . peeled potatoes by the pail, for your dinner . . . We didn't encourage cleaners . . . we did most of the cleaning . . . if you peeled so many pails of potatoes . . . you got half a slice of bread.[67]

It was believed to be in the 'moral interest' of the older girls to have little girls in the school to mother. In industrial schools were the girls ranged in age from 6 to 15 the older girls appointed to look after the little ones.[68] In reformatories like Chapelton, where the girls were over 14, former inmates now married were encouraged to bring their babies to the school. The advantage of having former inmates back to show off their tidy clothes and healthy babies was that 'really nice old girls coming about the school as a success themselves, talk to the girls and reason with them, and thus they form ideals'.[69] The superintendent, herself a trained nurse, instructed inmates in physiology and health nursing and bandaging techniques. She explained that the girls were 'very good to each other when they are sick.' By nursing each other they would acquire

> a knowledge they will carry with them in after life. They will forget the poetry or the grammar they learn, but they will not forget the bandaging, and the attention, and the poultice-making, that they do in a practical lesson with me.[70]

SUBSTITUTIONARY SUFFERING: LEARNING TO CONFORM

In practice the atmosphere of the school was not so loving or nurturant. Although they were intended to be non-penal institutions many relics of their penal ancestry survived, and inmates were watched as they would have been in prison.[71] The use of corporal punishment had decreased by the mid-century, but the new lighted and ventilated isolation rooms merely replaced the dark old cells. New approaches to punishment and elaborate systems of positive reinforcement and behaviour modification replaced older 'faster' forms, but were no less cruel or humiliating to children than five lashes with a leather strap.

In 1857, the matron introduced a somewhat sadistic system of justice into the Glasgow Girls' House of Refuge. Under her system of 'substitutionary suffering' girls who misbehaved were sent before a disciplinary tribunal of their peers. In one case a girl was judged 'guilty of striking a companion'; and two inmates were selected from among seventy volunteers to 'suffer the punishment in her stead'. According to the matron 'such discipline has a most salutary influence. Substitutionary suffering in another appeals to the better feelings, and moves deeply and with greater lasting effect than personal pain would.'[72]

Two generations of Maryhill superintendents used positive reinforcement in their schools. In 1896 the 'good girls' under Mrs Cameron could be distinguished from 'bad girls' by their red and blue hair ribbons. Bad girls wore brown hair ribbons.[73] In 1914, Catherine Dow maintained that a good system of merit marks and rewards (umbrellas for older girls and dolls and beads for younger), backed up by minor punishments such as food deprivation, made corporal punishment unnecessary. She reserved the right, however, to use isolation (not in excess of three days) for outbursts of bad temper.[74] Neither Cameron nor Dow objected to sending unmanageable girls to reformatories, where they could be kept longer.

The level of discipline varied greatly from school to school and it was more likely to reflect the individual superintendent's management style than any Home Office rules. The matron of Chapelton reformatory believed strongly in the preventative powers of whipping. She argued that many of the inmates were from abusive homes or transfers from other abusive institutions and simply did not understand anything else. Ironically, she found it justifiable to replicate the parental behaviour that so many child-savers found reprehensible in the girl's parents. In 1895, thirty-six out of thirty-nine Chapelton girls had been whipped ('on the hand mostly'). 'Thoroughly bad' girls, however, were taken to bed and stripped and beaten: 'I have a girl to hold her hands while she is being whipped' the matron revealed.[75]

Girls were usually kept in industrial schools and day schools until they were 14 and in reformatories until they were 16. Residential school pupils were then put on probation, or 'licensed out' as it was known, to a prearranged employment usually in domestic service. They were not technically free until their licences expired at the age of 18. Under the power of the 1891 Acts, children could be released without concurrence of their parents. The only exception, if it was an exception, was in cases of emigration, where the Secretary of State was required to consult with the parents, but their objections were not necessarily taken into consideration.[76] One Maryhill superintendent confessed that she seldom emigrated orphans. 'A child who is an orphan is very much easier floated at home . . . I only send out girls, as a rule, who have drawbacks in the way of bad friends.'[77] The law prohibited parents from inducing a child to escape licence and children who ran away were taken into custody when caught. By common law a parent was not entitled to claim control of a son after 14 years of age and a daughter after 16, so by the time a child was free of custodial care the parent had no legal right to interfere with her placement.[78]

The purpose of the licence was to give the child an opportunity to readjust to the community. In the case of an industrial school girl who had been in the school since the age of 6 or 7 this was a major adjustment. Dr Anne Watson, one of the most vocal critics of residential schools, argued that these schools did very little to prepare girls for the trials of life, consequently they were hopelessly 'ignorant of the ways of the world'. She recalled 'girls who have taken their wages to the women they were staying with after leaving the Industrial School and saying "How much is that?"'[79] The licence was also insurance against the interference of disruptive parents. Girls out on licence were regularly visited by the superintendent. It was intended that by the time her licence expired the inmate would be too settled in her work to abandon it to return home to 'parents, uncertain futures, and bad environments.'[80]

In essence, it was hoped that under the watchful eye and maternal guidance of the matron girls would learn to become little mothers and care-givers. According to Hunter-Craster, girls were considered to be morally reformed when they had 'learned to be of use to somebody.'[81] As future maids or mothers reformed girls fulfilled three functions; they would provide domestic help for middle-class women, they would make suitable wives for lower class men and be able to train their own families, and finally, they would serve as role models to other women of their class. Central to the regime of moral reform was the expansion of working-class women's domestic role. Reformed women would see themselves as more than contributors to the family economy through their paid work, but also as the true source of family emotional support and comfort.[82] As true agents of domesticity, reformed girls would lead working men home off the street and out of the pubs and more into line with their own masculine roles as fathers and husbands.[83] As a Scottish clergyman wrote:

> I feel persuaded that one of the best methods of making the allurements and excitements of the public house less attractive to the hard-wrought artisan . . . is to increase the attractions of his fireside by educating 'helps meet for him', instead of the tawdry, thriftless, ignorant wives that are too commonly met with.[84]

The lady child-savers were confident that respectability was within the grasp of any girls who could learn self-control, discipline, and above all chastity. The stigma of her reformatory past need not hold her back, but just to be sure, Hunter-Craster instructed her girls not to tell others where they had been, but she did advise them, 'in every case to tell their husbands before getting married.'[85] Regarding their after-care, the Secretary of State required the schools to keep in touch with inmates for three years following their release and the hospitality of the schools remained available to girls who continued to live respectably. The SNSPCC recognised that the regime of the schools did not enable all women to escape the cycle of poverty and they dealt with a significant number of infants whose teenage mothers had been through the system.[86] The SNSPCC established Social Schemes, Mothers' Meetings and Girls' Clubs to assist poor young mothers 'to struggle on'. They held Baby Competitions, with prizes for well-kept babies[87] and Home Employment Schemes for mothers:

> The object . . . is to keep the mothers more in their own homes during their spare time, which is so apt to be spent hanging about the closes gossiping with their neighbours . . . a great temptation to fall back into their former bad habits – and to give them some wholesome interest to occupy their minds, [piecework sewing] so that they may feel that by their own industry they can add a little to the husband's weekly wages.[88]

WORKING-CLASS REACTION: THANKFUL FOR THE HELP?

The state separated children 'at risk' from their parents on the grounds that their homes were intolerable, but the statistics placed before the parliamentary commissions in 1896 and 1914 indicate that almost 30 per cent of the inmates had to be returned home again after their detention because superintendents were unable to find suitable employment for them. It was also recorded with resounding disappointment that the majority of those for whom employment was secured returned home the minute their licence expired. The reason for this in the institution's view was 'parental interference'.[89] Obviously the children did not perceive the 'danger' in the same way their 'would-be-protectors did'.[90] The superintendents admitted that many of the girls were lonely and 'long for home'.[91] The failure to break down strong family ties deeply disturbed the child-savers. They regarded the affection these girls had for their parents as pathological. They could not make sense of this affection within the framework of their own cultural milieu, nor understand why it was so difficult to destroy.

In order to examine this contradiction more closely we must examine the role of the girls and their families in the incarceration process. Beginning with the families, Ignatieff argues that the poor 'were not passive victims and objects of the law: they used it for their purposes if they could.'[92] As M. A. Crowther's study of English workhouses reveals, 'the poor were suspicious of institutions, but nevertheless supported them: new hospital beds were filled as soon as possible; pressure on asylums and charitable homes continued to grow.'[93] In contradiction to her contemporaries' suspicions that the poor purposefully neglected their children in order to qualify them for industrial schools, Hepburn of the SNSPCC stressed that there was a 'certain amount of affection, even in the worst homes'.

> It is really quite surprising. When you look at the way in which many of them treat their children, or in some cases not actually ill-treat them but neglect them, you wonder at the amount of affection there seems to be underneath it, especially on the children's side.[94]

She also revealed that many parents 'greatly objected to their children being sent to the industrial schools,'[95] but in desperation many realised that it was best for the child. According to Hunter of the NVA, 'the position varies very much. Some parents would be thankful for the help, and others prefer to look after them themselves.'[96]

Evidence suggests that in a brave effort to 'protect them from the cruelty of others'[97] it was frequently the mothers and fathers who initiated their daughters' admittance into these institutions. In 1920 Lizzy Fuller's mother, whom the Maryhill Girls' register describes as a 'drunk' took her dirty, verminous little girls down to the police station and reported that someone had been sexually assaulting Lizzy's sister. Little came of the case, but 6 year-old Lizzy was placed in Maryhill Industrial School until she was 16 years old, and thus protected from an environment which her own mother recognised as unsafe.[98] People used these institutions in times of need, as a former day industrial school girl explains.

> We lost my mother and my daddy had to work and he was so independent he wouldn't leave us running around for neighbours to look after us . . . He found out about this school and he went down and inquired about it on his own.[99]

It is now recognised that the Victorian poor developed a variety of survival strategies that were incomprehensible to middle-class observers to cope with poverty, unemployment, illness and death. Bettina Bradbury argues that '[s]ome, when the future seemed particularly bleak and impossible, gave up their children' temporarily or permanently to kin, orphanages, and other institutions, 'taking them back again when the crisis passed or when they were old enough to work.'[100] Contrary to the child-saver's expectations that incarceration would destroy the family tie, the longer term consequence of this strategy actually favoured the survival of individual families. This does not mean that the residential and day school systems 'developed consensual support' among the working class, but that the problem of child welfare 'was a process in which state, ruling class and dominated classes participated.'[101]

The residential and day school systems and child protection agencies

worked on two levels: to break apart families in trouble, and, in cases
where the family was still functioning, it served as a (symbolic) reminder
of bourgeois child-rearing expectations.[102] Hepburn observed that the
SNSPCC had 'a certain amount of weight and good deal of influence with
parents'; and she used this power as a means of enforcing her will on
them. '[S]ometimes, if they give trouble, they are simply referred to the
[temporary] shelter, and they do not give any further trouble after they
have paid one visit there'.[103] She recognised that people feared the society.
Its inspectors were consequently very well received into the homes of the
poor'.

> Those that really want to do better look upon our inspectors as
> friends, and especially the women inspectors, and they welcome
> them to their homes . . . Of course, those who do not wish to do well
> receive us because they are afraid of us.[104]

In addition to fear of the SNSPCC there was widespread fear of the Parish
Inspector, as a Glasgow woman who grew up on the parish in the early
twentieth century recollects. Her mother would treat the family to
sausages on Thursdays, the day she received her money. 'He'd [the
inspector] be up at the house, saying, "You're living high to day!"'

> 'Well' [mother says], 'if I can't give my family a bloody decent meal
> when I get my money I'm a poor mother'. That's the words she
> used to him . . . you see they kept tabs on ya . . . It was just the way
> of liven then. Oh they had a lot of power over ya, they could take
> your children off you . . . They could take them, quite simple and
> [put them] in a home'.[105]

The day industrial school girl quoted above recalls that it was just this
fear that led her father to enrol her at the age of 9 and her 11-year-old
sister in the industrial day school after her mother's death in 1927.

> that is why my father put us in the school, '[if I don't] they will take
> my weans' off me' . . . So he put us in that school . . . Oh aye, he was
> worried, he didn't want his family sent away fa him . . . if he had
> went to his work, and left us running about the street, and no doubt
> somebody would have reported it, and they'd have went down and
> said 'Well you'er workin and cannae look after them' and take
> them away . . . They would take you quicker then than they would
> do now.[106]

These parents would have been regarded as ideal by the child-savers, as
they appeared to have adopted family-centred values and priorities. For
those with children in residential care, compliance with the institution's
wishes was often the only guarantee they had of continued contact with
their children. One superintendent confessed that she used parental behaviour on monthly visiting days as a test of a parent's suitability. 'If the
parents are good', she remarked, 'I always let them know about [the
licence], but if they are bad I do not.'[107]

Regarding the inmates' own desire to return to their families upon release, we must return to Ignatieff's assertion that the institution must be conceptualised as a social system of dominance and resistance ordered by complex rituals of exchange and communication. The interaction between middle-class women in the institution and the girls themselves demonstrate this resistance. As we have seen, the child-savers were bound by various gender, class and familialist ideologies and various beliefs about what constituted both appropriate work for working-class women and what constituted ideal family relations. Their approach to dealing with the problem of delinquent girls reflected their middle-class beliefs and their own experience of girlhood. Unlike middle-class girls who enjoyed leisure and the protection of a well-appointed family circle far into their 20s, working-class girls were expected to be wage earners at an early age.[108] Williamson argues that the 'conception of passive womanhood' espoused in these institutions was totally alien to lower-class inmates. 'It had no relationship to girls accustomed to a free, independent childhood.'[109] Domestic service was looked upon as the best means of rescuing girls from their plight, yet the statistics for 1912 revealed that of the sixty-five reformatory girls released between 1909 and 1911 only half were in regular employment in 1912. Watson recognised that domestic service was not a realistic option for all girls. She testified that there were a certain number of Aberdeen inmates who were not fit for it. 'They drift to the mills, or become what is known in Aberdeen as fish girls.'[110] A former student at Rose Street Day Industrial School recalled that she could not go into service, although her younger sister did, because her mother needed her wages. Hepburn claimed that many girls refused to go into service. 'Girls nowadays very much prefer to go to work and have their evenings free.'[111]

There was also resistance within the child-saving movement itself. Some middle-class women objected to certain institutional practices and women's part in them. For many conservative and radical men and women alike, women's reform activities were justified by the traditional 'women's sphere' argument.[112] As early as 1843, feminist opposition to the notion of 'women's sphere' could be heard. Edinburgh's Marion Reid wrote 'Let us hear no more of female influence, as if it were an equivalent to the rights which man possesses; for the possession of those rights, far from annihilating man's influence, gives it tenfold weight.'[113] At the parliamentary commission in 1886, Miss Mary Burton came forward and testified: 'My views are that these industrial schools do no good whatever to the children. . . . I think the children are none the better, but a good deal worse.'[114] Flora Stevenson used her testimony in 1886 to get sexual politics on to the public agenda. She demanded women's right to sit on the management boards of certified industrial schools and Hunter-Craster used the occasion of her testimony in 1914 to demand equal pay for female matrons and superintendents.[115] Most seriously, Dr Anne Watson, medical inspector of Aberdeen Female School, lost her job, a position she had held for ten years, because of her damaging testimony in 1914. She revealed that 'the girls we send out at 16 years of age to farm situations in the country are rather knocked about, and the result is a considerable amount of immorality . . . There is a ladies' committee, and I have spoken to them about it, but they all seem to shirk the difficulty.'[116]

CONCLUSION

It is obvious that no simple class and gender dichotomies can be drawn in this analysis of the child-saving agencies. Dominance and resistance can be observed at all levels. Middle-class child-savers united against working-class parents in an effort to protect working-class girls 'at risk' from the dangerous streets and in some cases their own homes. Working-class parents were not passive participants in the process. As one sociologist has recently pointed out, the Scottish poor 'knew perfectly well what was wrong with their existence.' Nobody in their 'right mind *wanted* to live in a slum tenement.'[117] He argues that tenement life has to be understood dialectically.

> The good and the bad, the progressive and the reactionary, the humour and the tears, the struggle and the defeat, the courage and the cowardice, the slum and the palace, were part and parcel of the same phenomenon. Virtue and evil co-existed in the tenements: they faced each other across a landing.[118]

At times poor women and men recognised that certain family members or neighbours might cause problems and they developed a variety of strategies to deal with these problems and to keep their children safe. Thus many of them also united against their own neighbours to protect their daughters from dangerous situations, even if it meant the 'temporary' loss of the child.By focusing on the dangers of the street, the child-savers used these institutions as an attempt not only to protect girls but to control female sexuality, which became sound grounds for incarcerating young girls in residential schools. Obviously these institutions did some good. They provided protection and a haven for a special class of girls on the run from male abuse and violence and a 'way out' for those who wanted it, but a far greater majority rejected the lady child-savers' efforts on their behalf and returned home the moment they were free.

The regime of moral reform in residential and day schools was based on a bourgeois model of the 'ideal' proletarian family and class-specific ideologies of girlhood and femininity. Lady child-savers recognised, and quite rightfully in some cases, that the family was not always the best place for some girls to be. Nevertheless their regime was based on familialist ideology that had as its roots a domestic role for women. This meant isolating inmates from their own working-class communities and placing them in exclusive contact with women of a higher class, who would train them in nurturing skills and housewifery. It was hoped that after adjusting to the overall standard of living, strict order and cleanliness in the schools, they would become dissatisfied with their family's standard of living. Thus whether they became servants or good wives, they would do so in accordance with middle-class notions of feminine propriety. The paradox of the system was that while work in child-saving institutions emancipated middle-class women from the domestic routine of their own homes, they were leaving their own homes in order to persuade working-class women to remain in theirs.

NOTES

1 Margaret May, 'Innocence and Experience: the Evolution of the Concept of Juvenile Delinquency in the Mid-Nineteenth Century' *Victorian Studies*, vol. 17 (1973–4) pp. 7. For a detailed comparison between Scottish and English industrial schools see: Andrew G. Ralston, 'The Development of Reformatory and Industrial Schools in Scotland, 1832–1872 *Scottish Economic and Historical History*, 8 (1988) pp. 40–55; My understanding of the residential school system and cultures of resistance has been broadened by Celia Haig-Brown, *Resistance and Renewal: Surviving the Indian Residential School*, (Tillacum Library, Vancouver, 1989).

2 First Annual Report of the National Vigilance Association of Scotland, 1910–11, p. 5.

3 Anthony M. Platt, *The Child-Savers: the Invention of Delinquency*, (University of Chicago Press, Chicago, 1969) p. 75.

4 Griselda Cheape, 'Helps and Hindrances in Rescue Work and Preventive Work', Reformatory and Rescue Union Report of Edinburgh Conference, 1911, p. 65.

5 Marilyn Gittell and Teresa Shtob, 'Changing Women's Roles in Political Volunteerism and Reform of the City,' *Signs*, vol. 5 (1980), p. 69.

6 Anne Summers, 'A Home from Home: Women's Philanthropic Work in the Nineteenth Century', *Fit Work for Women*, Sandra Burman (ed.), (Croom Helm, London, 1979) p. 45.

7 'Ladies' Meeting in Glasgow', *The Shield*, no. 216 (24 October, 1874) p. 207.

8 Michael Ignatieff, 'Total Institutions and Working Classes: a Review Essay', *History Workshop Journal*, vol. 15 (1983) p. 168–9.

9 Davin, Anna, 'The Precocity of Poverty', unpublished paper presented at the British Sociological Annual Conference, Edinburgh, 1988, p. 4.

10 Report from the Select Committee on Reformatories and Industrial Schools, PP. 1896 I, p. 16 [hereafter PP. S.C., 1896).

11 Report of the Glasgow Reformatory and Industrial Schools, [Glasgow Room, Mitchell Library GR 364.72], 1888, p. 6.

12 Leonore Davidoff and Catherine Hall, *Family Fortunes: Men and Women of the English Middle Class, 1780–1850*, (University of Chicago Press, Chicago, 1987) p. 23.

13 Deborah Gorham, '"The Maiden Tribute of Modern Babylon" Re-examined: Child Prostitution and the Idea of Childhood in Late-Victorian England', *Victorian Studies*, Spring (1979) p. 356; Bettina Bradbury, 'The Fragmented Family: Family Strategies in the Face of Death, Illness, and Poverty, Montreal, 1860–1885', in Joy Parr (ed.) *Childhood and Family in Canadian*

History, McClelland and Stewart, (Toronto 1982) p. 109–110.

14 Davin, 'The Precocity of Poverty', p. 4

15 Lynn Nead, 'The Magdalen in Modern Times: the Mythology of the Fallen women in Pre-Raphaelite Painting' in R. Betterton (ed.) *Looking at Images of Femininity in the Visual Arts and Media*, (Pandora, London, 1987) p. 76.

16 Davin, 'The Precocity of Poverty', p. 3.

17 J. Bertram, *Glimpses of the Social Evil in Edinburgh and Elsewhere*, (Charles Harvey, Edinburgh, 1864), p. 13.

18 Parish of Glasgow. Memorandum on a Social Evil in Glasgow and the State of the Law for Dealing with Certain Forms of Immorality, 1911, p. 58.

19 PP. S.C., 1896, p. 231; For a detailed account of the targeting and labelling of 'deviant and defiant' women see, Linda Mahood, *The Magdalenes: Prostitution in the Nineteenth Century*, (Routledge, London 1990).

20 Mrs Duncan McLaren, *Transactions of the National Association for the Promotion of Social Sciences*, Edinburgh, 1880, p. 395.

21 Catherine Hunter, matron of Chapelton Girls' Reformatory, Bearsden, Glasgow between 1893 and 1904. She married John Craster and became matron of Wellington Farm School from 1904 to 1914. PP. S.C., 1896, Q. 21, 886–9.

22 Calculated from PP. S.C. 1896, p. 214.

23 The remaining 4 per cent were taken up for 'other' offences. Calculated from PP. S.C., 1896, p. 211.

24 Calculated from PP. S.C., 1896, p. 124.

25 Steven Schlossman and Stephanie Wallach, 'The Crime of Precocious Sexuality: Female Juvenile Delinquency in the Progressive Era', *Harvard Educational Review*, vol. 48, (1978), p. 66.

26 Linda Gordon, *Heroes of Their Own Lives: the Politics and History of Family Violence*, (Virago, London, 1988), p. 205.

27 Frances Hepburn, Secretary of the Edinburgh Society for the Prevention of Cruelty to Children, Report of the Departmental Committee on Reformatory and Industrial Schools in Scotland, 1914, Q. 7919. [hereafter: PP. D.C. 1914].

28 Annual Report of the Scottish National Society for the Prevention of Cruelty to Children, 1911, p. 27.

29 Maryhill Industrial School Girl's Register, [Strathclyde Regional Archives Ded 7. 139.A1], (3 June 1914). The names of all subjects in this paper have been changed.

30 Florence Rush, *The Best Kept Secret: Sexual Abuse of Children*, (McGraw-Hill, New York, 1980).

31 Maryhill Industrial School Girls' Register, [SRA Ded 7.136 A1], 26 March, 1920.

32 Ibid., 11 May, 1923.

33 Ibid., 19 April, 1923.

34 Victor Bailey and Sheila Blackburn, 'The Punishment of Incest Act 1980: A case Study of Law Creation', *Criminal Law Review*, (1979) p. 714.

35 Anthony S. Wohl, 'Sex and the Single Room: Incest Among the Victorian Working Classes', in A. S. Wohl (ed.) *The Victorian Family*, (St Martin's Press, New York, 1978) p. 199.

36 Gordon, 1988, *Heroes of Their Own Lives*, p. 226.

37 Parish Council of Glasgow, 'Immoral Houses and Venereal Diseases', [Glasgow Room, Mitchell Library, C. 646054], 1911, p. 60.

38 Gordon, 1988, *Heroes of Their Own Lives*, pp. 219, 223.
39 'Immoral Houses and Venereal Diseases', Notes for Conference, Glasgow Parish Council of Glasgow, 1911, p. 4.
40 Mrs James T. Hunter, PP. S.C., 1914, Q. 3732.
41 Glasgow Parish Council, 'Immoral Houses and Venereal Cases', Notes for the Conference, Appendix 1, 1911, p. 19 [Glasgow Room, Mitchell Library, G.351.764].
42 Herbert Gray, The Scottish Council for Women's Trades. *Exempted Shops*, Report 11, Ice-Cream Shops, 1911, p. 7.
43 Glasgow Parish Council, Sexual Immorality and Prostitution in Glasgow, 1911, p. 10.
44 Maryhill Industrial School Girls' Register, (26 Feb., 1915).
45 Ibid., 27 Aug. 1920.
46 Ibid., 1 Jan. 1932.
47 Veronica Beechey, 'Familial Ideology' in V. Beechey and J. Donald (eds) *Subjectivity and Social Relations* (Open University Press, London, 1985) p. 99, 105.
48 PP. S.C., 1896, p. 31.
49. Miss Catherine S. Dow, Superintendent of Maryhill Industrial School since 1911. PP. D.S., 1914, Q. 4549.
50 Jane Silman, 'Food, Labour and Rest for Reformatories for Girls', *Prison and Reformatory Gazette*, (1 Feb. 1857) p. 37.
51 Mrs Hannah Elizabeth Harrison, Lady Inspector under the Home Office. PP. D.S., 1914, Q. 1055.
52 PP. S.C., 1896, p. 219.
53 Ibid., p. 43.
54 Ibid., p. 221.
55 Mrs Craster, PP. D.C., 1914, Q. 3530.
56 Harrison, ibid., Q. 1048–51.
57 Summers, 'A Home from Home', p. 59.
58 Harrison, PP. D.C., 1914, Q. 1068.
59 Mrs Cameron, superintendent at Maryhill School since 1881. She was at Green Street Day Industrial School before going to Maryhill, PP. S.C., 1896, Q. 7804.
60 Silman, 'Food, Labour and Rest', p. 39.
61 Hunter, PP., S.C., 1896, Q. 22,025, 22,028.
62 Craster, PP. D.C., Q. 3461, 3583.
63 Cheape, 'Helps and Hindrances in Rescue Work', p. 66.
64 Dow, PP. D.C., 1914 Q. 4462, 4471; Mary R. Philips, Treasurer of Dalry Reformatory, near Edinburgh and Miss Peane, teacher, Dalry Reformatory, D.C., 1914, Q. 5180.
65 PP. S.C., 1896, p. 230.
66 Ibid., p. 46.
67 Interview with former student of Rose Street Day Industrial School (1906).
68 Cameron, PP. S.C., 1896, Q. 7582.
69 Craster, PP. D.C., 1914, Q. 3480.
70 Hunter, PP. S.C., 1896, Q. 22,144.
71 PP. S.C., 1896, p. 23.
72 Silman, 'Food, Labour and Rest', 40.
73 Cameron, PP. S.C., 1896, Q. 7452.
74 Dow, PP. D.C., 1914, Q. 4414–29.
75 Hunter, PP. S.C., 1896, Q. 21,925–27, 21,931, 22,075.
76 Ibid., p. 66.
77 Cameron, PP. S.C., 1896, Q. 7528.

78 Ibid., p. 66.
79 Dr Anne Mercer Watson, Medical Officer Aberdeen Female School of Industry. PP. D.C., 1914, Q. 6510, 6557.
80 PP. S.C., 1896, p. 54.
81 Ibid., Q. 22,034.
82 See: Noeline Williamson, 'Factory to Reformatory: The Founding and the Failure of Industrial and Reform Schools for Girls in the Nineteenth Century New South Wales', *Australia and New Zealand History of Education Society*, vol. 9, (1980), p. 34; Kerry Wimshurst, 'Control and Resistance: Reformatory School Girls in Late Nineteenth Century South Australia', *Journal of Social History*, vol. 18, no. 2 (Winter 1984) pp. 278–9.
83 Summers, 'A Home from Home', p. 54.
84 Norman McLeod, *Notes on the Industrial Training of Pauper Children*, (Glasgow, 1853) p. 21.
85 Hunter, PP. S.C., 1896, Q. 22,009.
86 Hepburn, PP. D.C., 1914, Q. 7984–5.
87 Annual Report of the Edinburgh District of the Scottish National Society for the Prevention of Cruelty to Children, (1912) p. 22.
88 Annual Report of the Glasgow Division of the Scottish National Society for the Prevention of Cruelty to Children, (1912) p. 23.
89 PP. S.C., 1896, p. 54; PP. D.C., 1914, p. 70.
90 Gorham, 'The Maiden Tribute of Modern Babylon', p. 367.
91 Cameron, PP. S.C., 1896, Q. 7762.
92 Ignatieff, 'Total Institutions', p. 170.
93 M. A. Crowther, *The Workhouse System, 1834–1929: the History of an English Social Institution*, (Batsford Academic, London 1981) quoted in: Ignatieff, 'Total Institutions', p. 172.
94 Hepburn, PP. D.C., 1914, Q. 7939.
95 Ibid.
96 Hunter, PP. S.C., 1896, Q. 5789.
97 First Annual Report of the Scottish National Society for the Prevention of Cruelty to Children, (1885) p. 6.
98 Maryhill Industrial School Girls' Register, 19 March 1920.
99 Interview with former student at Rose Street Day Industrial School (1927).
100 Bradbury, 'The Fragmented Family', p. 110, 128.
101 Ignatieff, 'Total Institutions', p. 172.
102 Gordon, 1988, 'Heroes of Their Own Lives', p. 240.
103 Hepburn, PP. D.C., 1914, Q. 7957.
104 Ibid., Q. 7932.
105 Interview with a woman who grew up in the east end of Glasgow in the early twentieth century.
106 Interview with former student at Rose Street Day Industrial School (1927).
107 Dow, PP. D.C., 1914, Q.4575.
108 Gorham, 'The Maiden Tribute of Modern Babylon', p. 56.
109 Williamson, 'Factory to Reformatory', p. 39.
110 Watson, PP. D.C., 1914, Q. 6526; Ibid., p. 70.
111 Hepburn, ibid., Q.7992.
112 Gittell and Schtob, 'Changing Women's Roles', p. 69.
113 Marion Reid, *A Plea for Women*, first published in 1843. (Polygon, Edinburgh, 1988) p. 6.

114 Burton, PP. S.C., 1896, Q. 23,669.
115 Miss Flora Stevenson Member of Edinburgh School Board. PP., S.C., 1896, Q. 25,532; Craster, PP. D.C., 1914, Q. 3410–3609; p. 135–141.
116 Watson, PP. D.C. ,1914, Q. 6557, 6556.
117 Sean Damer, *Glasgow: Going for a Song*, (Lawrence and Wishart, London 1990) p. 92.
118 Sean Damer, p. 91.

SELECT BIBLIOGRAPHY

Bailey, V. and Blackburn, S. 'The Punishment of Incest Act 1980: A Case Study of Law Creation', *Criminal Law Review*, 1979, pp. 709–718.

Beechey, V. 'Familial Ideology' in V. Beechey and J. Donald (eds) *Subjectivity and Social Relations*, (Open University Press, London, 1985) pp. 98–120.

Bradbury, B. 'The Fragmented family: Family Strategies in the Face of Death, Illness, and Poverty, Montreal, 1860–1885', in Joy Parr (ed.) *Childhood and Family in Canadian History*, (McClelland and Stewart, Toronto, 1982), pp. 101–128.

Davidoff, L. and Hall, C. *Family Fortunes: Men and Women of the English Middle Class, 1780–1850*, (University of Chicago Press, Chicago, 1987).

Davin, A. 'The Precocity of Poverty', unpublished paper presented at the British Sociological Annual Conference, Edinburgh, 1988.

Gittell, M. and Shtob, T. 'Changing Women's Roles in Political Volunteerism and Reform of the City', *Signs* 5 (1980) pp. 67–78.

Gordon, L. *Heroes of Their Own Lives: the Politics and History of Family Violence*, (Virago, London, 1988).

Gorham, D. '"The Maiden Tribute of Modern Babylon" Re-examined: Child Prostitution and the Idea of Childhood in Late-Victorian England', *Victorian Studies*, Spring (1979) pp. 353–379.

Haig-Brown, C. *Resistance and Renewal: Surviving the Indian Residential School* (Tillacum Library, Vancouver, 1989).

Ignatieff, M. 'Total Institutions and Working Classes: a Review Essay', *History Workshop Journal*, 15 (1983) pp. 165–173.

May, M. 'Innocence and Experience: the Evolution of the Concept of Juvenile Delinquency in the Mid-Nineteenth Century', *Victorian Studies* 17 (1973–4) pp. 7–29.

Mahood, L. *The Magdalenes: Prostitution in the Nineteenth Century* (Routledge, London, 1990).

Nead, L. 'The Magdalen in Modern Times: the Mythology of the Fallen women in Pre-Raphaelite Painting' in R. Betterton (ed.) *Looking at Images of Femininity in the Visual Arts and Media*, (Pandora, London, 1987).

Platt, A. M. *The Child-Savers: the Invention of Delinquency* (University of Chicago Press, Chicago, 1969).

Ralston, A. G. 'The Development of Reformatory and Industrial Schools in Scotland, 1832–1872' *Scottish Economic and Historical History* 8 (1988) pp. 40–55.

Reid, M. *A Plea for Women*, first published in 1843. (Polygon, Edinburgh, 1988).

Rush, F. *The Best Kept Secret: Sexual Abuse of Children*, (McGraw-Hill, New York, 1980).

Schlossman, S. and Wallach, S. 'The Crime of Precocious Sexuality:

Female Juvenile Delinquency in the Progressive Era' *Harvard Educational Review*, 1978, vol. 48, pp. 65–94.

Summers, A.'A Home from Home: Women's Philanthropic Work in the Nineteenth Century', *Fit Work for Women*, Sandra Burman (ed.) (Croom Helm, London, 1979) pp. 33–63.

Williamson, N. 'Factory to Reformatory: The Founding and the Failure of Industrial and Reform Schools for Girls in the Nineteenth Century New South Wales', *Australia and New Zealand History of Education Society*, 1980, vol. 9, pp. 32–41.

Wimshurst, K. 'Control and Resistance: Reformatory School Girls in Late Nineteenth Century South Australia', *Journal of Social History*, 1984, vol. 18, no. 2 (Winter), pp. 273–287.

Wohl, A. S. 'Sex and the Single Room: Incest Among the Victorian Working Classes;, in A. S. Wohl (ed.) *The Victorian Family*, (St Martin's Press, New York, 1978) pp. 197–216.

4

THE PUNISHMENT OF WOMEN IN NINETEENTH-CENTURY SCOTLAND: PRISONS AND INEBRIATE INSTITUTIONS

RUSSELL P. DOBASH AND PAT McLAUGHLIN

Over the last two decades there has been an extraordinary and persistent interest in the history of crime and imprisonment. In Britain this revisionist history was heralded by the publication of E. P. Thompson's *The Making of the English Working Class*, in which Thompson analyses the way customary practices and traditional rights were gradually criminalised under the pressure of agrarian capitalism, beginning in the eighteenth century.[1] Building on the insights of Marx, Thompson and his colleagues have provided rich, detailed evidence of this process and demonstrated how the law and criminal justice apparatus were employed in the class struggles and antagonisms of this period.[2] They have shown how the physical punishments associated with monarchical power and paternalistic local justice operated to control and subdue the common people. Their generally Marxist historiography includes a consideration of the way these processes were mediated and at times altered by the struggles and demands of the people. Michael Ignatieff extended this analysis to a consideration of the ideological and social roots of the penitentiary in nineteenth-century England.[3] Ignatieff shows how the ideals of evangelical and utilitarian reformers were significant in shaping regimes within the modern penitentiary. As a result of these and other researches, there is considerable accumulated evidence of the general trends and in some instances specific local developments associated with the rise of imprisonment in nineteenth-century England.

The most influential thinker in this new revisionist history of the prisons has been Michel Foucault. Foucault's agenda was not solely or primarily the analysis of imprisonment, rather he sought to conduct a 'genealogy of the modern subject', to analyse the way discourses and social practices coalesced to constitute individuals. In *Discipline and Punish* he shows how by the nineteenth century the discipline or carceral society is being created as a means of producing the 'docile bodies' (subjects) necessary for industrial capitalism.[4] Individuation is a crucial element of this society, involving the creation of social and temporal compartmentalisation, the spatial ordering of tasks and individuals, explicit and detailed rules to separate, regulate and direct human action, and mechanisms for constant surveillance.[5] The penitentiary represents the apex of this process, combining the various elements of individuation into a totalising, all-encompassing experience geared to the alteration and moulding – the normalisation – of the human subject. Penitentiary regimes combined constant surveillance, regimented schedules of daily activity regulated by the clock, detailed rules to control all activities, and cellular confinement to break up the dangerous, immoral and contaminating masses thought to be associated with crime. In the penitentiary power and surveillance become continuous, relentless: 'The human body [and mind] was entering a machinery of power that explores it, breaks it down and rearranges it. . .'.[6]

Individuation did not, however, begin with the penitentiary, it has its roots in the disciplines and order associated with military formations. The English Bridewells and the Dutch *Tuchthusien* created during the late sixteenth and early seventeenth centuries were prototypes of the penitentiary, practising crude mechanisms of individuation and normalisation.[7] Social practices and discourses linked to individuation were also evident in eighteenth-century efforts to discipline the industrial, particularly factory, workforce. Nearly two centuries before Fordism and Taylorism, reforming entrepreneurs such as Josiah Wedgewood attempted to wrest control of the rhythm and organisation of the labour process from the common people.[8] With the intention of increasing efficiency and maximising production, they created formalised hierarchies of control, elaborate systems of rewards and punishments and explicit rules for differentiating workers and regulating the labour process. Through regimentation and training, Wedgewood sought to 'make such machines of the Men as cannot err'. The nineteenth-century penitentiary was merely the exemplar of these encompassing efforts.

Garland has recently argued that Foucault was wrong about the development of individuation.[9] Foucault and other revisionist historians locate the rise of systematic individuation in the late eighteenth and early nineteenth centuries. Garland locates its emergence in the late nineteenth and early twentieth centuries: 'I have begun to demonstrate that, at least for the British case, Foucault's thesis is incorrect'.[10] For Garland, the process of normalisation of the criminal emerges at the end of the nineteenth century and 'prison reform' now takes on a new meaning'.[11] Consequently prison regimes of this period are associated with 'hope' and 'moral regeneration'. Prison labour is no longer intended to have a punitive effect, rather it becomes the 'basic element of an educational and training regime'. The old discipline he asserts was intended to 'crush and break', the new discipline of this period is geared to 'correction and normalisation'. A new language develops which emphasises, 'supporting the inadequate, protecting the irresponsible and restoring the morally deficient to the fullness of good citizenship'.[12] A significant aspect of these developments was the attempt to remove from prison the mentally ill, inebriates and feeble-minded. 'In consequence', Garland claims, 'the prisons were left with all those persons whose offences were serious or frequent enough to warrant not correction or normalisation, but the punishment of imprisonment'.[13]

The present writers do not accept Garland's claims.[14] While he rightly identifies a change in discourses around crime and deviance during this period – the rise of a therapeutic rhetoric – we think he has somewhat misconstrued Foucault's arguments and placed an inordinate emphasis on discourse to the neglect of the social practices and technologies linked to the processes of individuation and normalisation. Garland appears to equate the 'positive' mechanisms associated with individuation and normalisation in penal discipline with 'humane', therapeutic discourses. Foucault employed the word 'positive' to identify those innovations in disciplinary discourses and technologies linked to the objectifying processes intended to produce new, reformed or altered individuals – exactly what the early penitentiary was intended to achieve. Positive mechanisms are not necessarily humane, as exemplified by the rigid solitary confinement associated with the separate system which was initially employed in the penitentiaries of nineteenth-century Britain. Our evidence and that of others leads us to conclude that the regimes and disciplines introduced into early nineteenth-century penitentiaries were intended to be transforming. This was not, of course, their sole function, just as the so-called 'training' and 'therapeutic' regimes of the past twenty years have been highly punitive, the reforming penal regimes of the nineteenth century were also geared to humiliation and punishment.[15] Nor does it mean that older reactions and forms of control, such as paternalism, were supplanted.

We also think Garland's concentration on official discourses and the relative neglect of social practices has led him to misconstrue developments in the early part of this century. We judge most of the discourses associated with criminal women in the late nineteenth and early twentieth centuries as far from 'caring' and humane and, as we show, women confined in inebriate reformatories during this period experienced anything but therapeutic and 'caring' regimes.

On a more fundamental level, Garland, like most other revisionist historians, has presented us with a gender-blind analysis of the discourses and social practices associated with imprisonment.[16] The same criticisms can be directed at Ignatieff, Thompson and his colleagues and Foucault. Considerations of the role of gender and patriarchal assumptions, if they appear at all, are only incidental to the analysis of crime and punishment in the nineteenth century. Uniquely, Thompson's rural landscapes are inhabited both by men and women, but he usually showed no explicit interest in the way gender shaped the commission of and reactions to crime and disorder.[17] It is only recently that social scientists and historians, primarily women, have begun to correct this silence. Deirdrie Beddoe provides a vivid account of the transportation of Welsh women and Portia Robinson has recently documented the experiences of British women once they were transported to Australia.[18] Estelle Freedman and Nicole Hahn Rafter have produced excellent histories of the imprisonment of women in the United States and Patricia O'Brien devotes a considerable proportion of her work on French prisons to the unique predicament of women.[19] Dobash, Dobash and Gutteridge have analysed selected aspects of the position of women in English and Scottish prisons in the nineteenth and twentieth centuries and demonstrated the continuity of penal ideals and practices of the past with current patterns. These mostly feminist-inspired works have built upon the few early descriptive accounts in existence and started the long overdue exploration of the history of the punishment and imprisonment of women.[20]

Despite the contributions of these works there is still much to be done. In this chapter we investigate a number of interlocking themes. We begin by briefly recounting the conditions of confinement characteristic of the early part of the century. One of the significant aspects of the development of imprisonment in nineteenth-century Scotland was the large proportion of women in the prison population. We present evidence of this pattern and consider early accounts of why women found themselves in prison. We then explore the penal practices associated with the rise of the penitentiary in the first half of the nineteenth century. In this analysis we show how new 'positive' technologies were intended to transform women into chaste, sober and industrious workers, illustrating how many of these new inventions were specifically, although not uniquely, aimed at women. We are particularly concerned to evaluate the significant role of labour in this transformative process.[21] We end the discussion of the imprisonment of women by considering the changes which occurred in the relationships between female prisoners and staff during this period. This analysis shows how initial paternalistic, even benevolent, relationships were transformed into more abstracted and distant approaches associated with the mechanistic approaches deemed most appropriate to transforming regimes. The final sections of the chapter are devoted to an examination of inebriate institutions, one of the supposedly progressive developments of the late nineteenth and early twentieth centuries. We demonstrate how inebriate institutions were not so much a part of the 'caring and rehabilitative' discourses identified by Garland, as they were an appendage and extension of the penal network.

THE PENITENTIARY

Creation of the penitentiary

The rise of the modern penitentiary for women and men in the 1840s was preceded by a period of intense debate and experimentation. A number of competing proposals emerged. The most influential were proffered by the evangelical reformers and the utilitarians, as represented by Bentham.[22] Evangelicals, such as Elizabeth Fry, proposed solitary confinement, religious instruction and exhortation, separation of the sexes and classification and useful labour. Bentham accepted all of these ideas, but his most important mechanism for transforming 'delinquents', whatever their age or sex, was constant surveillance.[23] Constant surveillance would be achieved through the simple technique of architecture. For this purpose Bentham offered his famous, or infamous, panopticon.[24] The important philosophical difference in the two proposals was in the mechanisms of transformation. Evangelicals sought to create the 'willing subject' through direct, personal engagement with the offender, whereas Bentham's plans emphasised abstract, impersonal techniques wherein the inmate is constituted as an object upon which transforming technologies and surveillance would be applied.

The creation of the penitentiary in the 1840s was preceded by a number of institutional experiments seeking to approximate these proposals. Many of these schemes were specifically aimed at women. Although Scotland was reticent to introduce institutional solutions for problems of crime, vagrancy and poverty, by the early part of the nineteenth century two model prisons had been erected and both primarily housed women. The Glasgow Bridewell, holding around 300 prisoners, was admired by foreign visitors. Elizabeth Fry, the most prominent reformer of women's prisons, praised it for its useful labour, education and cleanliness.[25] First erected in 1798, it was rebuilt in 1825 on an 'improved' form. The three storey Bridewell was designed to maximise surveillance. Built on the radiating-spoke plan with a central rotunda, 'the governor has a view of all the passages in the two wings lately built' and 'from morning to night the prisoners are under Inspection and Control, and are never for a Moment left to themselves'.[26] The improved institution was designed to avoid the contamination believed to be associated with the spread of crime by enforcing strict separation of prisoners through solitary confinement and classification. Within a year overcrowding made the system unworkable, enabling 'the prisoners to associate and combine and prevent[ing] proper classification. Because it allows criminals of different degrees of guilt to associate every day, and the more depraved to corrupt the less guilty. We find separate solitary confinement far more useful'.[27]

Edinburgh constructed its own Bridewell in 1795. It was the closest proximation to Bentham's panopticon ever built in Britain.[28] The most celebrated element of the Bridewell was its architecture. Four storeys high, each storey had thirteen working cells and thirty-six sleeping apartments, thus fifty-two working cells and 144 silent rooms. The architect Robert Adam was apparently much influenced by Bentham with whom he exchanged correspondence.[29] Following Bentham's views on constant surveillance Adam built the prison in the shape of a D with a central inspection tower, 'from which the prisoners are seen at work in the front working cells, without being aware when they are inspected'.[30] Even this 'celebrated' design had its flaws, for while allowing perpetual inspection from the central tower, it was also possible for prisoners to see each other. The immediate introduction of new technology enhanced individuation and prevented contamination. 'Most of the windows have lately been fitted up on the outside with reversed venetian blinds, which being fixed to look upwards, prevent the prisoners from having any communication with persons from without'.[31]

New positive architectural technologies were combined with processes of subjugation and reform. Female vanity was considered an important source of evil and crime and prison regimes were usually geared to its destruction. When women entered the Edinburgh Bridewell they were 'stripped, hair cut close, bathed, cleaned and placed in prison clothing (coarse linen shift, apron, and cap, woollen petticoat, and gown of drugget)' and set to work 'spinning, knitting stockings, picking oakum, weaving linen, cotton and wool, making list shoes'.[32] Women considered the 'most trusted' were 'set apart for cooking, washing and cleaning the prison'.

Despite these two 'noteworthy' exceptions most Scottish gaols in existence in the early nineteenth century were considered wholly inadequate. Fry's visit to Scotland in 1818 with her brother-in-law Joseph Gurney revealed widespread overcrowding and lack of classification, with the consequent 'herding' together of children and adults and men and women in the same cramped, filthy accommodation. In Aberdeen county gaol they found:

> a small room, about fifteen feet long by eight in breadth, set apart for female criminals. There were four women in it, a man (husband of one of them), and a child. The room was most offensively close and very dirty . . . the impropriety of the man being thus confined in company with women needs no remark.[33]

The Select Committee Report of 1818 found 'appalling' conditions in burgh gaols and found them 'insecure and incommodious'.[34] As late as 1835, commissioners enquiring into the state of the municipal corporations judged most institutions to be in a 'wretched state' and recommended abandonment or incorporation of smaller prisons into a more centralised system. One of the most persistent criticisms was idleness and lack of systematic labour: 'A great fault in all the prisons of Scotland is the total want of employment for the inmates'.[35] By the 1840s wider British developments and the efforts of the first Scottish prison inspector brought about a radical transformation of the penal estate in Scotland.

As the search for improved 'secondary punishments' (hanging being the primary one) intensified, William Crawford was sent to the United States in 1834 to inspect and report on penal developments. He inspected the two most widely touted regimes: the Auburn system combining

congregate, silent labour and solitary confinement at night and the Pennsylvania model devoted to perpetual solitary confinement and useful
cellular labour. Crawford opted for the Pennsylvania model as the most
efficacious system which would avoid the frequent physical punishments associated with infractions of the silent rule under the congregate
system. Yet even by this date prolonged solitary confinement was coming
under heavy criticism and in an attempt to avoid such criticisms
Crawford and his colleague Wentworth Russell dubbed their proposed
regime 'the Separate System'. In 1839 the Prisons Bill for Scotland
established the separate system as the preferred model for all forms
of imprisonment. Similar English legislation led to the building of
Perth prison as the central model prison for all of Scotland.

Filling the prisons and paternalistic accounts of female criminals

The 1840s until the end of the century was the era of the Great Confinement, with the population of Scottish prisons rising from 19,319 in 1840 to
60,503 in 1900. That increase holds good for both men and women.
Commitments of women rose from 7,105 per year in 1840 to 20,108 by
1900.

One of the most significant demographic aspects of imprisonment in
nineteenth-century Scotland was the proportion of women to men in the
prison population. Throughout the century women always constituted at
least 30 per cent of the population and at some points women represented
over 40 per cent of the entire population. Women in English prisons
apparently never constituted more than 25 per cent of the overall population and by the 1870s their numbers were a minute proportion of the
prison population. We can only speculate as to the reasons for this unique
and persistent pattern in Scotland and not in England and we will return
to this issue at the end of the chapter.

Women were sent to prison in the nineteenth century for the same sort
of offences for which they go to prison today, petty thefts and offences
associated with prostitution. Unlike today, however, a considerable proportion of Scottish women went to prison for offences against public
order: drunkenness, using obscene language, breaching the peace and
causing a nuisance. Prison reports in the 1840s indicate that women were
in prison because of lack of work 'owing to the want of manufactures'
with many in prison for prostitution, 'if a servant once loses her situation
with an injured character she has scarcely any other resource than prostitution'.[37] The matron of Perth prison observed, 'In a large number of cases
the prisoners, before entering on a course of crime, had been seduced;
and then, having lost character, had taken to drinking and begun to steal.
. . . Many of the old prisoners are, in my opinion, almost driven to crime
by destitution caused sometimes by their inability to labour, and sometimes by their being unable to get employment'.[38]

Frederick Hill, the first inspector of Scottish prisons, was especially likely to point to the 'great poverty and destitution in Scotland' and the lack of proper workhouses as significant elements in crime and prostitution. He pointed out that women were particularly vulnerable because of 'scanty wages' and their increasing exclusion from 'all the most lucrative employments', such as mining and printing. Consequently up to the end of the 1840s destitute and deserted women (and a few men), sought voluntary commitments to prisons as a source of relief. In 1843 'over 100 women applied to admittance to the Glasgow prison even though it applies the separate system in a rigorous manner'.[39] Hill's Seventh Report for 1842 included the following account of an imprisoned woman:[40]

> I was ill, and stupid, and doltish, my husband ill-used me and beat me; he left me and the child day after day to starve . . . I asked for a gill of whiskey without money to pay for it, and I did it purposely, as I told the baillie, to be sent here. My heart was broken with my husband's ill usage. He pawns my clothes for drink, and lies with another woman. I had rather be in prison all my life than do as my husband does – drink, drink, drink. He has beat me, turned me out of doors in the dead of winter, and tried to cut my throat.

By the end of the century the explanations of criminal women would shift from the paternalist focus on poverty and seduction to an emphasis on the personalities and the congenitally flawed morals of women, but the crimes remained the same. In 1900 the First Class Warder in charge of Greenock prison concluded that the crimes of most women were, 'Drunk and disorderly, and a good many are for shebeening and using abusive languages'.

By the sentencing standards of today most women served very short sentences, usually less than two months, a pattern evident throughout the century. A typical example of a certain type of female offender at the end of the century was a Glasgow woman imprisoned in Duke Street prison. In her early 30s, she had been imprisoned thirty or more times for periods of between three and thirty days, mostly for using obscene language or disorderly conduct.[41] Short sentences and the 'revolving door' of frequent imprisonment was a persistent concern of prison administrators and reformers. In 1845 the governor of Aberdeen Prison observed, 'if the offenders, while still young, were sent in the first instance for a long period, I have no doubt that many who now become confirmed criminals could be trained to habits of industry, and made honest members of society'.[42] Similar sentiments were expressed in 1865 by Harriet Martineau in the *Edinburgh Review*. She maintained that women who were 'once bad' become 'utterly hopeless' as a result of serving short sentences.[43] Reformers and prison officials were not arguing that women should not be imprisoned, rather they urged longer sentences so that the 'positive' reforming influences of the prison could be felt to their full effect.

The nature of imprisonment for women

Regardless of the length of their sentences, by the middle of the century the imprisonment of Scottish women usually involved the systematic application of rigid regimes aimed at punishment and reformation. It is important to note that, in contrast to England, the Scottish penal estate had been centralised and systematised by mid-century. The Prisons Bill of 1839 not only created Perth as the General Prison but also resulted in the establishment of a General Board of Directors of Scottish Prisons.[44] The Board of Directors were in direct control and management of Perth prison and were able to levy mandatory assessments for building and maintaining Perth and other prisons in Scotland. In the 1840s the General Board launched and supervised the building and rebuilding of the penal estate. By 1860 the number of prisons had been reduced from 170 to seventy-two with thirty-eight new prisons, eleven rebuilt on existing sites and fourteen enlarged and improved.[45]

Physical improvements were coupled with the introduction of new mechanisms of discipline, with the General Board attempting to ensure that institutions, 'train prisoners in good and industrious habits by effecting their complete separation from vicious society, and by affording them religious and moral instruction.'[46] There was to be little distinction in the regimes for men and women with the board specifying, 'Application of the Rules to Both Sexes – So far as is consistent with what is necessarily peculiar to each sex, every rule relating to male prisoners or to male officers, is to apply equally to female prisoners and to female officers'.[47] By early 1850s annual prison reports indicate considerable uniformity in the implementation of systematic regimes based on the principles, if not the exact details, of the separate system.

The 'ideal' penal regime for Scottish prisons as practised at Perth, included perpetual forms of degradation and subjugation aimed at preparing inmates for the reforming mechanisms enforced through a set of uniform and inflexible rules and regulations backed up by measured punishments. Individuation was to be enhanced through vigorous enforcement of the separate system involving near continuous individual cellular confinement, partitioned exercise yards, cubicle chapel stalls, and masks to be used on the infrequent occasions when prisoners were required to leave their cells. The congregate System was probably the most widely practised regime and although not as rigorous as the separate system it was still a potent mechanism for isolating and controlling prisoners.

Individual cellular confinement as practised under the two systems and cubicle chapels epitomise efforts of individuation. Cells become 'small theatres, in which each actor is alone, perfectly individualised and constantly visible'.[48] Cubicle chapels make the application of reforming technologies more certain as this description of the Perth chapel suggests:
The prisoners see and are seen by the chaplain, while they do not

see each other, an arrangement which not only prevents the less hardened from being corrupted by the more criminal, but secures all the advantages to be expected from the Gospel being proclaimed face to face to a needy audience. The behaviour of the prisoners, male and female, during both services is truly praiseworthy.[49]

The daily routine of discipline for women, whether in Glasgow or Perth or Inverness, was intended to be (and was) very much the same. The day ran to an explicit timetable, often to the accompaniment of bells. First bell 5.30 am: matron and warders rise and prepare for duty; second bell 5.45: warders reassemble and prisoners rise. By 6.am every prisoner was expected to have put out her 'night vessel', cleaned her cell, washed and be 'standing in her cell, ready to show herself to the matron on the ward'. Women worked until breakfast at 7.30 and, after a short break, resumed their labours. The women would work in silence, with short intervals for meals, until 7.30 or 8.pm when the order was given to 'sling hammocks'. They could then read approved texts for a short time before the last bell sounded at 9 pm.[50]

In contrast to Garland's claim that labour only became a reforming technique in the early twentieth century, the evidence is clear that most penal labour in nineteenth-century prisons was intended to be a technique for moral and social transformation. Frederick Hill was an ardent supporter of useful, reformative labour and women imprisoned in Scottish prisons were generally involved in productive and socially necessary labour. Predictably women were engaged in a great deal of socially necessary labour, including cooking, baking, cleaning and, most importantly, laundering. A large proportion of women prisoners were employed in washing, drying, ironing and folding clothes and linens for both women's and men's prisons. Female convicts were also responsible for cleaning prisons, although it is not clear whether or not they were required to clean the men's sections.

Women were required to sew, knit and weave in their cells and in groups under the congregate silent system. In 1842 the matron of Edinburgh prison noted, 'I got on with my prisoners remarkably well last winter, because we had a very busy winter of various kinds of work, most of which was well paid. My prisoners were tasked daily and their diligence and spirit were delightful. . . There was no idleness in getting up in the morning; each was more anxious than another to get to their work.'[51]Although at times there was an apparent lack of work for male inmates, women usually had domestic and productive work to do. As the Departmental Committee Report of 1900 indicates, 'cooking and laundering work is always to be had, and sewing of various kinds.'[52] The routine of silent labour was interrupted only for teaching, preaching and exercising. Everything was geared towards instilling patterns of sobriety, orderliness and punctuality. Judging by the evidence of the prisons themselves, this regime made most (though by no means all) women quiescent for the short time they were in prison but did little to effect a change in their behaviour once released.

By the mid-1840s English Home Office officials and members of the Scottish judiciary began to object to the useful labour practised in Scottish prisons. In 1842 the Home Secretary Sir James Graham pronounced he had 'no great faith in the efficacy of *reformatory* prison discipline . . . WHAT WAS NEEDED WAS HARD LABOUR'.[53] During his tenure Hill successfully opposed the introduction of purely 'useless' punitive labour.[54] However, with continuous pressure from the Director of British Prisons, Joshua Jebb, and the introduction of a new Scottish inspector, the crank was eventually introduced at Perth and eight county prisons. Purely punitive labour was never very prominent in Scottish prisons, particularly since the sale of prison-produced commodities defrayed a considerable proportion of prisoners' maintenance.

Labour was an integral element in the modified separate system operating at Perth in the last quarter of the century. Women were certainly employed in unpleasant, although productive, work such as picking oakum, but the major orientation of the period involved useful productive labour. Productive labour combined with rigorous classification and the use of a progressive stage system, constituted a clear example of the more exacting processes of human accounting and hierarchical judgement associated with the carceral society. In the first six months of her sentence, Stage I, a woman was required to pick oakum or coir in her cell for ten hours a day 'tasked in proportion to her powers'. Picking oakum, a dirty and tiresome task, served as a humiliating punishment intended to strip women of their vanity and to encourage them to welcome the more interesting labour associated with subsequent stages. After successful completion of the first six months women would move to the first reformatory class, Class II, where they would be employed in 'sewing, knitting or other feminine work, unless in the case of a refractory or illconducted prisoner who shall be continued at the employment of teasing oakum or coir for such period as should be thought proper'.[55] By this time the monolithic rule of silence had been somewhat relaxed and women in Class II were able to associate with up to three other prisoners, 'during which period they are to be allowed to talk on proper subjects'. Women who progressed to Class III were allowed to converse at meals and exercise but were required to remain silent for the remainder of the day while 'employed in sewing, and knitting, and needlework, and such other fitting occupations for women as can be found for them'.[56]

Staff and prisoners

Evidence such as this suggests that labour was the major mechanism for reforming female (and male) prisoners throughout the nineteenth century, although some punitive labour was introduced after the 1850s. The continuity of these practices seems indisputable. However, there were, of course, important changes in Scottish prisons during the century. We detect an important shift in the the relationships between prison staff and inmates, changing from personal paternalistic approaches aimed at producing the willing subject to more monolithic, depersonalised efforts associated with more objectifying processes. It is even possible to detect such a shift in the work and writings of Elizabeth Fry in the first quarter of the century. Fry's early work at Newgate was associated with 'gentle persuasion', 'kind' religious ministration, scripture reading and education. Women prisoners were to be involved in their own transformation, were considered worthy of consultation and convict monitors were to be appointed from the ranks of imprisoned women. Reforming imprisoned women should involve bringing them together in order to 'express sympathy' and to 'soothe them with words of gentleness and kindness as a means of gaining their trust and co-operation'. As a member of Fry's Association for the Improvement of the Females at Newgate said, 'it has been our constant endeavour to associate them with ourselves in the object . . . all rules are first submitted to them and receive their voluntary consent'.[57]

By 1825 when Fry published her *Observations on the Siting, Superintendence and Government of Female Prisoners* she had clearly changed her tune. Uniquely for penal reformers she continued to urge engagement with prisoners but her views had developed to include continuous surveillance, hard useful labour, systematic punishment, complex systems of classification, and progressive stage programmes with continuous judgements of progress expressed through a mark and badge system. These more developed proposals went far beyond the rather loose and benevolent systems she envisaged and introduced into Newgate and other prisons for women. More abstract and certain mechanisms were needed wherein female staff were to be a 'consistent example of feminine propriety and virtue' and practise 'vigilance and impartiality in dealing with prisoners'. Despite Fry's endorsement of more abstract mechanisms, when 'professional' women staff were introduced into Scottish prisons in the mid-nineteenth century they appear to have practised the more direct, personal approach associated with her early work.

The duties of the matron were clearly set out in many of the Prison Reports and included the 'imparting of moral and religious instruction to the female prisoners'.[58] During this early period it seems clear that female warders and matrons were seen as integral elements in attempts to create a 'moral order' geared to transformation. It also seems likely that female staff were often, in the words of Freedman, 'their sisters' keepers'.[59] Early annual prison reports often included descriptions of the positive ben-e-volent relationships between prisoners and staff. For example, the matron of Stirling prison reports, 'The more I try by persuasion and gentle manners to convince the prisoners of the errors they have committed, the better I succeed'.[60] Hill continually stresses benevolence and guidance as the best approach to reformation, 'The tone of the [female] warders, no less than that of the matron and teachers, in speaking of the prisoners, is uniformly that of a desire to benefit them, and of their strong conviction that it is by mildness and kindness that they are most successful in managing prisoners'.[61]

Paternalistic benevolence extended beyond the walls of prison when matrons and governors took girls and women into their houses as servants. Some went even further. The governor of Paisley prison reported:[62]

> A young woman, aged twenty-six, had conducted herself so well in the prison, and showed so earnest a desire to do right, and to avoid returning to Glasgow, where her crime was known, that on her liberation the matron not only procured her employment in Paisley, but with the aid of benevolent persons whom she had interested in the young women's welfare, furnished a small room for her and became security for the rent.

Hill's reports indicate that prisoners expressed similar feelings and responded well to such methods. For example, a woman in Glasgow prison is reported to have said, 'Miss Cameron is a mild nice girl over us, she has a soft word on her tongue to us, and shuts the door and opens it cannily; she does not gar it bang through one's head till one's all in a tremble'.[63] We can be sure that Hill's reports exaggerated the kind and benevolent attitude of his female staff and the positive responses of inmates, yet the frequency of such reports leads us to conclude that paternalism was an important element in early penal relationships. Such a pattern of hierarchical relationship would not be surprising in light of the social relationships between the classes at this time.

By the end of the century greater 'professionalism' and efforts to make staff cogs in the penal machine radically altered relationships. Unlike the early annual reports, those produced in the last quarter of the century rarely mention relationships between staff and prisoners and when they do staff complain about the direction of penal developments. In 1895 the matron of Ayr prison noted, 'Our prison warders are, you may call, moral nurses, but they have never any time to get beyond discipline'.[64] The matron of Duke Street prison complained about the rigidity of the discipline and noted 'that it is most desirable to humanise the system as far as possible'. William Sievwright, the chaplain of Perth prison around the turn of the century, praised the institution but also criticised certain aspects of its harsh regime, 'the silence is very ominous and foreboding . . . THEY ARE COMPELLED TO LABOUR yet in very hateful labour teasing oakum, teasing or plaiting coir for mats, mat-making, or sack-sewing', all 'enforced by stern rules which threaten punishment . . . if not accomplished'.[65]

Although we have yet to locate any direct first-hand evidence of the reactions of Scottish women during this period, we do have an excellent, fulsome account of a woman convicted of murder who served fifteen years in an English prison. She noted the impact prisons had on both staff and prisoners. For staff:

> within their walls can be found, above all places, that most degrading, heart-breaking product of civilisation, a human automaton. All will, all initiative, all individuality, all friendship, all the things that make human beings attractive to one another are absent . . . sympathy is no part of their official duty, and be the warder never so tender in her domestic circle, tenderness must not be shown toward a prisoner.[66]

For prisoners, surviving imprisonment 'depended upon unresisting acquiescence – the keeping of . . . sensibilities dulled as near as possible to the level of the mere animal state'.[67] 'Supervision is never relaxed,' she notes, and because of strip searches [an estimated 10,000 during her imprisonment] 'I was never allowed to forget that, being a prisoner, even my body was not my own'.[68]

Florence Maybrick's Own Story is unique in the annals of prison literature, but her account rings true for Scotland, particularly for those women serving long sentences. Paternalistic relationships and benevolent discourses appear to have disappeared from the prisons of this period. In its place was a more monolithic penal system and early 'therapeutic' discourses which marginalised women who committed crimes as beyond the kin of normal women, ruled by their aberrant biology and heredity.

EXPLAINING CRIMINAL WOMEN

Nineteenth-century accounts of the crimes of women often emphasised their unique biological features, particularly their physiognomy.[69] One mid-century account of a woman convict is exemplary:[70]

> A physiognomist might have guessed much of her character from her countenance – it was so disproportionate and revolting. A white-faced ape would have been something like her and there was a look in her black eyes which made one shudder to account.

By the end of the century 'scientific' accounts were developing which emphasised the link between congenital, inherited inferiority, moral degeneracy and crime. Maudsley and Tredgold believed that criminals were 'morally defective' because of the congenital inheritance of malfunctioning brains.[71] Despite the emerging claims to scientific, medical rigour these discourses were riddled with the morality and prejudices of the period. Maudsley wrote that a woman who committed crime, 'completely loses all sense of shame, modesty, self-respect and gentleness, all her womanliness, and becomes violent, cruel, outrageously blasphemous, and impudently immodest; in fact, a sort of fiend with all the vices of woman in an exaggerated form, and with none of her virtues'.[72] In Tredgold's topological approach to crime women were classified as 'facile types' who were 'lacking in will power' and 'unable to steer a right course'.

Tredgold and Maudsley were physicians involved in the charting of problems of mental degeneracy, and only marginally interested in crime. Other emerging professions, particularly clinical psychologists and criminologists, would make crime and deviance one of their major areas of concern. During the first quarter of the twentieth century, two prominent practitioners, Havelock Ellis and Cyril Burt, wrote explicitly about the criminality of women. Ellis associated criminality with 'insensitivity to pain' and 'constitutional laziness'.[73] Women involved in crime 'suffered' from an 'excess of pubic . . . or facial hair' and exhibited a 'male-like appearance'. Like all women, he claimed, they suffered from 'emotional instability', but they were uniquely, 'masculine, unsexed, ugly abnormal women.' Burt argued that delinquent girls inherited 'undeveloped sentiments' and 'aboriginal modes of response'.[74] Women and girls, he claimed, were ruled by their biology particularly during 'puberty and periodicity'. Puberty he felt was a particularly dangerous time because girls became potential threats to community morality and the reputations of 'innocent' adult males.

The bulk of these discourses were English based, but this does not mean they did not influence Scottish thinking and a few Scottish medical practitioners made similar claims. J. F. Sutherland's *Recidivism*, published in 1908, is an explicit example of a Scottish physician's views of criminality.[75] Sutherland had been a prison medical officer and at the time of publication of his book was serving as Deputy Commissioner in Lunacy for Scotland. His book reflects the turn of the century concern for recidivist offenders – 'habitués' – and the homeless vagrant. According to Sutherland, most habitual petty offenders were women who were 'degenerate, feebleminded, mentally perverted and obsessed in various directions . . . passive, idle, debauched, parasitic, and unproductive'.[76] He claimed that prostitution was a typical habitual crime, 'synonymous with drunkenness, dress, and indolence, these having perhaps, as much, or more, to do with it than *lust*' [our emphasis].[77] Traditional physiognomy was invoked when Sutherland claimed, 'The furtive, restless eye, a look of boldness, cunning and determination, is specially characteristic of prostitutes'.[78]

These discourses were profoundly linked to the National Eugenics Movement. Unlike some other British eugenicists, Sutherland rejected 'radical' solutions such as sterilisation and opted instead for 'isolation'. While endorsing 'social amelioration', his penal solutions for crime primarily echo early nineteenth-century approaches, 'in the order of their importance, cellular or associated confinement, hygiene, discipline, industry and [restricted] diet'.[79] The major mechanism for straightening the twisted minds and bodies of degenerate 'habitués' was labour. 'Most prisons', he urged, 'might well be turned into labour settlements, labour colonies, industrial reformatories, and inebriate retreats'.[80] Whatever the specifics of these late nineteenth and early twentieth theories and solutions for crime, there was very little concern for 'care'.

INEBRIATE REFORMATORIES

Institutional 'care' for women

New, 'reforming' discourses were an integral aspect of the penal landscape in the closing decades of the nineteenth century and the first quarter of the twentieth. New institutions were also created at this time and some were especially directed at the habitual offender.[81] The inebriate reformatory was such an institution. Inebriate reformatories were embedded in the new treatment and 'caring' discourses of the period, but as we will show their practices and technologies reflected the gender and class-based assumptions of the period. Although reformatories were not specifically intended for the reception and confinement of women, we shall also show that at least in Scotland they were used almost exclusively for the confinement of women.

Throughout history there have been unique institutions for the confinement of women. Some acted as refuges from patriarchal abuses and poverty, while others were specifically penal.[82] During the nineteenth century institutions were created or consolidated that were intended to confine and rehabilitate women and girls in order to prevent the irreversible slide into sin and crime. Magdalene Institutions provide perhaps the best-known examples.[83] There were a number of variations on that theme – the Home for Deserted Mothers established in Glasgow in 1873, for example, cared for the 'first-time fallen', women who had become pregnant by their first sexual experience. Inebriate reformatories reflect the legacy of these institutions and are a prime example of institutional reform directed at women. The promoters of 'asylums for drunkards' clearly felt that the rationale that lay behind the development of confinement for criminals, fallen women, and the insane could be (should be) just as readily applied to the habitual drunkard.

As the institutional option developed during the nineteenth century – throughout what has been called the age of the great confinement – the level of dissatisfactions with traditional penalty increased. Reformers and penal authorities alike were concerned that more should be done about the control of women, especially young, sexually active women. Evidence of discourses on the control of women can be found in the stream of tracts and essays published throughout the period. At the close of the century the argument was that the standard practice of bringing women charged with public order offences (drunkenness, prostitution, etc.) before the courts and imprisoning them, albeit for short periods of time, only added to their corruption. Reformers did not object, however, to detaining such women in other, supposedly more caring, surroundings. Eliza Orme, writing about 'Our Female Criminals' in 1898, gives some of the flavour of the debate. As Orme saw it, 'the most pressing need is to remove habitual drunkards from the local prisons'.[84] Removed from the prison, but not freed from control. Such women, it was suggested, should be 'locked up in a hospital' until cured and upon release 'trouble and even expense should be incurred to guard her from [the] first temptation of finding herself free of control'.[85] The favoured solution involved persuading women to 'volunteer' for a regime of moral and industrial re-education in one of a number of non-statutory institutions. Section 24 of the Inebriates Act 1898, for example, provided that anyone convicted of certain drink-related offences and who had at least three convictions for similar offences in the preceding twelve moths, could 'agree' to go to a Certified Inebriate Reformatory, for 'a term not exceeding three years'.

By the late nineteenth century there were an increasing number of non-statutory agencies providing for the care, rehabilitation and control of women. Initially the focus had been on women's sexual activities. By the end of the century, however, the remit had expanded to provide for female felons, habitual drunkards, juvenile offenders, and so on. The idea had been to rescue women from the criminal justice system (prison), but in practice their efforts led to an extension of control and an expansion of judicial supervision. Cohen identified a similar paradox in the community control movement of the 1970's.[86] Attempts by community groups to reduce the size, scope, and intensity of formal systems of control – destructuring the criminal justice system to use Cohen's terminology – actually produced an expansion of the system. What happened in the latter half of the nineteenth century was that more women, in particular more working-class women, came potentially within the institutional gaze and response. In 1890 there were 15,000 commitments to Glasgow prisons, of whom 10,000 were women.[87] Instead of reducing the amount of stigmatisation, labelling and overcrowding in prisons, the expanding range of options brought more women into the carceral net.

Sober houses, reformatories and retreats

A significant element in the expansion of the carceral net was the activities of the caring professions. It becomes clear that they did not merely inform responses, they became deeply enmeshed in the processes of implementation. The 'caring' professionals, like the legal and criminal justice establishments, became an integral aspect of social control. Then, as now, the area was characterised by a good deal of conceptual confusion and disagreements about such things as the nature of the problem and appropriate response strategies – there were a number of discourses in fact. The major theme which comes across, however, concerns the relationship between the control of crime and the treatment of individuals.[88]

The influence of the medical profession, for example, is clearly evidenced at one level in the provision of treatment facilities in retreats where people could obtain help. The mainly private retreats offered facilities for the well-to-do – usually male clients with a drink problem. An advertisement for one such retreat – Vaughan Private Sanatorium in the Dunbartonshire hills – gives a flavour of life in private institutions:

> The House is a handsome stone building, containing large airy rooms, and every modern convenience . . . The Reading and Smoking room is particularly comfortable, while, for those patients who prefer a little exercise along with their pipe or cigar, there is a good Billiard room . . . (S)urrounding the House are six and a half acres in extent comprising wood, shrubberies, lawns, fruit and flower gardens, besides 700 feet of glass hothouses.[89]

It was the proud boast of this sanatorium that there was 'no restraint on patients'. The same could not be said for those less fortunate whose only hope of 'treatment' lay in being admitted to the public lunatic asylum, 'chargeable to the Parish' (that is, under the provisions of the Poor Law) or to one of the new inebriate reformatories. They would certainly not find a place in a licensed retreat.

In Scotland in 1909, according to the Inspector of Retreats, there were only three licensed retreats: 'All three . . . conducted by private enterprise, and all three. . . . designed to meet the requirements of the upper and middle classes'[90] The few facilities which did cater for the 'lower classes' were operated by voluntary organisations, religious and quasi-religious charities for the most part, who were more concerned with moral rather than medical well-being. In any case, there were never more than a handful of these voluntary 'unlicensed retreats' for working-class inebriates. This situation, it was clear to many people, did nothing either to reform or deter the persistent offender. Indeed, as the Inspector for Scotland under the Act observed, the recognition of this fact underlay the provisions of the Inebriates Acts:

> The intention of the (1898) Act is not explicitly stated, but presumably it is (1) To protect the community against inebriate offenders; (2) to provide facilities for their reformation. The implication from the terms of the Act, is that both these objects are better attained by relatively prolonged detention than by repeated committal, which has been proved useless by long experience.[91]

Without the active involvement of the medical profession the inebriate reformatories might well not have been established. The ideology which underlay the initiative was apparently therapeutic. Policy documents at least give the impression that the intention was to translate the medical ideology into practice. In a Scottish Office circular of February 1899, the Secretary for Scotland 'earnestly hoped':

> that a fair and reasonable experiment of the Act may prove, not only that a large percentage of these unfortunate inebriates are capable under careful and humane supervision of reformation and restoration to useful lives, but that ultimately both the imperial and the local Exchequer and local funds will in this way be relieved by a

sensible decrease in the population now located in our prisons and poorhouses.

It is interesting (and curious) to note that – whether talking about inebriate reformatories or the current enthusiasm for community care – the equation of financial savings with the adoption of a more humanitarian approach to social problems seems to be an enduring theme.[92]

Two certified inebriate reformatories – Girgenti, 'The Glasgow Home', and Greenock – formed the major provision in Scotland under the Inebriates Act. The buildings at Greenock were already well equipped for their purpose, having operated as a refuge for 'fallen women' since 1853. The most striking feature of these inebriate reformatories – indeed nonstatutory provision in general – was the way in which they were created as unique institutions for dealing with women. The 'therapeutic' service was provided for women, almost to the exclusion of men. The ratio of men to women in the certified inebriate reformatories was about 1:32. At Perth the ratio was nearer 1:3, although after the closure of the male division of the state reformatory in 1915, no more men were admitted to any part of the reformatory system.

Focusing on drunken women

The emphasis on women is significant not simply for the insight it provides on the importance of gender in the operation of the system, and indirectly on the position of these women in society, but also because it goes some way towards explaining the problems encountered by the reformatories in their attempts to contain inmates. Carswell offers a simple explanation for the disproportionately high level of women – poverty.[93] The usual method of dealing with minor offences, then as now, was to impose a fine. Those who could pay the fine, or who were prepared to forfeit their bail, escaped 'the system' comparatively unscathed. Those who could not usually faced no more than a short prison sentence. Carswell suggests that sheriffs favoured this option for men because they were reluctant to separate a breadwinner from his family for a prolonged period of time:

It is a serious matter to take a breadwinner away from his family. The worker who gets drunk on a Saturday night and pays his fine of seven shillings and sixpence on Monday morning is not a suitable man to take away and shut up for three years.[94]

The women, however, had not infrequently severed their family ties and with them, in the eyes of respectable society, their right to be considered as 'real women'.

What was more influential than these considerations was the continuing pre-occupation in late Victorian society with (and fear of) women's sexuality. The family continued to be seen as the mechanism *par excellence* through which sexuality (read: women) could be controlled. In the popular imagination, the women we are talking about were equated with sexual promiscuity and prostitution and, as such, were considered to be beneath contempt. They challenged the 'familist' view of the world and the cults of domesticity and true womanhood by their 'wanton behaviour'. They threatened the very fabric of the society and had, therefore, to be controlled. As with criminal women, they could be cast as 'the other', the 'outsiders', who by their very existence and distinction promoted the 'normal', domesticated female.

Women in general, and women of the 'lower working class' in particular, were vulnerable to the kinds of pressures exerted by the courts, if for no other reason than, as Carswell implies, they had often only very limited financial resources. Could this be why women constituted a greater proportion of the Scottish prison population than their English sisters? Were they less able to pay their fine? While certainly not the only answer, this must provide a partial explanation of this persistent pattern. Like men, women could be sentenced to inebriate reformatories, but because of social perceptions of their outcast status and associated poverty they were also more likely than men to be *sent* to inebriate reformatories. Beyond these judicial considerations, there might have been another, more pragmatic reason, for the differential emphasis on women. It was more than coincidence that two of the reformatories had earlier been Houses of Refuge for Fallen Women. Could it be that, just in that moment as Victorian attitudes towards prostitution were becoming ambivalent – especially about the need to 'lock up' prostitutes – the Houses of Refuge saw in the Inebriates Act an opportunity for bureaucratic survival and, perhaps, for the continuation of the fight against prostitution as part of some 'hidden agenda'[95] At Greenock and Seafield in Aberdeen they seized the chance. The Magdalenes made way for their drunken sisters.

Reformatory life: ideas in practice

The operation of the various reformatories raises many questions. What was life like for the women? What were the strategies and technologies adopted by these institutions in an effort to 'care for and control', and reform, the women? How successful were the institutions in reforming those individuals committed into its care? Whatever the ideological judicial intentions associated with inebriate institutions, it is important to explore how they operated and the role of penal and/or therapeutic mechanisms. Crucially, where is the evidence of any meaningful therapeutic intervention? The regime cannot be defined as therapeutic just because the discourses of those who set them up say it was. What differentiates the punitive from the therapeutic must be evaluated in terms of the day-to-day practices of the institutions.

From the reports we have, it seems that most reformatories employed very similar uniform, almost regimented, standards of institutional life. The strategy of reform favoured by the institutions can be summed up in one phrase – 'prayers and piecework'. Even the fairly short period of recreation allowed to the inmates was given over to the demands of the factory or the pulpit. Recreation periods were generally times of self-improvement – learning the skills of literacy and numeracy in which many of the inmates were seriously deficient and which were increasingly important in the industrial world outside the reformatory. Such free time as remained was taken up by visits from the ladies' committee, lectures (usually on Biblical themes), concerts and 'amusements, such as draughts, dominoes, ping pong, etc'. All very familiar to those inmates who had been in prisons.The emphasis on 'moral treatment' which structured the institutional environment, reflects their origins in the asylums for the mentally ill.[96] The ideology and the therapeutic practices of the psychiatrist (alienist) dominated thinking on institutional care from the mid-nineteenth century through to the First World War. The lunatic asylum continued to be a principal location for the non-criminal treatment of women. It is not too surprising, therefore, that when medical enthusiasts of non-statutory institutions thought about how they might construct the institutional environment, they turned to the model of the lunatic asylum for inspiration. The annual report of the Girgenti Home for 1906 illustrates the point, bringing together what were seen as the essential elements of treatment.

Treatment is essentially the same as that for mental disorders, because inebriety is closely allied to insanity in causation, etc. 'A healthy mind in a healthy body' is the whole aim of the treatment. To gain this we must have (a) total abstinence (b) the removal of predisposing and exciting causes (c) the restoration of the general tone of body and mind (d) full employment of body and mind. I believe in keeping the inmates in constant employment, and as much as possible in the open air.[97]

The 'treatment' offered in most institutions (including prisons) had little to recommend it to the modern advocate of the therapeutic community. There was no counselling beyond the more or less constant religious exhortations which served mainly to impress upon the wrongdoer her 'guilt' in the eyes of both society and deity. Nor, curiously enough, does there seem to have been a full-time medical presence in many of the reformatories. The case of the first inmate of Girgenti serves as a tragic example. This woman was badly burned in uncertain circumstances (possibly an accident or a suicide attempt). Despite being only a few miles from the nearest town, it was two days before she was seen by the medical officer. Shortly afterwards, she died of her injuries. Had qualified medical staff been readily available, while she may not have survived, she would surely have been removed to hospital much sooner.

In general, the therapeutic practices associated with the reformatories were simple and straightforward, relying on 'moral treatment' with labour at its core, rather than medical science. It is interesting that, for all the therapeutic ideology and despite the active involvement of some medical men, there was very little emphasis on drug therapy.

Dr Cunningham, the medical officer at the Girgenti Home, did run one drug trial. On the recommendation of a medical friend, he gave twenty-two patients a daily dose of a mixture of quinine, ammonium and aloin, plus a tablet of 'atrophine sulphide'. The 'willing patients' suffered sickness, vomiting, general stomach upsets, and attacks of diarrhoea (aloin being a bitter and fairly strong purgative) during the month-long experiment, but their general health and mental well-being was said to have greatly improved. Two years after this experiment, however, all but three of the 'patients' had relapsed. So it was back to the Bible and reliance upon the therapeutic and reformative value of hard work, and the benefits of a well-balanced diet.

The work regimes of the reformatories were very similar to those established in prisons. They focused, predictably, on the domestic tasks that were necessary for the upkeep of the institution and the production of a few commodities which supposedly prepared the inmate to return as a useful member to society. Gardening, sewing, knitting, cooking, cleaning, making doormats and doing laundry (especially the latter) – these were jobs the women were set to do: jobs intended to equip them for a role as household servant, wife and mother. Even the most cursory glance at the available inmate files, however, gives the lie to the official view, making it plain that many of these women had abandoned their families, or had been rejected by them, long before they entered the system.

It is difficult to escape from the comparison of many of these non-statutory institutions with prison. There are the rules and regulations; the similarity in the regimes with their emphases on religion and work; some even had a system of release on licence. Given that the realities of reformatory life did not match the formal therapeutic discourse, we might assume that this contradiction would result in a concern about institutional practice. Yet rather than focus on the limitations of the regimes, many commentators shifted the discourse to the personal attributes of their 'clients'. All of the reformatories, to a greater or lesser degree, complained about the 'clients' that were referred to them by the courts. They all had an ideal 'client group' in mind, one that offered the institution (and the individual) the best hope of effecting a reformation. The ideal inmates, in Carswell's opinion, were:

> persons who, while habitual drunkards, are of such character and disposition that it may be reasonably expected, if cured of their intemperance, they would be able to take their places in society as self-supporting citizens.[98]

The preference for young, reasonably 'uncorrupted', well-motivated inmates is an echo of penal discourses of the past and present, but it is in marked contrast to the actual pattern of receptions which favoured the admission of older, more chronic, offenders. The reformatories, however, were either public institutions or were dependent on public funding. They were in effect required to accept anyone, even those whose prognosis was considered to be hopeless.

Widening the carceral net

The degree of interaction between the various institutions of 'treatment' and/or control is very marked in places, precisely because they share a common client group. Looking at this interpretation gives some indication of the overlap that existed between formal and informal control, even in the most routine aspects of an individual's life. The 'revolving door' – which has proved such an evocative image in the context of contemporary discussions of institutional care – was already spinning freely in the closing years of the nineteenth century. The poor, the mentally ill, the inebriate, the petty offender, the prostitute, all were stigmatised and confined within a complex and expanding network of institutions.

The progress of individuals within this institutional network can be traced through the sparse entries in the files. The following history of events in the life of one woman presents an extreme, but by no means atypical, illustration of the institutional nexus between the hospital, the prison, the reformatory and the asylum. After a number of short prison sentences, in 1901 this woman was sent to the Girgenti Home and here her journey through the institutional network begins:

10 October – transferred to State Inebriate Reformatory, Perth.

4 April – 'The P.C. [Prison commissioners] have the honour to report that Isabella Thompson, at present an inmate of the State Inebriate Reformatory at Perth, has become insane'.

21 October – Removed to Woodilee Asylum, Glasgow, where, 'Beyond a slight blunting of the finer intellectual and moral faculties', the psychiatrist could find 'no sign of insanity'.

10 June 1903 – Returned to State Inebriate Reformatory.

14 September – Re-admitted to Woodilee Asylum, Glasgow.

16 July 1904 – Liberated.

18 July – Arrested (drunk and incapable) fined 2/6d (15p) or three days' imprisonment.

8 November – Transferred from Duke Street Prison, Glasgow (sentenced seven days for using obscene language) to Woodilee Asylum.

5 December – Discharged from Woodilee Asylum.

28 June 1905 – Sentenced to seven days' imprisonment (drunk and incapable).

30 June – Transferred from Duke Street Prison to Woodilee Asylum, Glasgow as 'insane and dangerous'.

5 July – Discharged from Woodilee Asylum on expiry of prison warrant. Readmitted same day 'chargeable to Parish'.

From court, to prison, to lunatic asylum, to inebriate reformatory, and back to the court. The progression does not seem to be explicable in terms of any socio-medical diagnosis, or even some crude classification, rather it was related to the role of the institutions in controlling/treating such women.

To judge these institutions on their success, or lack of it, in the rehabilitative field, is to accept perforce that the therapy was the main institutional aim. For some contemporary commentators the inebriate reformatories have been seen as a testimony to the seriousness of medical interest in the problem or as examples of the emergence of 'caring' institutions.[99] Viewed from this position, the history of the reformatories appears as an essentially benign, even progressive series of events perhaps confounded by unfortunate, or unintended, consequences. However, having explored the official record, we would suggest an alternative explanation. The reformatories formed part of a much broader interlocking carceral network. Although they were not penal institutions, the reformatories had a good deal in common with the penal estate. The regime, the emphasis on 'prayers and piecework', the system of release on licence, even the concern with diet and 'moral treatment', all find parallels in other areas of the carceral world. They were adjuncts to, rather than a radical departure from, the extant policies of the criminal justice system. and, whatever the fine phrases about 'fair and reasonable experiments', this was clearly meant to be the case.

CONCLUSION

The treatment of women in prison in the nineteenth century was shaped by gender assumptions about the potential of women who were trained primarily in domestic service and the production of textiles. Women were also subjected to the technologies associated with individuation and normalisation as exemplified in rigid regimes, moral and religious exhortation, systems of elaborate rules, and forms of confinement and regulation which sought to separate them from the contaminating influences of fellow offenders. In the first few decades after the creation of the modern penitentiary these objectifying processes were often mediated by the more personal and paternalist reactions of female staff. By the end of the century the evidence suggests that the numbers of prisoners and an alternative approach resulted in more abstracted, distant relationships between staff and prisoners. Around the turn of the century new discourses constitute women offenders as a race or class apart from 'normal' chaste women. They also stress the need for new 'caring' forms of reacting to women. New institutions such as inebriate reformatories develop at the same time, yet they do not reflect a 'caring' orientation.

The therapeutic and caring discourses emerging at the turn of the nineteenth century, and the professionals who proposed them, did not necessarily bring about improved conditions and lessen the control over women. In many ways they constituted an extension of the power to punish. Foucault has demonstrated how the behavioural and social sciences have, through the coming together of power and knowledge, actually extended the processes of objectifying individuals. Through examination people are scrutinized and 'scientifically' selected for diverse 'treatments'. Their lives are distilled into the abstracted 'case' for use by the powerful. As employed within the institutional nexus of prisons and reformatories these tendencies reduce the possibilities for genuine concern and assistance, closing off the potential for change.[100]

In the 1920s Mary Gordon, a prison medical officer and inspector, remarked on the total absence of a caring and reformative atmosphere in British prisons for women. 'A prison . . . has no use for the emotions: expressions of feelings are as much out of place as pistols would be: the prisoner's part is to do as she is told, and consume her own smoke'.[101] Penal discipline, she observed did not reflect the new therapeutic discourses. 'In 1922 our discipline, and restraint of prisoners under it, is about as humane or scientific as to render a caged animal irritable and savage by confinement, and then to treat its irritability, or nervous exasperation, by tying it up and beating it'[102]

Possibly the most significant aspect of the new 'treatment' orientation in this century has been to expand the nature of control in women's prisons. Nineteenth-century penalty focused on the control of the minds and bodies of women, today prisons for women are additionally concerned about the regulation and reformation of emotions. The concern to control the emotions of imprisoned women is not unsurprisingly shaped by conceptions of the proper emotions for women. In 1952, after serving a sentence in an English prison, Joan Henry wrote that officers were 'expressionless monotones' who 'always require a sense of ebullient cheerfulness'.[103] A recent intensive investigation of Cornton Vale prison, the only Scottish institution for women, revealed that female prisoners are more closely observed and controlled than male prisoners.[104] Women in Cornton Vale are also required to present a cheerful countenance, yet authentic displays of emotions are to be avoided. Cornton Vale, however, has not escaped the legacy of the nineteenth century. All prisoners must labour and they are punished if they refuse to work.

NOTES

1 E. P. Thompson, *The Making of the English Working Class* (Gollancz, London, 1963).

2 See for example, D. Hay, P. Linebaugh, J. Rule, E. P. Thompson and C. Winslow (eds), *Albion's Fatal Tree* (Allen Lane, London, 1975).

3 M. Ignatieff, *A Just Measure of Pain: The Penitentiary in the Industrial Revolution, 1750–1850* (Macmillan, London, 1978).

4 M. Foucault, *Discipline and Punish*. Translated by Alan Sheridan (Allen Lane, London, 1977).

5 Ibid.; H. L. Dreyfus and P. Rabinow, *Michel Foucault: Beyond Structuralism and Hermeneutics* (The University of Chicago Press,

Chicago, 1972); P. Rabinow (ed.), *The Foucault Reader* (Penguin, Harmondsworth, 1984).

6   Foucault, *Discipline and Punish*, p. 137

7   See for example, J. Thorsten Sellin, *Pioneering in Penology. The Amsterdam Houses of Correction in the Sixteenth and Seventeenth Centuries* (University of Pennsylvania Press, Philadelphia, 1944); P. Spierenberg, *The Emergence of Carceral Institutions: Prisons, Galleys and Lunatic Asylums 1550–1900* (Erasmus University Press, Rotterdam, 1984); R. P. Dobash, R. Emerson Dobash and S. Gutteridge, *The Imprisonment of Women* (Basil Blackwell, Oxford, 1986).

8   See N. McKendrick, 'Josiah Wedgewood and Factory Discipline', *The Historical Journal*, vol. 4, no. 1, pp. 30–55; E. P. Thompson, 'Time, work-discipline and industrial capitalism', *Past and Present*, vol. 38, 1967, pp. 56–97; R. Bendix, *Work and Authority in Industrial Society* (University of California Press, Berkeley, 1972).

9   D. Garland, *Punishment and Welfare,* (Gower, Aldershot, 1985).

10 Ibid., p. 31.

11 Ibid., p. 30.

12 Ibid., p. 248.

13 Ibid., p. 243.

14 While Garland has done an admirable job of detailing and analysing the discourses of this period, we think he has exaggerated the distinction between this period and the nineteenth century. This is particularly the case for labour. As we argue later in this chapter useful and productive labour has always been an element of the modern penitentiary and it was always seen as a reformative activity. Certainly punitive labour has always existed but the material demands for the upkeep and maintenance of the prison and the production of commodities have always been more important than punitive ideologies. It could be that Garland reaches these conclusions after having consulted the works of liberal and radical reformers such as the Webbs, who, for political reasons, tended to emphasise the spread of punitive labour in prisons in the late nineteenth century. For a more informed account of labour in this period see, R. S. Hinde, *The British Penal System* (Duckworth, London, 1951).

15 Similar 'contradictions' are evident in the philosophy and practices of the Scottish Children's Panels. As Robert Hughes, Under-secretary of State for the Scottish Office, pointed out in 1975, 'Their duty to act in the best interests of the child was by no means incompatible with action other people would regard as punishment'. *Tmes Educational Supplement*, Scotland, 1 April 1975.

16 For a critical analysis of the gender-blind nature of contemporary criminology see, A. Morris, *Women, Crime and Criminal Justice* (Basil Blackwell, Oxford, 1987).

17 See for example E. P. Thompson, 'The moral economy of the English crowd in the eighteenth century', *Past and Present*, vol. 50 (February, 1971), pp. 76–136.

18 On the crimes of women see: J. M. Beattie, 'The pattern of crime in England, 1660–1800', *Past and Present*, vol. 62, 1974, pp. 47–95; J. M. Beattie, 'The criminality of women in eighteenth century

England', *Journal of Social History*, vol 72, 1975, pp. 80–116; D. Beddoe, *Welsh Convict Women* (Stewart Williams, 1979); P. Robinson, *The Women of Botany Bay* The Macquarie University Library Pty. Ltd., New South Wales, 1988).

19 E. B. Freedman, *Their Sisters' Keepers: Women's Prison Reform in America, 1830–1930* (University of Michigan Press, Ann Arbor, 1981); N. H. Rafter, *Partial Justice: State Prisons and Their Inmates, 1800–1935* (Northeastern University Press, Boston, 1982); P. O'Brien, *The Promise of Punishment: Prisons in Nineteenth Century France* (Princeton University Press, Princeton, 1982).

20 For earlier straightforward and generally uncritical accounts of the imprisonment of women see: E. C. Lekkerkerker, *Reformatories for Women in the United States* (J. B. Wolters' Uitgevers-Maatschappij, Batavia, The Netherlands, 1931); A. D. Smith, *Women in Prison* (Stevens, London, 1962).

21 R. P. Dobash, 'Labour and discipline in Scottish and English prisons: Moral correction, punishment and useful toil', *Sociology*, vol. 17, no. 1, 1983, pp. 1–27.

22 See Ignatieff, *A Just Measure of Pain* for a discussion of these ideals.

23 See Foucault's discussion of the panopticon society in *Discipline and Punish*.

24 R. Evans, 'Bentham's Panopticon', *Architectural Association Quarterly*, vol. 3, pp. 21–37.

25 J. J. Gurney, *Notes on a Visit Made to Some of the Prisons in Scotland and the North of England in Company with Elizabeth Fry* (Longman, London, 1819).

26 Lord Advocate's Report, 1826, p. 104.

27 Ibid.

28 For a comprehensive analysis of nineteenth-century penal architecture see R. Evans, *The Fabrication of Virtue, English Prison Architecture, 1750–1840* (Cambridge University Press, Cambridge, 1981).

29 See T. Markus, 'Buildings for the sad, the bad and the mad in urban Scotland', in T. A. Markus (ed.) *Order in Space and Society: Architectural Form and its Content in Scottish Enlightenment* (Mainstream, Edinburgh, 1982).

30 Lord Advocate's Report, p. 22.

31 Lord Advocate's Report.

32 Lord Advocate's Repot, p. 44.

33 Gurney, *Notes on a Visit*.

34 Quoted in D. F. Smith, 'Scottish prisons under the General Board of Directors, 1840–1861', *Albion*, vol. 15, no. 4, winter 1983, pp. 296–317.

35 Lord Advocate's Report.

36 *Fifth Report of the Inspectors, Prisons of Great Britain, Volume IV. Scotland, Northumberland, and Durham*, 1840.

37 Ibid., p. 54.

38 *Second Report of the Inspectors*, 1837, p. xix.

39 *First Report on the Execution of the Criminal Law – Especially Juvenile Offenders and Transportation*, 1847.

40 *Seventh Report of the Inspectors of the Prisons of Great Britain*, 1842, p. 71.

41 The evidence further suggests that women on average received shorter sentences than men. In 1900 88 per cent of women had

sentences of sixty days or less. For men the figure was 64 per cent. At the other end of the scale, sixteen per cent of men were sentenced to six months or more, but only 3.3 per cent of women received comparable sentences.

42 *Tenth Report of the Inspectors*, 1845, p. X.
43 H. Martineau, 1865, 'Life in the criminal class', *Edinburgh Review*, vol. CXXII, pp. 337–371.
44 Smith, 'Scottish prisons'.
45 Smith, 'Scottish prisons', p. 296.
46 Quoted in Smith, op. cit.
47 *Prison Board of Directors Second Report*, 1841, p. 68.
48 Foucault, *Discipline and Punish*.
49 *Seventh Report of the Inspectors*, Appendix VI, 1842, p. 57.
50 *Board of Directors*, 1844.
51 *Seventh Report of the Inspectors*, 1842.
52 *Report from the Departmental Committee on Scottish Prisons*, 1900, p. 23.
53 Quoted in Smith, 'Scottish prisons', p. 297.
54 F. Hill, *An Autobiography of Fifty Years in Times of Penal Reform* (ed.), Constance Hill (Bentley and Son, London, 1893).
55 Appendix to Parliamentary Report, 1878–9, p. 1225.
56 Ibid.
57 Gurney, *Notes on a Visit*, p. 164.
58 *Ninth Report of the Inspectors*, 1844, p. 9.
59 Freedman, *Their Sisters' Keepers*.
60 *Fifteenth Report of the Inspectors*, 1850, p. 41.
61 *Eighth Report of the Inspectors*, 1843, p. 29.
62 *Ninth Report of the Inspectors*, 1844, p. 12.
63 *Seventh Report of the Inspectors*, 1842, p. 70.
64 Parliamentary Reports, Minutes of Evidence, 1900, p. 20.
65 W. Sievwright, *Historical Sketch of the General Prison for Scotland at Perth* (Wright, Perth, 1894), pp. 105, 275.
66 F. E. Maybrick, *Mrs Maybrick's Own Story. My Fifteen Lost Years* (Funk and Wagnalls, 1905) pp. 66, 70.
67 Maybrick, p. 104.
68 Maybrick, p. 121.
69 For a discussion of nineteenth-century theories of female criminality see Dobash, Dobash, and Gutteridge, chapter 5, *The Imprisonment of Women*; C. Smart, *Women, Crime and Criminology: A Feminist Critique* (Routledge, London, 1973).
70 Robinson, *The Women of Botany Bay*, p. 67.
71 See for example H. Maudsley, 'Review of female life in prison', *Journal of Medical Science*, vol. 9, 1863, pp. 69–87.
72 Maudsley, op. cit., p. 67.
73 H. Ellis, *The Criminal* (Scott, London, 1901, first published in 1891).
74 C. Burt, *The Young Delinquent* (University of London Press, London, 1919).
75 J. F. Sutherland, *Recidivism: Habitual Criminality, and Habitual Petty Delinquency* (William Green, Edinburgh, 1908).
76 Ibid., p. 1.
77 Ibid., p. 19.
78 Ibid., p. 44.
79 Ibid., p. 75.
80 Ibid., p. 80.

81 In some states in the USA special women's reformatories were created to house the most respectable and redeemable women. Black and poor women continued to be sent to the often squalid county and state jails and prisons. See Rafter, *Partial Justice*, for a discussion of this pattern.

82 For a discussion of the philosophical bases of refuge for women see chapter 3 in R. Emerson Dobash and Russell P. Dobash, *Women, Violence and Social Change* (Routledge, London, 1992).

83 W. Tait, *Magdalenism* (Edinburgh, P. Richard, 1840); for a contemporary account of the Scottish situation see L. Mahood, *The Magdalenes: Prostitution in the Nineteenth Century* (Routledge, London, 1990).

84 E. Orme, *Our Female Criminals*, 1898.

85 Ibid., p. 791.

86 S. Cohen, *Visions of Social Control*, Polity Press, Oxford, 1985.

87 Presbytery of Glasgow, Report of Commission on the Housing of the Poor in Location to Their Social Condition, 1981, p. 31.

88 P. McCandless, 'Curses of civilisation: Insanity and drunkenness in Victorian Britain', paper presented at the International Group for Comparative Alcohol Studies meetings on the Social History of Alcohol, Berkeley, CA., 1984.

89 Glasgow Room, Mitchell Library, Glasgow.

90 *Report of the Inspector for Scotland, Under the Inebriates Acts*, 1910.

91 *Report of the Inspector for Scotland, Under the Inebriates Acts*, 1907, p. 834.

92 A. Scull, *Decarceration* (Prentice-Hall, Englewood Cliffs, NJ, 1977).

93 J. Carswell, 'The working of the Inebriates Act', *Journal of Mental Science*, October 1901, pp. 1–14.

94 Ibid., p. 7.

95 J. R. Walkowitz, *Prostitution and Victorian Society: Women, Class and the State* (Cambridge University Press, Cambridge, 1980).

96 On moral treatment see, E. I. Carlsen and N. Dain, 'The psychotherapy that was moral treatment', *American Journal of Psychiatry*, vol. 117, pp. 519–524.

97 Annual Report of Girgenti Home, 1906, p. 19.

98 Carswell, 'The working of the Inebriates Act', p. 9

99 Garland, *Punishment and Welfare*; J. Orford and G. Edwards, *Alcoholism* (Oxford University Press, Oxford, 1977).

100 See Dobash and Dobash, *Women, Violence and Social Change* chapter 7, for a discussion of the social and political consequences of conceptualising women who experience persistent violence as in need of therapy.

101 M. Gordon, *Penal Discipline* (Routledge and Sons, London, 1922), p. 175.

102 Ibid., p. 190.

103 J. Henry, *Who Lie in Gaol* (Gollancz, London, 1952), p. 21.

104 Dobash, Dobash and Gutteridge, *The Imprisonment of Women* chapter 6.

SELECT BIBLIOGRAPHY

Beddoe, D., *Welsh Convict Women*, Stewart Williams London, 1979.

Dobash, R. Emerson and Dobash, R. P., *Women, Violence and Social Change* (Routledge, London, 1992).

Dobash, R. P., 'Labour and discipline in Scottish and English Prisons: Moral correction, punishment and useful toil', *Sociology*, vol. 17, no. 1 (1983) pp. 1–27.

Dobash, R. P., Dobash, R. Emerson and Gutteridge, S., *The Imprisonment of Women*, (Basil Blackwell, Oxford, 1986).

Evans, R., *The Fabrication of Virtue, English Prison Architecture, 1750–1840*, (Cambridge University Press, Cambridge, 1981).

Freedman, E. B., *Their Sisters' Keepers: Women's Prison Reform in America, 1830–1930*, (University of Michigan Press, Ann Arbor, 1981).

Garland, D., *Punishment and Welfare*, (Aldershot, Gower, 1985).

Gordon, M., *Penal Discipline*, (Routledge, London, 1922).

Gurney, J. J., *Notes on a Visit Made to Some of the Prisons in Scotland and the North of England in Company with Elizabeth Fry*, (Longman, London, 1819).

Henry, J, *Who Lie in Gaol*, (Gollancz, London, 1952).

Hill, F., *An Autobiography of Fifty Years in Times of Penal Reform*, Constance Hill (ed.), (Bentley and Son, London, 1893).

Ignatieff, M., *A Just Measure of Pain: The Penitentiary in the Industrial Revolution, 1750–1850*, (London, Macmillan, 1977).

Lekkerker, E. C., *Reformatories for Women in the United States*, (J. B. Wolters', The Netherlands, 1931).

Mahood, L. *The Magdalenes: Prostitution in the Nineteenth Century*, (Routledge, London, 1990).

Markus, T. A. (ed.), *Order in Space and Society: Architectural Form and its Content in the Scottish Enlightenment*, (Mainstream, Edinburgh, 1982).

Maybrick, F. E., *Mrs Maybrick's Own Story. My Fifteen Lost Years*, (Funk and Wagnalls, New York, 1905).

Morris, A., *Women, Crime and Criminal Justice*, (Basil Blackwell, Oxford, 1987).

O'Brien, P., *The Promise of Punishment: Prisons in Nineteenth Century France*, (Princeton University Press, Princeton, 1982).

Rafter, N. H., *Partial Justice: State Prisons and Their Inmates, 1800–1935*, (Northeastern University Press, Boston, 1982).

Robinson, P., *The Women of Botany Bay*, (Macquarie University Press, New South Wales, 1988).

Smart, C. *Women, Crime and Criminology: A Feminist Critique*, (Routledge, London, 1973).

Smith, A. D., *Women in Prison*, (Stevens, London, 1962).

Smith, D. F., 'Scottish prisons under the General Board of Directors, 1840–1861', *Albion*, vol. 15, no. 4 (1983) pp. 296–317.

Sutherland, J. F., *Recidivism: Habitual Criminality, and Habitual Petty Delinquency*, (William Green, Edinburgh, 1908).

Thompson, E. P., *The Making of the English Working Class*, (Gollancz, London, 1963).

Walkowitz, J. R., *Prostitution and Victorian Society: Women, Class and the State*, (Cambridge University Press, Cambridge, 1980).

5

'SPROUTING WINGS?': WOMEN AND RELIGION IN SCOTLAND *c.* 1890–1950

CALLUM G. BROWN AND JAYNE D. STEPHENSON

INTRODUCTION

The history of women and religion in Britain is a much neglected field of study. Neither in the study of religion and the churches, nor in feminist studies, has there been significant research into the historical dimensions of women's religious experiences. So scant is this field of inquiry that there exists virtually no agenda of issues nor sets of hypotheses for analysis from which to set new research.

Equally, the sources of evidence so far opened up by historians in their study of religion demonstrate the difficulties in accumulating material with which to research. As Gail Malmgreen has noted (in what is so far the only book devoted solely to the analysis of women and religion in Britain), the sources upon which historians of religion have relied 'are maddeningly uninformative on matters of gender'. She continues: 'We have no idea, yet, how women's religious beliefs and practices might be correlated with social class, age, marital status, geography or educational background.'[1] A very small number of studies have 'turned up the corners' of the blanket of ignorance: studies of women preachers and of women's role in philanthropy, studies of leading religious figures, and the role of women in the English temperance movement.[2] Beyond these boundaries, the historiography is extremely thin – and especially so in Scotland.[3]

The most profound ignorance prevails in relation to religion and working-class women. The studies listed above, and the vast majority of the others not cited, concern themselves with the most highly visible, and often the wealthiest, of women involved in religious organisations and campaigns. The relationship between middle- and upper-class women and organised religion reveal very little about the very different sets of economic, social and cultural situations within which working- or lower middle-class women formed relationships with religion. Equally, with the exception of notable oral history work by Rickie Burman amongst Jewish women in Manchester,[4] we know little of variations in religious experience between women of different ethnic groups.

In these circumstances, this chapter must of necessity have modest aims. It exploits two types of historical evidence which *can* throw light upon the role of religion in the lives of working-class women: oral history testimony and autobiographies. Using the first of these predominantly, we explore in this chapter the varieties of religious experience of Scottish women between the late nineteenth and mid-twentieth centuries. We seek to establish the extent and nature of women's links with organised religion (both churches and religious voluntary organisations), drawing on the evidence of both childhood and adulthood to explore the religious constituents in women's lives. The evidence we dwell on is that from working-class women – those most neglected in the existing literature.

THE HISTORIOGRAPHICAL FRAMEWORK

Discussion of the importance of religion in the lives of working-class women has been subsumed in wider debate about working-class religion generally. This debate has failed to produce a consensus view.[5] Instead, historians have generated a series of views which cannot be easily polarised. In part, superficial evidence – such as statistics of religious adherence and social composition analysis – has been open to varying interpretation. The traditional view, held by church and general historians, has been that the growth of industrial and urban society in the nineteenth century alienated the working-classes from middle-class-dominated churches and caused church adherence to decline.[6] However, new research by social historians of religion has challenged this view, indicating that the majority of church members and churchgoers of all denominations belonged to families in which the male head of household was working class (and notably of the skilled working class), and secondly that church membership did not start to decline until the first decade of the twentieth century, and then only slowly until the late 1950s.[7]

Evidence of high levels of working-class church adherence in modern Scotland (as in Britain as a whole) has tended to lend support to an older concept of artisan religious 'respectability'. In this concept, 'respectability' was allegedly not found amongst the lower working class – those families where male heads of households held unskilled jobs like labourer or carter, and those families who were very poor. The aloof independency of 'respectable' artisans, and the evangelising energy of the Victorian middle classes in city slums, seems to many historians to point to the 'unrespectability' and irreligious habits of the lower working class and the poor. This correlation between wealth and social status on the one hand, and respectability and religious adherence on the other, has dominated historians' consideration of working-class religion. Whilst wealth and status were influential factors affecting church connection, the role of religion in industrial society is not to be understood solely by studying the churches, but by the study of religion's place within popular culture as a whole.

When considering working-class women and religion, the significant research undertaken in the United States has not been matched in Britain.[8] The most fruitful indications, interestingly, have come through the use of oral history and autobiography. Hugh McLeod, in a pioneering examination of both male and female testimony in three English oral history archives, alluded to some important distinctions between the two in their religious experiences.[9] Most significant, perhaps, was the evidence that respondents in all regions of England recalled greater churchgoing by their late-Victorian and Edwardian mothers than by their fathers. However, McLeod did not report such a gender difference for Scotland nor for Wales – regions in which churchgoing for both mothers and fathers was very high. For example, in the Potteries, north Midlands and north-east of England, respondents reported that 40 per cent of mothers and 20 per cent of fathers were 'regular' churchgoers; in Scotland and Wales the figures for both mothers and fathers were over 50 per cent.

This does not mean that a gender difference did not exist in Scotland – notably in later decades of the twentieth century. Certainly, by the 1960s it was being reported that well over 70 per cent of all churchgoers in both the Church of Scotland and the Roman Catholic church were women. More generally, there seems to be cause for believing that women's participation in religious organisations and events has often been higher than men's. High female participation has been noted in Scottish religious riots of the Napoleonic period. Equally, the church-promoted local-veto plebiscites conducted in the 1920s and 1930s to instigate local prohibition of alcohol (popularly remembered as the 'dry' areas) suggest that the female working-class vote was numerically decisive for the 'religious temperance' side.[10]

Oral history and autobiography from working-class women has been employed in another approach to the subject. The nature of proletarian women's neighbourhood and community life, and the centrality of the concept of 'respectability', has been illuminated in a number of studies.[11] These have suggested that religion was an important factor in the construction of the culture of plebeian women, infusing daily life and popular values with religious or quasi-religious ideals. In part, churches expected women to sustain moral behaviour in families where male behaviour (primarily of fathers) was often compromised by exposure to drink and to 'unhealthy' environments like the public house. But in part also, it can be argued, working-class women sustained an indigenous concept of 'respectability', quite independent from church interference.

It is in these issues that this chapter seeks to make a preliminary exploration within the Scottish experience.

WOMEN AND THE SCOTTISH CHURCHES

Like most other institutions of civil society, churches have traditionally been a male domain. Before the second quarter of this century, no organised denomination in Scotland permitted women to be full clergy. The first to do so was the Congregational Union in 1929 followed by the small and very liberal Presbyterian United Free Church in the 1930s. The largest Scottish denomination, the Church of Scotland, only admitted women as ministers and elders in the late 1960s, but has since found that it has a growing dependence on women to meet its 'manpower' needs; in 1986, while women made up less than 10 per cent of full ministers, they made up 23 per cent of probationers.[12] Since 1929 the Roman Catholic church has had the second largest adherence in Scotland and by 1984 the largest number of Sunday attenders, but has traditionally confined women's official professional functions to that of nuns within the segregated religious orders; the secular priesthood in that church, as also in the much smaller Scottish Episcopal Church, remains all male.

The Presbyterian tradition which has dominated in the majority of Scottish churches has often been seen as oppressing women. From John Knox's exhortation against 'the monstrous regiment of women' in the sixteenth century, Calvinism in Scotland had many facets which appeared peculiarly barbarous towards women. Parish kirk sessions of minister and male elders spent most of their time in judicial cases investigating fornication; single women accused of fornication could have their breasts milked for 'evidence' of pregnancy, and might expect to be interrogated during the pains of childbirth to reveal the father's name.[13] The witch-hunt craze in Scotland, which between 1570 and 1680 was one of the worst in Europe, exploited fear of women as a means of a wider social control.[14] Yet some historians have suggested recently that the Presbyterian heritage was less anti-women than has often been thought. James Young has demonstrated that Calvinism was not so uniquely anti-women, whilst Leah Leneman has suggested that the kirk session system – despite its apparent barbarity – actually operated a paternalistic concern for single women and their bastard children by putting emphasis on finding paternal child support.[15]

However, as late as the 1920s there were women who recalled the threat of kirk session interrogation for fornication – even when they did not adhere to the Presbyterian church. Christian Watt had been born into a fisher family in the village of Broadsea near Fraserburgh in 1833, and gave birth in the 1850s to an illegitimate child whilst her 'promised' husband (a 'bond of handfast' marriage, later confirmed in traditional manner before a sheriff) was away at sea. While her father was Church of Scotland, Christian followed her mother as a Congregationalist; yet, the kirk session of the local Church of Scotland still claimed a parish-wide remit in its control of popular morality. She recalled in her memoirs how the elders – 'that bunch of hypocrites' – planned to call her before it on a 'libel' of fornication, and how she intended to 'wreck the session': 'I would ask to appear in the body of the kirk not the vestry, and I would start on one elder, a Fraserburgh business man who had in the past been known to frequent bawdy houses in Aberdeen.' For all her bravado, Christian makes clear that the prospect of the church case was a daunting one, and she seems relieved that it did not proceed. However, retribution was made when the Church of Scotland minister allegedly influenced the local registrar to disregard the sheriff's confirmation of marriage and record the child's birth as illegitimate.[16]

The Church of Scotland, as the established or state church until 1925, had powerful influence in the local parish. Even the apparent 'secularisation' of local government in the nineteenth century did not eliminate this influence. The parish councils (1896–1929), school boards (1873–1919) and *ad hoc* education authorities (1920–1930) were dominated by ministers and church elders, acting as surrogate kirk sessions in pursuing female poor relief recipients for spending money on drink and for sexual 'scandal', and haranguing mothers for allowing their husbands to be drunks and for their children to play truant from school.[17] Despite strong continuities between the eighteenth and twentieth centuries, the Presbyterian churches' prosecution of women for sexual immorality practically disappeared after 1870. In part, the kirk had belatedly come to acknowledge that a 'godly society' of the type which the early reformers had striven for, could not be attained in a modern urban society. But in part also, the enforcement of sexual morality was no longer being sought through moral force but through moral suasion – through the influence in popular leisure and life of religious organisations and notions of 'respectability'. It was as a diffusive rather than an enforced Christianity that influence was to be exerted, and especially through women.

WOMEN IN RELIGIOUS ORGANISATIONS

In 1891, Scottish Presbyterian Sunday schools had enrolments representing 52 per cent of Scottish children aged between 5 and 10 years. With the addition of other Protestant Sunday schools and Catholic church provision for children, the true figure of children's Sunday connections with organised religion was probably considerably higher. In addition, from the 1870s until the 1920s there was a plethora of weekday religious and church-operated organisations for children – some devotional like Christian Endeavour groups, but many more were temperance organisations (like the Bands of Hope for Protestants and the League of the Cross for Catholics). For older children and young adults there were the Girls' Guildry, the YMCA, and the YWCA, and for adults the Women's Guild and a variety of dramatic, literary and sporting associations and clubs. The period between 1880 and 1920 was the highpoint for church-based organisations and recreational activities.[18]

We have seen how Hugh McLeod, using the Thompson–Vigne oral history archive, concluded that 50 per cent of Scottish respondents claimed their mothers were 'regular' churchgoers. The testimony of the eighty elderly women born between 1894 and 1926 which is stored in the

Stirling Women's Oral History Archive provides an opportunity to assess the extent of church connection from a wider range of statistics and using a larger sample of Scots women. The respondents in the archive were socially and occupationally broadly representative of the local female occupational structure in 1921. Thirty-four per cent had held jobs as domestic servants, 23 per cent had worked in textile manufacturing, 15 per cent in each of retailing and clerical work, 24 per cent in other manufacturing, agricultural and mine-related occupations, 17 per cent in other service occupations, and 15 per cent in miscellaneous jobs.[19] Furthermore, unlike some oral history archives, the Stirling respondents were recruited overwhelmingly through 'secular' organisations rather than churches, thereby reducing the likelihood of an unrepresentively high proportion of interviewees coming from strongly religious backgrounds.

The vast majority of the respondents were brought up in late Victorian and early twentieth-century households in which Christian practice was strong. Of the fifty-five who gave responses to standardised questions on parental churchgoing, fifteen (27 per cent) stated that both parents attended church 'every Sunday', a further twenty-two (40 per cent) said they attended 'regularly', six (11 per cent) that their fathers only attended regularly or every Sunday, five (9 per cent) that their mothers only attended regularly or every Sunday, and only seven (13 per cent) that neither parent attended church.

The seventy-one respondents who defined their parents' religious affiliations (if any) expressed them as follows: forty-six (65 per cent) were Church of Scotland or United Free Church (most respondents failing to distinguish these two denominations which amalgamated in 1929); five (7 per cent) were Episcopal, four (6 per cent) were Catholic and a similar number Baptist, three (4 per cent) were Congregationalist, two (3 per cent) were Methodist, one set of parents (in-migrants from Morayshire) were Free Presbyterian, three (4 per cent) attended mission halls, three attended unknown denominations, and five (7 per cent) had no religious affiliation. Thus, out of seventy-one respondents, seventy-six separate denominational affiliations were mentioned for parents – the extra five being accounted for by multiple 'affiliation' on the part of two sets of parents, and by different religious affiliations on the part of three sets of parents. The multiple affiliations resulted from attendance at the Church of Scotland or United Free Church for Sunday morning worship, and attendance at Baptist churches and mission halls in the evening.

With 67 per cent of respondents recording that both parents attended church either regularly or every Sunday, and a further 20 per cent saying that one parent attended, it is not surprising to find very high levels of religious participation by the respondents themselves. Indeed, as children and as young adults, the women invariably attended religious organisations irrespective of their parents' religious habits. Of the seventy-six non-Catholic respondents, fifty-two (68 per cent) stated that they attended Sunday schools. Amongst these were four of the seven respondents whose parents were non-churchgoers and members – including the one woman who said that her parents were atheists. Amongst those who did not attend Sunday school, one woman's church – the Free Presbyterian Church – opposed this institution, one mentioned Bible class but not Sunday school, one lived in a small rural community with no Sunday school (though it did have a church-based Girl Guides), and two failed to mention Sunday schools despite attending church with highly religious parents. If we ignore these distorting categories, the proportion attending Sunday school rises to 73 per cent. In addition, all four Catholic women recorded that as children they attended church every week.

In addition to Sunday school, the Stirling women mentioned other religious or quasi-religious organisations to which they belonged as children and as teenagers. Prominent amongst these was the Band of Hope, the Protestant children's total abstinence organisation which in 1908 had 147,000 Scottish children enrolled and 'pledged' to abstinence. A total of twenty-seven of the Stirling respondents (or 36 per cent of non-Catholics) attended the Bands, and a further seven (9 per cent) mentioned other temperance organisations (the White Ribboners and the Good Templars). A total of ten (13 per cent) had belonged to the Brownies, Girl Guides, Girls' Guildry or the Girls' Association (each of which was strongly religious in tenor and invariably church-based), eleven (14 per cent) were in their church choir, and one was in Christian Endeavour.

Broadly speaking, the respondents retained the religious affiliation of their parents, though there was a significant drift of nine respondents from the Church of Scotland and the United Free Church to the Brethren (three respondents), the Salvation Army (three), the Baptist church (two) and the Methodist church (one respondent). In most of these cases, the women were affected during their teenage years by the highly evangelical atmosphere of the 1920 and early 1930s – and notably for three who were brought up in mining villages where the Brethren attracted them.

Assessing the women's religious commitment as they grew older is extremely difficult. On a general level, membership of religious voluntary organisations never reached anywhere near the scale of childhood membership; a small number mentioned membership of the Woman's Guild and of church choirs. Church attendance was much more rarely discussed in recalling their adult years, though for perhaps a fifth of them it is implicit rather than explicit that going to Sunday worship has been a regular part of their lives since childhood.

The picture this gives is of an upbringing in the first four decades of this century spent in a highly religious environment. None of the eighty respondents mentioned even the existence of non-religious or non-temperance organisations during their youth. They make plain – as some of the following extracts do – that churches and religious voluntary organisations were the only ones available for girls and young women before the Second World War. Even as adults, church-based organisations like the Woman's Guild, mothers' groups and church choirs predominated; only a handful of women mentioned 'secular' organ-isations like the Co-operative Women's Guild and the Miners' Welfare, and none mentioned sports clubs for women. As adults before 1940, leisure-time activities had three pivots: informal recreation with workmates, the cinema and dancing with one or two close women friends, and church or temperance organisations. Even then, as the testimony shows, dancing was often organised by temperance organisations, and the   cinema was not available to many village dwellers. As the testimony which follows shows, religious leisure for women was a vital ingredient of early twentieth-century diffusive Christianity.

THE ROLE OF CHURCH CONNECTION

The level of women's religious activity when they were young emerges from oral testimony not merely in quantitative but also qualitative terms. The sheer domination of leisure time by church and related 'recreation' is expressed in the vast majority of testimonies. Although we have little comparable men's testimony, and though it is not the aim of this chapter to draw comparisons with male experience, the accounts offered by women do suggest important characteristics of women's lives both as children and as adults from which religion emerges as a distinctive life-shaping experience.

Childhood memories are dominated by the Sunday school. Interestingly, the most vivid recollection is not of the ordinary weekly meetings but of the annual 'summer treat'. The recollections of Mrs N.2 (1906)[20] are typical of a very large number of women born in the century:

> We used to go in a cart, and we'd a tinny – a tin mug – it was round your neck, you know, with a ribbon or string or something. And oh, it was lovely getting hoisted up into the van. There were seats, you know; they'd put the seats in the van. And we didn't go very far. It was some field if it was dry; if not, we were in the hall. But in the field there was racing. It was great, the racing, you know. I enjoyed it.

The Sunday school outing a few miles into the countryside, together with the annual *soirée* of buns and oranges, were clearly highlights in the juvenile calendar. But the yearly treats were rewards for good attendance at the Sunday school throughout the year, and were emblematic of a much stronger and more sustained church connection. Asking respondents how they spent their Sundays as children between 1900 and 1930 produces a similar near uniformity of memory. Mrs I. 3(1904) recalled:

> Yes, I can tell you how I spent Sundays. We got up in the morning, I went for the milk, came back, had our breakfast, went to Sunday school at half-past ten, came back, went to church about half-past

eleven, came back home and had our lunch, which would be soup maybe, pudding, bread, cheese maybe. I can't remember. Back again to an afternoon session at the church, and back home. And if we weren't tired of it by that time, we went back with my father at half-past six at night, or one or other of them took us back at night. So, that is how our Sundays were spent until we reneged.

This pattern of highly religious activity on Sundays was not an exception but for very large numbers of Protestant girls the norm. As Mrs K.3 (1906) observed, 'as a child you just accepted that was the way of life. And your friends all went to Sunday school as well . . . everybody went to Sunday school as a matter of course'.

Family commitment lay at the root of such high religious participation for around a fifth of the children. Many recalled a strict sabbath of no games, no 'secular' reading, and Bible readings at home. Daily prayers were also frequently recalled. Mrs N. 3 (1910) recalled:

A: I was at the Sunday school when I was two years old. I got taken with my two elder sisters. And we went to the [Brethren] Gospel Hall in Port Street . . .

Q: So you took up your mother's side of the religion?

A: Yes.

Q: You didn't go to . . .

A: No, we all did. We all went to my mother's. My father eventually left the Church [of Scotland], and he came an odd time at night to my mother's church. But he never joined it. But we went to Sunday school, and then we went when we got older – when we got to about fifteen – we went to Bible class. And we went to church at night. So we always went to church.

Even those like Mrs E.4 (1923) who were still in their teens when the Second World War broke out recalled a hectic weekly schedule of religious events:

We went to church every [Sunday] morning and every evening from the time we were two years of age. And we stayed on and went to Sunday school. And as we got older we went to Bible class. And our outings during the week were Christian Endeavour on the Monday, . . . Band of Hope on the Friday and Saturday night meetings. That was our lives.

Parental direction, and the want of alternative attractions, were elements in the intensity and extent of such church activity. But part of the attraction of religion, though, was pageantry. In many ways the church service and the meetings of religious voluntary organisations offered an atmospheric 'community theatre' in which children as well as adults could participate. Religion was pageantry, and as young girls the women respondents came to enjoy it for its theatrical opportunities. Mrs V.1 (1914) recalled:

Well, Sunday was my day because . . . on a Sunday morning I got dressed, you had a Sunday outfit you see. You only wore it on a Sunday; no other day except Sunday. Well, I went to my two pals; they went to the Catholic church. So I went with them to Mass on a Sunday morning so as I'd have my Sunday clothes on. When I got home I'd go to [Protestant] church with my mother. And then when I came home from that I kept on my clothes because I was going to the Sunday school and then we went to Bible class at night. And the reason I went to all that was because I got wearing my Sunday clothes.

Children from otherwise religiously indifferent families sought out religion just as keenly as those who were pressed into attendance by parents – as with Mrs W.2 (1916):

[I went to] Sunday school, yes. And at nights the Hebron Hall or any – you know – any meeting houses at night-time. The Sunday evenings my pals and I, you know, we would go to the Sunday school, then maybe five or six o'clock we'd go to the meetings at night . . . We went to the Baptist church too sometimes in the evening . . . we didn't think about religion in the house.

Others remember additional enticements to their religious participation. Born in a mining village, Mrs Q.2 (1912) remembered:

You went to church, and then you came home had something to eat, and you went to the Brethren in the afternoon – Sunday school. They let you go in there. You got these tickets, you know, verses on them, and that, you know, to learn. And maybe a cup of tea and a cake. I think it was the cake we went for. And then to the evangelistic meeting at night. That was really all we had – all our pastime you know. 'Cause my parents were strict that way. They wouldnae let you play ball or games outside on a Sunday – no, no.

However, the 'treats' were by no means always free, as Mrs U.1 (1898) made plain:

Well, we used to go, a chum and I, we used to go to a wee Holy Meeting up at the top of Baker Street . . . We got a cup of tea for a penny, I think. And then she sent us all a Christmas card at Christmas time.

Private Sunday schools, organised in schoolrooms, hired rooms or in people's own homes were common in working-class parts of early twentieth-century Scottish cities. Mrs K.2 (1906) recalled her Sundays:

Oh well, we went to church and then . . . we went to Sunday school. The Sunday school was at four o'clock, and in fact down at the mill there, there was an English family lived in the big house, and she started a Saturday Sunday school. And we used to all go down there on an afternoon. She'd this wee room and we sang hymns an' that, had a wee cup of tea. Quite enjoyed that.

Mrs. E.3 (1923) recalled another private school, but one with a less socially elevated location:

Sunday we went to Sunday school. Before we went to Sunday school – I think you'd to be five to go to Sunday school – there was a hut just down from the Blocks that belonged to Mr Marshall. He had a grocer's shop. Now, I don't know if he was a lay preacher or what he was, but it belonged to him. And we all went to the wee Sunday school there. And as I said, the Pilgrims came with tents, and we went to the tents to sing tunes. And we went from there to the church – the big Sunday school – when we were five.

Weekday meetings were just as important in the memories of many children. Religion provided a week-round focus of devotion and recreation. Mrs N.2 (1906) summed up:

Sundays were at church quite a lot. Church and the Sunday school. Then when I got older the Bible class it was. But there was a lot of the church. And Monday was the Band of Hope. I always remember that . . . the Band of Hope. Tuesday was the Girl Guides. You know it seemed to be all church things.

The Band of Hope was organised either in congregations or in separate branches. Its tenor was strongly religious, and just as the Sunday school led onto Bible class, so the Band was often the beginning of a youthful career in temperance organisations in which secular entertainment became an enticement as girls entered their adult years. Mrs H.3 (1902) recalled:

A: The Band of Hope – well you used to have hymn-singing, and you used to get magic lanterns – you know what – the old-fashioned kind of magic lantern. And different things. Yes, we had a good time at the Band of Hope.

Q: Was that on a Sunday as well, or was that . . . ?

A: No, that'll be through the week, the Band of Hope was on through the week. The same as what the [Good] Templars were. As I got older I was in the Templars, and we used to have some good nights there too. I mean, it was a good night.

Q: So was that a sort of step on from the Band of Hope?

A: Well, it was a different crowd that had that – the Templars. You see, you didn't drink or you don't drink or anything. But we used to have some good nights. Enjoyed them, dancing and all the rest of it.

But it would be wrong to see religious and temperance occasions as merely sources of tea, cakes and dances. Secular enticements apart, there was tangible pride in dramatic processions and displays of what was perceived as moral righteousness. As well as attending religious services of a variety of denominations, Mrs U.3 (1913) remembered the strong teetotal movement in her mining village:

And oh, there was a temperance thing [of] which my father was horrified – the White Ribboners. And I went to the White Ribboners, and they had a parade. My father didn't know that I had been going to the White Ribboners. But he was standing at the corner when he saw us coming down with the white banners, and somebody said: 'My Archie, see who's leading it?' He says: 'Aye, an' I'm going to the pub tonight'. My mother was horrified, she was, with him saying that. But she said 'It doesn't matter. She was doing her best.' And I signed this White Ribboner thing. I was as good as anyone that lived . . . signed the pledge.

In this way, part of the attraction of 'religious theatre' was that the individual could play a central rôle. Whilst the teetotal pledge was a badge of righteousness in the Band of Hope, the White Ribboners and the Good Templars, the conversion experience was an important focus of drama in evangelistic meetings. Mrs W.1 (1913) recalled being a 'Sunbeam' as a young child at the Salvation Army:

> The Salvation Army people were always wanting to convert you and they used to say: 'Now, put up your hand anybody that wants to be saved'. So you would look along the line to see who wanted to be saved, and if you thought you were safe you'd put your hand up and you'd go forward. Sometimes you were all embarrassed, but still you went forward, and they put up a prayer for you, and you were saved.'

Molly Weir recalled a similar situation when she attended the annual Tent Missions of Jock Troup at Springburn in inter-war Glasgow. She described how Jock Troup was such 'great value' as a preacher that he could 'make the flames of hell so real, we felt them licking round our feet, and the prospect of heaven so alluring we often stood up to be saved several times during the week'.[21] This phenomenon was evidently widespread, and much more prevalent amongst girls and young women than amongst boys or men. During the Billy Graham 'Crusade' in Scotland in 1955, of the 20,000 people who came forward 'to make decisions for Christ', 70 per cent were women, 73 per cent were under 30 years of age, and 11 per cent were under 12 years.[22]

In addition to the Tent Missions, Molly Weir attended a variety of religious events on a regular basis: the Church of Scotland with her parents, the Salvation Army with her grandmother, and evangelistic meetings for nothing but 'the sheer enjoyment'. She does acknowledge, however, that she and her chums went indiscriminately to Protestant, Catholic and Methodist churches 'just because one gave tattie scones, the next sausage rolls and the other gave pies'.[23] Young women sought out religious events and organisations quite independent from parental direction, inducing what to the modern eye seems an unusually ecumenical or multi-denominational approach to religion. It is a prominent characteristic of oral testimony and autobiography from women in Scotland that they attended services and religious events of many different creeds. Mrs U.3 (1913), a woman whose family were Church of Scotland, recalled:

> A: We had the same thing in the Methodist church. We weren't

Methodist, but they ran a – I can't remember what they called it, it was a kind of youth club. And then there was Pentecostal people ran a Band of Hope. It was for nothing, you see. And you went to it and you sang these Moody and Sankey hymns. And if you were well behaved you got something at the end of the year. Again that was nothing' [to pay].

Q: So, it didn't really matter what denomination you were?

A: Oh no, you just went. It didn't matter what it was. Oh, I went to a Catholic thing. Now what was the name of it?

Mrs N.2 (1906) attended the Church of Scotland and Sunday school on Sundays, the Band of Hope and the Girl Guides on two days of the week, but also attended Salvation Army meetings 'because it was something different from the ordinary church'. The evangelical events in the Salvation Army, in independent mission halls, in Brethren gospel halls, and in annual revival 'tent meetings', offered a more intense and highly popular form of worship than was generally available in the Church of Scotland or the United Free Church. Just as Molly Weir recalled the excitement of Jock Troup's Tent coming to Springburn, Mrs G.1 (1924) remembered the annual Band of Hope Tent coming to her mining village:

I think it was called the Band of Hope. Came to Fallin. And they put up a huge tent, and you sang all these lovely wee jolly choruses, which were different from the church hymns – in this big tent. And you listened to the preacher. And they would be there for a few weeks. . . . Maybe about once a year they came.

Mrs Y.3 (1901) recalled attending evangelical meetings attracted by 'Sankey's hymns . . . He had lovely hymns. They used to hold it in the Arcade in Stirling. It was a music hall, but on a Sunday it used to be for the singing of hymns. . . . The Alhambra.' Several Stirling respondents cited the attraction of Ira Sankey's hymns at mission and gospel halls and at the Band of Hope. Introduced to Scotland during the Moody-Sankey revival of 1874, most middle-class-controlled congregations of the Church of Scotland and United Free Church dispensed with them before 1900, but working-class mission halls and 'tents' retained these until the middle of the century as a major attraction for worshippers.

The mixing of Protestant and Catholic children at religious services is very striking from women's testimony. Just as Mrs V.1 (1914), already cited, 'was born, and brought up as a Protestant' but 'went with [her chums] to Mass on a Sunday morning so as I'd have my Sunday clothes on', so Mrs H.1 (1907), another Protestant, attended the Catholic church with her friends:

A: But not many of my brothers and sisters went. They didn't like that. They went to the English church Sunday school. But I went. And all my chums. Some was Protestant, some was Catholic. But I went with them just the same. Just to the Catholic chapel. And I went to the Protestant, just with them to be

> chummy, you know. There was no fighting and doing what
> they do now – never.
>
> Q: Did anyone think that was wrong that you should be going to
>   the different churches?
>
> A: My father didn't object as long as you went someplace, he
>   said.

One respondent recalled how she was totally ill-informed about the
sectarian divide between Catholic and Protestant, and about the intense
history of political division in Ireland which underpinned it. After a
childhood of mixing with Catholics when 'it made no difference while we
were young', Mrs I.3 (1904) recalled work at a laundry in Milngavie:

> And the machinery was going good style, and they were singing all
> the time – Catholic songs, political songs, I used to come home and
> sing them, and he [her father] used to almost go for me: 'Stop that at
> once, don't sing that here'. [She sang] 'At Mountjoy one Monday
> morning/Still upon the gallows tree/Kevin Barry gave his young
> life/For the cause of Liberty.' . . . And this was, I think my father
> said, a Fenian song . . . which I didn't know what 'Fenian' even
> meant. Oh, that was one of the things that . . . oh, they all sung it
> joyfully, because the Roman Catholic element was in the majority
> in that place. And if you didn't go with them, well it was just too
> bad for you. That was just about the size of it.

But memories of childhood recalled little in the way of friction between
Protestants and Catholics, Catholic children recalled a Sunday not dis-
similar to that for the Protestants; Mrs B.1 (1907):

> Well, you went to Mass in the morning. You had dinner. And when
> it was a good day you went for a walk. And you finished up in
> church at night again – Benediction, what we call Benediction at
> night . . . Oh, I remember that the Sunday best was special dresses
> with velvet.

Because none of the Catholic women recalled attending other churches,
the surprising impression of oral history testimony is of far greater religious participation by Protestant women, arising from the attendance at
different denominations. Mrs W.1 (1913) remembered:

> We went to an awful lot of religious meetings in those days. Not I
> think for any religious feeling, but the fact . . . material gain, you
> know. We got a wee bag with maybe different things in it – cookies
> and things in it, and that was a sort of draw. Not that we were
> hungry; we werenae as bad as all that, but just it was something
> different – of getting something for maybe a penny or something.
> There was a wee Railway Mission at the end of the street where
> Millar's Garage is now – a lovely wee Mission hall. . . . And then
> y'see when we went to the different Sunday schools – I went to the
> South Church Sunday school because my parents were away in St
> Ninian's church, y'see. I chummed with the same wee girl going up

to school. . . . And then I was in the Salvation Army again. My
friend joined the Salvation Army, I didn't, but I was a Sunbeam for
a day or two. [Laugh] I used to belt out: 'A sunbeam a sunbeam,
Jesus wants me for a sunbeam.' . . . I must have been 10 or 11 or
something by that time. Oh yes, it was all religion. And another
thing. Another friend, another pal of mine, her father was a care-
taker of the Baptist church. Now we went to the Baptist church
meetings. I don't know why we didnae sprout wings! [Laughing]

TRANSITION   TO   ADULTHOOD

The role of religion in the lives of working-class women clearly diminished as they passed through adolescence into adulthood. The imposing
schedule of Sunday schools and children's mission meetings which a
large proportion of women born in the first quarter of the century recall
was not sustained. Nevertheless, religion continued to play an important
part in their young lives.

In some occupations, a form of 'religious respectability' was expected
of young women from working-class backgrounds. This was particularly
so in domestic service, which as much as a third of all women experienced in the first third of the century. Mrs T.1 (1906) remembered:

We were encouraged of course to go to church. We were allowed to
go to church maybe every second Sunday anyway. And I remember when I was quite young we were encouraged to join the church
then. And I was about 16 when I joined the church, you know,
when the minister took a class of us. Several of us would go at an
appointed time to the minister, to the manse, and we got instruction on joining the church. And we had set things to learn. We
learned the Creed. We had to repeat the Creed to him, and there
were several bits of scripture that we had to learn. And then that
was us a member of the church for life.

Another domestic servant, Mrs Q.2 (1912), recalled a similar set of rules in
the house where she worked, but she evaded the church.

Q: Did your employer tell you how you should spend your time?
A: They were always looking after your welfare, you know. No,
     we started going out every Sunday. It was every second Sun-
     day we got. But we started – the housemaid and I – going
     every Sunday down to the village of Milngavie. . . . Well,
     instead of going to church, we walked down to Milngavie, and
     we were back in time for the church coming out, and they
     never knew. We went down to get the Sunday papers, you see.
     Oh, I didnae want to go to church every Sunday, no.

Churchgoing was, indeed, virtually the only permissible leisure pursuit
for young women in domestic service. Mrs G.4 (1918) was a tablemaid
amongst the large staff in a 'big house':

A: Every second Sunday . . . we were off in the morning. And we

used to go to church on a Sunday morning when we were off.
The people that owned the house, they used to take the staff
that was off down in the car to the church, and we came back
and we went on duty then to ten o'clock and the others were
off in the afternoon. The following week it was vice versa. . . .

Q: Did your boss tell you how you should spend your time off or
was that completely up to you?

A: Oh no, but old Mrs A., she liked you to go to church on Sunday
morning if you were off . . . the day we joined the church she
gave us a church hymnary.

Though the pressures to attend church were greatest for domestic
servants, church connection also remained important for those in other
occupations. Amongst other things, the church remained during the first
half of the century an important venue for 'respectable' entertainments,
and a place for meeting boys and men. Mrs C.2 (1912) joined the church
while she was working in her teenage years as a hairdresser:

Went to church, yes, went regularly to church. So did all the boys
and all the girls. We all went to church. I remember we got an older
man from the church to come with us, and we did a moonlight hike
over the Pentlands, and we had a moonlight picnic on top of the
Pentlands.

When asked about their leisure time as working adults, many of the
Stirling respondents referred to religion, Mrs I.2 (1907):

Q: So, did you spend your free time away from work at the mill
by going to dances and things like that?

A: Parties or social evenings that they used to have for maybe the
Bible class, or the Sunday school, or the choir. When we were
in the choir, the church choir, we used to have a bus run every
year. . . . We attended the church and the Bible classes, and I
mean it was a sort of routine we had, we had been brought up
to.

And similarly with Mrs O.3 (1912):

Q: Going back to when you first started working [in a laundry],
how did you spend your free time away from work. Did you
go to dances?

A: No. I was always involved in the church. There were meetings,
different meetings, on. You weren't allowed out every night in
any case.

Q: And how did you spend your Sundays when you were working?

A: The same as when I was a child: church and Sunday school,
Bible class and such like, singing in the choir and all that sort of
thing.

The majority of the eleven Stirling respondents who joined the junior
choir in their congregations graduated to the senior choir. The Sunday

school led on to Bible class, and on reaching the age of about 20 several respondents acted as Sunday school teachers or Girl Guide leaders.

But others recall how they stopped their church connection on reaching working age. Mrs E.3 (1923) started work at a bottle-works and finished with the church: 'I think I kind of broke it, aye, I think I kinda fell away then. Ken how you get to that age? And aye, I think I fell away frae church then.' After marriage, church connection became even more tenuous for many women. Indeed, motherhood established a distinctive pattern of church connection for women. Though their religious faith may have been unaffected, domestic confinement practically eliminated weekday church and secular events, and was also the cause of diminished Sunday church attendance, Mrs H.3 (1902) remembered:

Then after I had joined it [the church], well I'd be two years married before my son was born. Well, you just couldn't get out the same.

Oral testimony suggests that marriage and motherhood caused a form of 'separate sphere' in women's lives during the first half of this century. Despite evidence of higher churchgoing rates amongst adult women compared to men, significant numbers of oral respondents commented on how churchgoing suffered through domestic demands. Some women recall their fathers being keener churchgoers than their mothers because of the need to look after small children and, more generally, because of the domestic responsibility of preparing Sunday meals – even when, because of sabbatarianism, this was merely re-heating food prepared the previous night. Mrs I.3 (1904) remembered her mother's situation:

My father was a more – he practised his religion more than my mother. My mother didn't go out much because she had the family to bring up.

In some country districts, special provision was made by the church and landowners for wives of estate workers. Mrs R.1 (1912) recounted the situation on the large west Stirlingshire estate where she was brought up:

The morning service in the Buchanan church was held in the morning for adults, and in the afternoon at three o'clock there was the Sunday school. And the minister – the mothers that couldn't go in the morning, went in the afternoon. And they had their service while we were having our Sunday lessons. At the back of the church we went to, and the mothers sat and the minister gave them their service.

For some mothers, domestic confinement was combined with the responsibility of religious education of the children. Mrs V.1 (1914) reported that her mother, who had twelve children, 'had to get a chapter of the Bible read every day, but not on a Sunday. But every single day there was a chapter of the Bible read, and we'd all sit and listen to her.'

The breaking of church connection was induced by several factors. Mrs U.3 (1913) recalled how as a domestic servant she started to feel socially alienated from her own Church of Scotland.

Afterwards I came away from the church because in some houses
the ministers came to the front of the house, the back wasn't – they
didn't seem to consider it. Plus, I worked in a Catholic house. This I
never forgot because the nursery staff – the governess, the two
nannies and the nurserymaid – were all Catholic. If a new nurserymaid came, or a new nanny, they were only a week in, the priest
came to see they were all right, and to see if they needed any help in
visiting or anything. Did the minister come to any of the houses I
was in? No. But I realised afterwards as time went on you have to
have roots of some kind. Where better than the church? But I
certainly went off it from 16 to wartime.

Social alienation also arose when Presbyterian churches amalgamated,
resulting in working-class members being thrown into a choice of
entering middle-class congregations or of seeking other denominations.
The United Free Church congregation that Mrs C.1 (1907) attended
closed in the 1930s, and she recalled how the social tenor of the
alternatives was unwelcoming. When the one she chose itself closed,
'for a long time I never had my lines in any church'. She later decided to
join a well-established local congregation with a distinctly middle-class
composition:

I put my lines in the Viewfield church eventually. So I went to the
Viewfield church a good bit, but I don't know – sometimes you
thought you were taking somebody's seat. You used to have your
own seat in the church – your name was at the end of it. But they
don't do that now. You can go to any seat. The first seat I went to
when I went to the Viewfield church – here it was somebody's; it
was filled up. The same the next. So here I noticed this one at the
very back. There was never anybody in it. So [I] just thought [I'd]
get [myself] in there. So I was in there for a long time. And Mrs A.
and her husband used to speak. But I don't know what it was –
because you werenae brought up in that church or no. The ones
that I knew were very nice, but I always felt sort of, och. I still keep
myself a member, and I go to communion. I go up and down once
or twice. I always keep up my church. But I mostly just go up to the
Baptist chapel.

This phenomenon of 'keeping up' membership of the Church of Scotland
whilst making regular (and sometimes more frequent) attendances at a
more evangelical denomination was widespread amongst Protestant
women respondents in both childhood and adulthood. The Baptist and
Methodist chapels, the Brethren, the Salvation Army and mission halls
were frequently cited as places where Presbyterians attended regularly,
often for Sunday evening worship.

But for a small minority of women, work combined with political
awareness to alienate them from religion. Mrs I.3 (1904) joined the Independent Labour Party and her religious upbringing started to disintegrate:

'Religion didn't mean an awful lot to me. I was beginning, I think, at that time, to sort of penetrate – to penetrate is the only word I can think on at the moment – religion.' She subsequently became active in the labour and trades union movements, and lost interest in religion.

THE CHURCHES AND WORKING-CLASS WOMEN'S CULTURE

The recollections of Scottish oral respondents, together with the limited autobiographical material, emphasises a widespread and ready acceptance of church-based religious and quasi-religious activities in the recreational life of early twentieth-century working-class women. At a minimum, the evidence of the preceding pages suggests that women's lives both as children and as adults were strongly influenced by the tenor and recreational structure of organised religion. Whether in church or in religious voluntary organisations, women were drawn into the ambit of the Christian religion, and there was an implicit adherence to concepts of 'respectable' pastimes.

Interpreting the significance of this to women's history can be problematic. In a study of the Women's Christian Temperance Union in the United States in the late nineteenth century, B. L. Epstein has argued that the organising and campaigning role of middle-class women gave rise to a 'proto-feminism' that combined protest against female subordination with a commitment to puritanical morality. As promotors and evangelisers of women's 'social purity', Epstein concludes:

> The WCTU can be seen as having pushed the women's culture of the time to its limits. The politics of the WCTU demonstrate not only the possibilities but the limits of a culture that accepted the structure of the nineteenth-century middle-class family and, by extension, the subordination of women; the WCTU went as far as it could in pursuing the feminist and progressive possibilities of this culture.'[24]

In short, the morality of the temperance message came from a middle-class vision of liberating working-class women by *perfecting*, not eroding, their domestic confinement in their 'separate sphere'. As such, this message had limited appeal, and restricted the practical political possibilities of this Victorian bourgeois feminism.[25]

British parallels may be drawn to this. L. L. Shiman has explored the rôle of women in the English temperance movement in the Victorian period, and provides a similar picture of middle-class women, deprived of work opportunities by domestic confinement, developing voluntary careers in the religious temperance sphere.[26] This strategy of social reform is best exemplified in the White Ribboners organisation, mentioned earlier in the Scottish evidence. It derived its name from the white ribbon bow which was the distinctive badge of members of the British Women's Temperance Association, founded in the late 1870s in emulation of the American Women's Christian Temperance Union studied by Epstein.[27]

One of the few temperance organisations limited to women, the White Ribboners sought to attain 'purity' in the midst of poverty, poor housing and degradation: as Mrs U.3 (1913) recollected of when she walked at the head of the White Ribboners' parade in her mining village watched in bewilderment by her pub-going father, she saw herself 'as good as anyone that lived – signed the pledge.'

At the same time, the religious-temperance dominance of working-class women's recreation was an important aspect of social control. The larger Protestant churches and some of the independent religious voluntary organisations were conducted by middle-class patrons, directing their work at the working classes. In a few cases in the Stirling evidence, the direct hand of the 'boss class' may be detected. The Railwaymen's Mission events for children in Stirling were superintended by the station master; Mrs K.2 (1906) was taught in her 'Saturday' Sunday school by the wife of the mill manager; and Mrs E.3 (1923) was taught in the infants' Sunday school by the local grocer in her mining village. Most impressively, perhaps, the Band of Hope in the factory textile community of Bannockburn in the 1920s was conducted by two spinsters, a Miss Mitchell and a Miss Wilson – the latter belonging to the family that owned the principal mills in the village. Mill-workers' children were the main participants in the Band. 'On the Friday night it was the Band of Hope', recalled Mrs B.2 (1907), 'and that hall would be packed from end to end with youngsters. You see, these were the only things we had.' Mrs M.2 (1915) remembered the two ladies and the queues to get in to see their lantern slides 'because there was no village cinema and that was the only village cinema we had in those days'. Mrs P.1 (1913), another Bannockburn woman, remembered: 'Oh it was packed in these days, everybody went to the Band of Hope, no matter which church you were; there were no divisions or anything'. In this way, the women of the factory-owning class ran the Band as a unifying agency in the community.

Perhaps even more plausibly, the puritanical content explicit in such organisations can be interpreted as inculcating 'middle-class' values useful to the maintenance of good order in capitalist society, and to the recreation of a sober and industrious labour force. In this, the churches certainly looked upon girls and women as playing a crucial role. In the 'war against vice' (sexual immorality, gambling and drunkenness), women were regarded as having a moralising effect on the main source of these vices – men. As wives and as daughters, women were seen to be of great potential in reforming the behaviour of working-class husbands and fathers. The content of moral stories was invariably targeted at women, as in magic lantern stories – the typical medium of the Bands of Hope. These were composed of a series of storyboards, shown as slides, in which the evil effects of drink upon family life were enacted. The slide shows at the Band of Hope in Springburn in Glasgow between the wars were well remembered.

In Fountainwell Road there was a church where we used to go to the Band of Hope – the 'Bandy' as we called it. And there you would get a bun and they would have lantern lectures showing the sins of drink – where the man just couldn't go past the pub when he got a bit of money – and where eventually he was able to go past the pub and became a teetotaller.[26]

The lantern show often portrayed the effects of male drunkenness upon wife and children, and emphasised the centrality of women's domestic role. In Stirling, Mrs X.2 (1920) remembers the lantern slides at the Band of Hope:

You would see the mother would probably be in bed, and she'd either just had an addition to her family or she was ill with tuberculosis. And you usually saw the father who had been drunk, and it was always perhaps the eldest sister was looking after a big family. And this was brought home to you about – you know – drink, you know, how it was the downfall of your – . So, with the result that when you would go to these things, you know, you'd sometimes come away with you face all tear-stained.

Mrs C.1 (1907) recalled the same type of event at her local Mission Hall: 'This is where they used to show films, sort of Christian films like 'The man that drank too much and never gave his wife the money for to feed the children'. Mrs S.3 (1902) remembered a portrayal of the woman as the culprit in the Band of Hope lantern shows: 'A drunk woman or something, being taken out of a pub. And all that kind of thing, you know. Just funny things; you got a laugh. You were young and you got a laugh at it.'

Despite the apparent explicitness of social control, there remains a need to understand the appeal of, and active participation of working-class women in, evangelical and moral crusades such as these. In relation to drink, as Elspeth King has suggested, working-class women – as wives, mothers and as daughters – stood to gain a great deal from a temperance environment. The churches' temperance organisations offered an attractive proposition to those who were often the victims of drink and drunkenness. King quotes a report on wife-beating from an agent of the Glasgow City Mission:

Out of the twelve families I visited today, I do not think that more than one women is living at peace with her husband. The men . . . are all drunkards and abuse their poor wives when under the influence of strong drink. These poor decent women . . . said they could not live with their husbands; that rather than be murdered by them, they were thinking of separating from them, even although they should have to beg their own and their children's bread.[29]

The temperance movement had to balance conflicting objectives. While attacking the drinking habits of the husband and father, it also wished to preserve – and perfect – the nuclear family. Equally, the purity message aroused conflicting emotions in the receivers. While women's temperance walks through working-class communities were designed to bring moral conflict to a resolution within families, did Mrs U.3 (1919) perceive her presence at the head of the White Ribboners' parade in Stirlingshire as an indictment of her father, or merely as a general display of being 'as good as anyone that lived'? When he saw her there, he certainly understood it as a statement of protest at his pub-going habits – the leading girl in the parade possibly standing out as supposedly the greatest victim of 'the demon drink'. Family conflict was mediated by the mother; horrified at her husband brazenly announcing to bystanders that he was going to the pub that night, she nonetheless placated him: 'It doesn't matter. She was doing her best'. And to cap the ambiguities, perhaps there was a touch of pride in both father and mother at their daughter's prominence in the parade.

Plainly, the issue of whether or not the purity message was accepted in working-class families is not a simple one, for the message had complex implications. Mrs U.3's memory of the incident suggests that girls and women were elevated to the position of moral guardians, giving them a sense of pride and self-worth perhaps denied them in other spheres of activity. The pageantry of the parades and meetings, and the solemnity of the pledge-signing ceremony, could be a beacon in an otherwise bleak and perhaps mundane experience. Yet, though the temperance message might be accepted as a righteous one, it sought to generate conflict in the family by recruiting women and girls as agents for reforming the drinking habits of husbands and fathers.

Woman might be the nominated moral guardian in the working-class family, but in the community at large she was also to be found as evangeliser. Working-class women were not merely the passive recipients of religious and temperance campaigns. As adults, they participated as Band of Hope, Girl Guide, and mission leaders, and as Sunday school teachers. Mrs B.2 (1907), the daughter of a ploughman, became a clerkess in a butcher's shop, and graduated from Sunday school and Bible class to Sunday school teaching. She spent three nights a week as an adult in church activities – one at a planning meeting for Sunday school teachers – and undertook mission work amongst the children of the very poor in the 'Top of the Town' area of Stirling.

> It was up Baker Street, and these days it was a poor area. But we used to have at Christmas, the Sunday before Christmas we had a gift service and they could bring good toys. They didn't need to be new, and then they were parcelled up and everything. And the teachers, oh for years – Christmas forenoon, Christmas day – I spent delivering these parcels. Oh, some of the places were unbelievable – up dark stairs and oh, some of the people of course were very dirty and other were. . .spotless, you could have taken your food off the floor. . . I mean, they hadn't a thing practically but their place was spotless. It made you awful humble, and as I say we did

that all these years. I became a Sunday school teacher. . .for fourteen
year, and I helped in the Life Boys. . . . We had a big Mission in
Baker Street [for fifty children], and they were really poor. . . Two
days before Christmas we gave a concert for these kiddies and had
a Christmas tree and all got a parcel. And then on Christmas Eve it
was the turn of the Sunday school, and we did it again.

Though such women as Mrs B.2 were not from the lower working classes,
they were much more *of* the proletariat than of the class from which the
bourgeois volunteers came. There is in this extract an affinity with those
she visited, an ability to recognise and distinguish the 'really poor', and to
be 'humbled' by those who kept their homes as well – if not better – than
she did. Her religious offerings acknowledged that her morality was
already in place as the values of plebeian life, and unlike the middle-class
visitor she did not bring a fruitless message of social redemption, merely
religious worship, some events for the children and a few treats.

CONCLUSION

The disappearance by 1900 of the system of kirk session justice, as experienced by Christian Watt in the north-east, left religious influence on
working-class women as a diffusive rather than an enforced Christianity.
In this context, the Stirling testimony shows that women had religious
freedoms. As children, working-class women often had an indigenous
enthusiasm for religious events, and independently sought out and made
choices as to which organisation and occasions they attended. The spectacle of religion, especially as presented in the greater proletarian atmosphere of the Baptist, Brethren, mission and evangelistic organisations,
was more emotionally as well as socially appealing than the 'ordinary'
and mundane events at the Church of Scotland and United Free Church.
The drama and pageantry of evangelical religion was also to be found in
the parades and lantern shows of the temperance organisations. In these,
women were encouraged to see their unique role as arbiters of their
families' morality – the agents both for respectability and for family
harmony. The religious-temperance environment offered women a legiti-
mation of their worth in a society in which other fountains of self-esteem
may have been few in number.

As adults, women might be pressurised into church membership and
attendance by employers in domestic service, but they sustained means
of independence and even resistance to such compulsion. Those who
sought a place in a church were conscious of social snobbery and élitism,
and either circumvented it by attending other churches or by deliberately
distancing themselves from organised religion. But in the inter-war
period at least, the smaller evangelical denominations – the Baptists, the
Brethren and mission organisations – seem to have benefited from being
identified as more proletarian in composition, control and ambience.

Overall working-class women's testimony shows a vibrancy and devotion to religious activities in the first half of this century. The bland hymns and socially ordered snobbery of morning worship at the Church of Scotland was compensated by attendance at more evangelical, emotional and rousing evening services at the minor churches. There was an excitement to be savoured from the lively congregation, the revivalist preacher, the Sankey hymn, and from standing up to be 'saved'. In a context where alternative 'secular' women's recreational organisations were extremely thin on the ground, and where alternative commercial pastimes like the cinema and dancing were only slowly becoming available, religion and temperance remained vital spheres in which working-class women could gain access to leisure. Religion provided a means for working-class women to 'sprout wings' of angels, to stand as the symbols of moral purity; it was not, however, the means to 'sprout wings' of liberation from male subordination.

NOTES

1   G. Malmgreen (ed.), *Religion in the Lives of English Women 1760–1930*, (Croom Helm, London 1986), pp. 1–2.

2   Most notably O. Anderson. 'Women preachers in mid-Victorian Britain: some reflections on feminism, popular religion and change', *Historical Journal* xii (1969); F. K. Prochaska, *Women and Philanthropy in Nineteenth Century England*, (Clarendon Press, Oxford, 1980), and the articles contained in Malmgreen, *Religion in the Lives of English Women*.

3   For instance, only nine items are listed under 'Religion' (with a further seventeen under 'Women and Foreign Missions) in *Women in Scotland: An Annotated Bibliography*, (Open University (Edinburgh, 1988). All but one are biographies, hagiographies, architectural guides or church publications.

4   R. Burman, '"She looketh well to the ways of her household": the changing role of Jewish women in religious life *c* 1880–1930', in Malmgreen, *Religion in the Lives of English Women*, pp. 234–259.

5   See H. McLeod, *Religion and the Working Class in Nineteenth Century Britain*, (Macmillan, London, 1984).

6   This view is propounded for Scotland in T. C. Smout, *A Century of the Scottish People 1830–1950*, (Collins, London, 1986), pp. 181–208.

7   P. L. Sissons, *The Social Significance of Church Membership in the Burgh of Falkirk*, (Church of Scotland, Edinburgh, 1973), and C. G. Brown, *The Social History of Religion in Scotland since 1730*, (Methuen, London, 1987).

8   For example, R. R. Ruether and R. S. Keller (eds), *Women and Religion in America* Vol I. (Harper S. F., New York, 1982).

9   H. McLeod, 'New Perspectives on Victorian working-class religion: the oral evidence', *Oral History Journal* 14 (1986), pp. 31–49.

10 K. Logue, *Popular Disturbances in Scotland, 1780–1815*, (John Donald, Edinburgh, 1979), pp. 168–76, 191–217; E. King, *Scotland Sober and Free: The Temperance Movement 1829–1979*, (People's Palace Museum, Glasgow, 1979), pp. 17–18.

11 Ellen Ross, 'Survival networks: women's neighbourhood sharing in London before World War One', *History Workshop* 15 (1983); J. Obelkevich, *Religion and Rural Society: South Lindsay*

1825–75, (Clarendon Press, Oxford, 1976); and J. D. Stephenson, 'The influence of Christian social teaching on the lives of working-class women in Britain, *c* 1850–1950; the autobiographical evidence', unpublished BA dissertation, Department of History, Lancashire Polytechnic 1984. See also the important material in J. Seabrook, *The Unprivileged,* (Penguin, Hardmondsworth, 1973), and M. Phayer, *Sexual Liberation and Religion in Nineteenth-century Europe,* (Croom Helm, London, 1977), especially chapter 4.

12   Calculated from data in *The Church of Scotland Yearbook 1986.*

13   C. G. Brown, *The Social History of Religion in Scotland* p. 95.

14   C. Larner, *Enemies of God: The Witch-Hunt in Scotland,* (Chatto and Windus, London, 1981).

15   J. D. Young, *Women and Popular Struggles: A History of British Working Class Women 1560–1984,* (Mainstream, Edinburgh, 1985); L. Leneman, 'Two sides of a coin: women's position in early-modern Scotland', paper delivered to Conference of the Scottish Social and Economic History Society, Glasgow, 1988.

16   D. Fraser (ed.), *The Christian Watt Papers,* (Paul Harris, Edinburgh, 1983), pp. 67–8, 124.

17   J. Littlejohn, *Westrigg: The Sociology of a Cheviot Parish,* (Routledge and Kegan Paul, London, 1963), pp. 41–2; C. G. Brown, 'Education', in J. Hood (ed.), *The History of Clydebank* (Parthenon, Carnforth, Lancs 1988), p. 44.

18   C. G. Brown, *The Social History of Religion,* pp. 135–208.

19   These figures do not add up to 100 per cent because of multiple occupations. For a more detailed review of the occupational composition of respondents, see J. D. Stephenson and C. G. Brown, 'The view from the workplace: women's memories of work in Stirling c. 1910–c.1950', in E. Breitenbach and E. Gordon (eds.), *The World is Ill Divided: Women's Work in Scotland in the Nineteenth and Early Twentieth Centuries,* (Edinburgh University Press, Edinburgh 1990)

20   Except where otherwise indicated the oral testimony which follows comes from the Stirling Women's Oral History Archive, Smith Museum, Stirling. Respondents are identified by a code followed in parentheses by their date of birth.

21   M. Weir, *Best Foot Forward,* (Hutchinson, London, 1972), pp. 69–71.

22   T. Allan, *Crusade in Scotland: Billy Graham* (Edinburgh, 1957).

23   M. Weir, *Best Foot Forward.*

24   B. L. Epstein, *The Politics of Domesticity: Women, Evangelism, and Temperance in Nineteenth-century America,* (Wesleyan University Press, New York, 1981), p. 146.

25   Rickie Burman has argued, using oral testimony, that amongst the Jewish immigrant community in England the status of women declined as Jewishness became decreasingly expressed in the synagogue and increasingly in the home – represented by women having to prepare *kosher* food and by having to adhere to Sabbath observance in its preparation. R. Burman, 'She looketh well to the ways of her household'.

26   L. L. Shiman, '" Changes are dangerous": Women and temperance in Victorian England,' in Malmgreen (ed.), *Religion in the Lives of English Women,* pp. 193–215.

27   E. King, *Scotland Sober and Free,* pp. 17–18; Epstein, *The Politics of Domesticity,* pp. 115–146.

28 Testimony of Mr M. Suttie, quoted in *Two Communities: Springburn and Kirkintilloch: A Chronicle of Glasgow Overspill,* (Strathkelvin District Libraries , Kirkintilloch, 1983), p. 10.

29 Quoted in E. King, *Scotland Sober and Free,* p. 17.

SELECT BIBLIOGRAPHY

O. Anderson, 'Women Preachers in Mid-Victorian Britain: some 'reflections on feminism, popular religion and change', *Historical Journal,* xii, 1969.

C. G. Brown, *The Social History of Religion in Scotland since 1730,* (Methuen, London, 1987).

B. L. Epstein, *The Politics of Domesticity: Women, Evangelism and Temperance in Nineteenth Century America* (Middletown, Connecticut, 1981).

E. King, *Scotland Sober and Free: The Temperance Movement 1829–1979,* (People's Palace Museum, Glasgow, 1979).

H. McLeod, *Religion and the Working Class in Nineteenth Century Britain* Macmillan (London, 1984).

H. McLeod, 'New Perspectives on Victorian working-class religion: the oral evidence', *Oral History Journal,* XIV , 1986.

G. Malmgreen (ed.), *Religion in the Lives of English Women 1760–1930,* (Clarendon Press, London, 1986).

M. Phayer, *Sexual Liberation and Religion in Nineteenth Century Europe,* (Croom Helm, London, 1977).

R. R. Ruether and R. S. Keller (eds.), *Women and Religion in America* (New York, 1981).

T. C. Smout, *A Century of the Scottish People 1830–1950,* (Collins, London, 1986).

Women in Scotland: An Annotated Bibliography, (Open University Press, Edinburgh, 1988).

J. D. Young, *Women and Popular Struggles: A History of British Working Class 1560–1984,* (Mainstream, Edinburgh, 1985).

6

THE SCOTTISH WOMEN'S SUFFRAGE MOVEMENT

ELSPETH KING

INTRODUCTION

There is a distinction to be made between *women's history* and *women in history*. One looks at women's lives, work, leisure and culture patterns while the other, with a predetermined male agenda, looks for instances where women appear, or can be found, in relation to the history of men. It is my regret that this chapter is in the second category. Given the lack of historical study and academic interest in the Scottish suffrage movement, both female and male, this contribution can be nothing more than a straight chronicle of what happened, when and how.

Students new to Scottish history, or to the history of the women's suffrage movement in general, could be forgiven for thinking that there was no women's suffrage movement in Scotland, or that it was of so little consequence as to be beneath mention. Scottish events are mentioned only incidentally in London and Manchester-based contemporary accounts. The subject has suffered from the double disadvantage of being Scottish and feminist, and therefore of marginal interest to publishers. Militant suffragette Helen Crawfurd (1877–1954) for example wrote her autobiography within a European framework, keeping local references to a minimum, so that it would be of 'wider' interest. Thirty-five years after her death, it is still unpublished.[1] If she had managed to publish, it would perhaps have spurred both Flora Drummond and Theresa Billington-Greig to complete theirs, and women such as Janet Barrowman who went to prison and lost their jobs for the suffrage cause might have been encouraged to record their experiences.

Scottish academics have taken as much interest as Scottish publishers. In I. G. C. Hutchison's weighty and otherwise thorough *Political History of Scotland 1832–1924 – Parties Elections and Issues* (Edinburgh, 1986) women's suffrage is not an issue. Women's suffrage does not feature in the relevant volumes of Edward Arnold's *New History of Scotland*. Even in Christopher Smout's *A Century of the Scottish People 1830–1950*, women's suffrage rates only a brief mention, in the context of a discussion on horse and dog racing. In James D. Young's *Women and Popular Struggles* (1985)

Scottish suffragettes are dismissed as participants in a British movement, and lacking in 'sympathy for the plight of working-class women'.

In short, the lack of attention given to the Scottish women's suffrage movement is a historiographical scandal. Apart from my own pamphlet of that title (see footnote 2), published in haste in 1978 to commemorate the fiftieth anniversary of the Representation of the People Act, the only other work on the subject is in Rosalind K. Marshall's *Virgins and Viragos* (1983).[2]

Given the almost daily coverage of suffrage activities in the newspapers in the years before the First World War, it is difficult to comprehend why only eighty years later, the issues have come to be regarded as esoteric and unimportant. 'Suffragettes May Break Windows' ran the advertisement in Glasgow's *Forward*, 'but I am the wee boy that can put them in. James H. Caldwell, Glazier and Glass Merchant, Eglinton Street...' Caldwell's sense of humour brought him business, for he ran the advertisement for over a year. In the period 1912–14, in particular, the Scottish suffragettes were highly successful in keeping their cause in the news. There were many such periods when the case for women's suffrage was never out of the news. When J. G. Holyoake came to lecture in Glasgow in 1856 on the 'Civil Freedom of Women' he spent much time avoiding the phrase the 'rights of women', because he said such phrases were so overused, worn and outmoded as to be meaningless.[3]

The way in which people perceive the political issues of their time, and the manner in which these issues are later treated by historians can be very different. From the point of view of the preservation of material culture for example, the most common objects relating to nineteenth-century political history offered as donations to our museum collections are franchise objects. In Glasgow most common of all are the badges issued by the Glasgow Liberal Association to the male participants in the great Franchise Demonstration to Glasgow Green on 6 September 1884. Next are the objects carried or worn in the demonstration, and the banners which the demonstration generated. Many of the trades unions had banners specially made for these occasions.

From newspaper reports, oral sources, and the way in which these objects were handed down from generation to generation, it is easy to ascertain that the men who participated in the demonstrations of 1832–3, 1867 and 1884 felt that they were making history, taking part in one of the great epoch-making events of the century. In the last few years, three 1832 banners have been acquired by the People's Palace. These were kept and treasured in families for so long that their original purpose had been all but forgotten. For the individuals who used them, the demonstration was the event which changed their world. Historians do not view the franchise struggle in the same light.

It is a little over sixty years since women obtained the vote on the same terms as men. Largely thanks to the women's liberation movement of the

1960s and 1970s, the struggle is still in our collective popular consciousness, fuelled by books and television drama. While the original participants have passed on, they had the same feeling about making history and about preserving parts of it. Some took decisions after the First World War to deposit banners and artefacts with the library set up in memory of Millicent Fawcett.[4] Those who came together in Glasgow in 1949 to celebrate the twenty-first anniversary of the Representation of the People Act decided to deposit the few bits and pieces they had kept in the People's Palace.[5] There are still relatives of suffragettes who treasure small collections of memorabilia and will not part with them, and who feel the satisfaction of knowing that their grandmother or great-grandmother 'made history'.

Women's historical consciousness is a fragile and delicate plant which has been choked and overrun by the tares of male prejudice and the official history curriculum in school and university. There is little indication of historical awareness from one generation to the next. The women who in 1902 formed the Glasgow and West of Scotland Association for Women's Suffrage thought they were breaking new ground, and were probably unaware of the achievements of the 1870s and 1880s. Those who were petitioning for the suffrage cause in the 1870s and 1880s gave no sign of having any knowledge of what had happened in the 1840s and 1850s. Those reporting the female Chartist societies of the 1840s seemed to believe that women's political societies were something new.

On rare occasions, because of their own family history, some women were aware of the historical past. Alison Gibb, who received a six-month sentence in March 1912 for militant activity, was a descendant of William Skirving (d. 1795) who was given a fourteen years' transportation sentence in 1793 for broadly similar beliefs.[6] In any given generation however, there is no great sense of feminist historical continuity. Eunice Murray of the Women's Freedom League was the unofficial historian of the women's movement in Scotland in her time. She summarised the history of the women's suffrage movement, 1832–1908, in two articles in *Forward*,[7] from which it is obvious that she had no knowledge of the feminist Owenite disciples who followed Alexander Campbell, or of the female Chartist agitation. As a Liberal, Eunice Murray was not particularly searching for a radical perspective on suffrage history however; her interests lay elsewhere.[8]

By comparison, readers of *Forward* at that time were well served with information of male political history. Willie Stewart was writing articles on Thomas Muir, Baird and Hardie; Dr G. B. Clark was writing his reminiscences of the Highland Land League, and Tom Johnston was serialising his studies of the Scottish aristocracy and the working class. The ceremonies commemorating Baird and Hardie were taking place then as they do today, and the practice of holding dinners in memory of Robert Owen and Tom Paine had not yet died out.

As far as the history of the Scottish women's suffrage movement is concerned, our knowledge is still at the stage defined by feminist historians elsewhere as 'compensatory history' – the rediscovery of our foremothers.[9] It is a first base which must be passed before we can progress to the next stage. The following fragmentary and imperfect narrative is therefore offered as a beginning.

THE EARLY YEARS

It is inconceivable that women were not always involved in the struggle to extend the franchise. When William Skirving was sentenced to fourteen years' transportation for agitating for universal suffrage and annual parliaments in 1793, it was recognised as a death sentence. As a token of this, strands of his hair and that of his wife were woven together for the bezel of a mourning ring which went with him to Australia.[10]

Women were involved in large numbers in the movement for political reform in the years leading up to the first Reform Bill. Until the word 'person' was qualified as 'male person' in the Reform Act of 1832, there were expectations that the franchise might be extended to women on the same terms.

Lack of Scottish radical newspapers in this period probably meant that Scotswomen adopted the practices and pageantry of their English sisters, which were well reported. One reform society tended to copy another. In August 1819 the *Glasgow Courier* reported, for example, that the Stockport Female Reformers had obtained a cap of liberty which would be presented at their next public meeting 'as our sisters at Blackburn did at theirs'.[11] Before long, similar ceremonies were taking place all over Lowland Scotland. At a radical meeting in Ayr there were

> about thirty Female Reformers who accompanied them carrying flags with various inscriptions; a very handsome girl named Calderwood, at the head of the females, carried a fine blue ensign, and another good-looking girl, the Cap of Liberty and delivered them in due form to the President. These two girls, with some others, had a most interesting appearance, being handsomely dressed for the occasion, in black silk gowns with white scarfs and highly decorated head-dresses, white, studded with black knots, to represent the mourning for the persons killed at Manchester.[12]

In rural Galston, the formula was the same:

> During the proceedings, the Female Reformers from Galston, accompanied by a band of music arrived. When they came within twenty yards of the hustings, a vocal band sang 'Scots wha hae wi' Wallace bled' and on moving on 'solemn and slow' to the music, a deputation of female reformers mounted the hustings and one of them placed a splendid cap of liberty on the head of the chairman, and another presented a flag inscribed 'Annual Parliaments, Universal Suffrage, Election by Ballot' and reverse 'Arise Britons and

assert your rights'. A third presented an address from the Galston Female Reformers Society, consisting of 279 members. When the cap of liberty was placed on the head of the chairman, the meeting gave three cheers.[13]
The same scenes were reported in Paisley and Johnstone at about the same time, much to the disgust of the conservative press.

> The first of these occasions which excited our disgust and regret, was the exhibition of females, not only regularly formed in various of the processions, but actually bearing standards and mounting the hustings to invest the fellow who acted as president with the revolutionary cap. We know nothing of the characters of these women, but there was a time when the most abandoned of the sex in this part of the country would have blushed at such an exposure.[14]

When the Bridgeton Political Union celebrated its third anniversary, the formula was the same:

> Among the company was a considerable number of well-dressed females, which added a novelty and grandeur to the scene . . . a deputation from the female Reformers . . . were ushered in amidst the loud plaudits of the assembly. One of them presented a beautiful flag to the Preses [President], bearing the inscription 'A present from the Females in Bridgeton to the Union'. The figures were on one side a female addressing a young man, 'go where freedom calls you', on the other, a mother presenting her son the Bill of Rights. Motto: 'For this your fathers bled, nourish it and cherish it'. Another of the females carried a splendid cap of liberty, which she placed with great gravity and formality on the head of the Preses. . . . Both these actions were accompanied with suitable addresses from the respective females.[15]

The greatest of these meetings, involving some 30,000 people, took place at Clayknowes on the east side of Glasgow on 1 November 1819. The badly built platforms were crowded and shaky, and besides the men, there were

> perhaps about forty females, some of them with infants in their arms . . . we were truly grieved to see females in the procession; their character and dispositions being naturally so averse to any such public exhibition of their persons.[16]

The ceremonial at Clayknowes involved some fifty flags and eight caps of liberty. During 1819 at least, the presence of women reformers and the enactment of such pageantry seemed to be an inextricable part of the procedures of the reform societies. Because the newspapers report the activity of women reformers in this context only, we should not assume that their function was a decorative and ceremonial one. Two hundred and seventy-nine women in Galston could not have been held together by ceremony alone.

It is only on rare occasions that women political participants are mentioned by name in these reports, and the references are tantalisingly short. A police informant at the Clayknowes meting stated that:

> the only one of the females known to the declarant was Mrs Brown, wife of James Brown, weaver in Donald's Land Tobago Street – she is a middle-aged Irish woman . . . the women were all well dressed.[17]

Sadly, no caps of liberty or banners from this period are known to survive.[18] Memories then, as now, were short. Twenty years later when a newly formed working-men's association in Eaglesham was holding its first *soirée*, the male veterans of 1819–20 were present, and it was noted as 'the first Radical meeting at which the females of the village graced the cause and movement.'[19]

CHARTISM, ANTI-SLAVERY AND SOCIALISM

The violent repression after the 1820 rising stamped out the revolutionary tendency in Scotland for a generation. Great efforts were made to present the movement for parliamentary reform as moderate, respectable and safe, and as far as Chartism was concerned, this meant presenting the women involved as helping their male relatives to attain universal suffrage. Whilst 'universal suffrage', could be taken at face value, many societies spelled it out as the extension of the franchise 'to every man in Great Britain and Ireland, twenty-one years of age, sane in mind and unconvicted of crime'.[20]

Some of the Female Societies may have felt otherwise. The Female Political Union of Dunfermline, established in November 1838, regarded political economy as being comparable to domestic economy: 'National affairs is but an aggregate of household affairs . . . that until woman becomes an independent creature, not the subservient slave of man, but a fit companion and assistant in all his undertakings . . .' would the reform be effected.

Apart from Dunfermline, a Female Union was in the process of formation in Perth, and another existed in Forfar. The Female Union in Kirriemuir with 330 members appears to have been the largest, the *Montrose Review* commenting on the 'singular and somewhat novel sight in our neighbourhood (of) so many matrons with their daughters, congregated for political purposes'.[21]

It is unlikely that these four Female Political Unions on the east coast existed in isolation. When others are reported elsewhere, the same tone of surprise is always adopted with the implicit suggestion that it is a first-time event. At a meeting of the Partick Universal Suffrage society in August 1839 for example, over 600 were present, 'the fair sex forming no inconsiderable part of the audience'. The chairman was very happy to see such an assemblage of the ladies, joined with the stout hearts and strong arms of the men of Partick, come to lend a helping hand in the great work of national emancipation.'[22]

In many reports, the Female Unions are relegated to a supporting role.

In Barrhead for example, 'the females unanimously resolved to support their radical brethren in getting up a Chartist store, in aid of the plan of exclusive dealing'.[23] The Female Chartists of Glasgow were addressed thus:

> Dear Sisters – your appearance in the political arena at the present juncture has given rise to much rebuke, as well as seeming disgust. Some think that you are being created for nothing but the domestic circle and would give you no other education than housewifery . . . It is well known that you were designed by the great Creator to be a helpmate to man, to share with him in his griefs, his toils, his happiness and his sorrows. Can you do all this at home? Can you console him whose spirit is weighed down by the weighty yoke of tyranny, whose hard-earned wage cannot support you and your family?[24]

There is an assumption by male Chartists that the male wage should be a family wage, and that the 'natural' sphere of women is the home. The Gorbals Female Universal Suffrage Association was told that women were being forced to become beasts of burden and that the purpose of the Association should be to 'aid us [i.e. the male association] to emancipate the working classes from bondage'.[25]

Consistent relegation of the women Chartists to 'helpmate' status was undoubtedly a contributory factor to the length of the protracted struggle to obtain the franchise on equal terms. The women accepted this, and it is apparent that in some instances the men effectively ran the female societies. The Gorbals Female Universal Suffrage Association had male 'guardians'; its chairwoman, Agnes Lennox, asked for

> our warmest thanks to the guardians from the male Association who have given us their valuable assistance in managing the affairs of this Society; although working men – some of them venerable in years, they have not scrupled to spend two or three hours of their time per week . . . in assisting to conduct the affairs of this Society and in promoting the welfare of the members.[26]

It is difficult to obtain information on individual Scottish women Chartists, but there is frequent mention of Agnes Lennox of the Gorbals Female Association, which was reputedly one of the largest, with a committee of forty members and admired and respected 'even in England'. She was denounced as 'a brazen-faced jade' in the *Glasgow Constitutional*,[27] and consistently praised in the *Scottish Patriot*, where she was reported as chairing meetings, signing petitions, and even singing Chartist songs.[28]

At the same time, women were involved in the work of the various anti-slavery and emancipation societies. Indeed, some male Chartists thought that women had won this particular war and urged women 'to obtain for the white slaves that what they had already obtained for the black – freedom', pointing out that 'Nobly did you do your duty at the time of the agitation of the obtaining of freedom to the Negroes; then what can hinder you from doing your duty now?'[29]

These remarks were made some months prior to the International Slavery Convention in London in 1840, when it became clear that the women had been fighting for the emancipation of black men only. Seven American female delegates were forbidden to speak on the platform, and were excluded from the convention on grounds of sex. The movement split on the 'woman question'. The schism was deeply felt in Glasgow, where the vice-president of the Emancipation Society publicly resigned because the other officers did not support the exclusion of women at the London Convention. In an effort to win him back, the Glasgow Emancipation Society only succeeded in alienating their female supporters.

'Neither our Society nor all the Anti-Slavery Societies in the world put together have anything to do with the general Rights of Women, nor are we, as a Society, either one way or another committed on the subject. We neither approve nor disapprove', wrote President William Smeal. The Glasgow Ladies' Auxiliary Emancipation Society split into opposing factions on account of this vacillation.[30]

Those women who may have realised that working to 'emancipate the working classes from bondage', or indeed, the black slaves, was not necessarily the way to help break their own chains, could join the Owenite socialists. In the 1830s and 1840s, socialism could not be described as a mass movement. Nevertheless, Glasgow was regarded by Owenite missionaries as 'one of the strongholds of socialism . . . our northern bulwark' and thanks to the Hall of Science there, Matilda Roalf's book depot in Edinburgh, and the well-organised tours of the lecturers and missionaries throughout Scotland, socialist principles must have been familiar to many. Having thrown aside religious preconceptions in the search for the New Moral World, equality of the sexes was one of the main planks of Owenite socialism. This much-desired condition was described by a Scottish suffragette some seventy years later as 'the freeing of the womanhood of the people'. The Owenites sought a complete change in society, and regarded women's enfranchisement as a necessary part of the process whereby the sexes would attain equality. It was always the Owenite feminists who threw down the challenge to parliamentary candidates in public meetings in the 1830s and 1840s.

Barbara Taylor's in-depth work has made the period and the issues available for the first time to our generation.[31] Tracking down the various female lecturers who operated in Scotland is a task which is yet to be undertaken. Given the financial state of the Owenite organisations, it is probable that most of them supported themselves through their lecturing, or by other means. Agnes Walker, for example, 'a young lady of little over 20 years' was employed by the Glasgow Mechanics Institute to give a course of lectures in 1834. She was obviously an Owenite socialist:

She announced that in her next lecture she would discuss the 'riddle of Sampson' and other topics, in the course of which she is to enter into one of her favourite doctrines of asserting, if not the supremacy, at least the perfect equality of her sex to that of the male, and vindicating her sex from the bondage in which they had been held for the last 1800 years.[32]

Mrs A. S. Hamilton seems to have travelled Scotland as a phrenologist and lecturer in the 1830s–50s offering phrenological charts at a shilling a time, giving educational advice based on phrenology, and full consultations costing five shillings.[33] In 1834, she describes herself as 'A Female Reformer, who is on tour through Scotland' and a graphic account of her lecturing style was given in the local paper:

The reformation of her own sex she declares to be one of the grand objects of her labours. She complained very loudly, and in no very delicate terms, of the tyranny with which males lorded it over the females, and advised the latter to be ruled no longer. In handling this part of the subject, she said the apostles were taught to become fishers of men and (shaking her fist towards the women) she added 'I will teach you how to become the fishers of men' – a sentiment which elicited great laughter and approbation from the female part of the audience, in which she heartily joined . . . She then went on to detail her proceeding at the late election at Paisley. She said, the men there told her that if she were allowed to propagate her principles, the women would take the country to themselves, and the men would be forced to flee to America; but she told them that she did not care, 'the truth' was her object, and by that she would stand or fall.[34]

Lecture tours of this kind could be exhausting and debilitating, especially if they provoked opposition. The Scottish lecture tour of Emma Martin (1812–1851) in the winter of 1844–5 was her last.[35] In some places, she was physically attacked; in most places she was harassed, or found herself banned. In Arbroath she was arrested and temporarily imprisoned. Some weeks later, her presence in a church in the Gorbals created a near-riot, when 6,000 turned up to see her. She was arrested again, and fined £3 by the magistrates on the following day.[36] To add insult to injury, she was accused by Alexander Campbell ([1796–1870] the founder of the Co-operative Movement, and Owen's right-hand man in Scotland) of bringing the cause into disrepute, a charge which she vigorously denied.[37] Tired and disillusioned, she trained as a midwife to support herself and her four daughters only to find herself banned from practising in certain places when she refused to profess Christianity.[38]

Glasgow-born Fanny Wright (1795–1852) adopted socialism in America after she met Owen at New Harmony in 1824. She set up her own Owenite community at Nashoba, Tennessee.[39] Her actions and teachings were known and appreciated throughout the Owenite world. At an atheist dinner in Glasgow in 1844 'Miss Frances Wright and all female advocates of civil and religious liberty' were the subject of a special toast.[40]

1867–1900 THE MIDDLE-CLASS CONTRIBUTION

When an amendment to the Reform Bill of 1867, which would have enfranchised women on the same terms as men, failed, there was a surge of interest in the question of women's suffrage. Suffrage societies were formed in Manchester and London and on 6 November 1867, a new Scottish Women's Suffrage Society met in Edinburgh. The first president was Priscilla McLaren, wife of the radical Edinburgh MP who championed Scottish rights in the Commons, and daughter of anti-Corn Law campaigner Jacob Bright.[41]

Middle-class women began to recognise the necessity of enfranchisement for the first time. Between 1867 and 1876, two million signatures in Scotland were obtained for petitions in favour of the suffrage cause.[42] By 1878, canvassing for signatures was proceeding in every major town. Petitions were also sought from various different classes of people – advocates, solicitors, bankers, architects, ministers, physicians and headmasters – to strengthen the cause.[43] Many aristocratic ladies, like Lady Frances Balfour and Ishbell, Countess of Aberdeen (1857–1939) took up the suffrage cause, as did many notable university professors who wished to obtain higher education for women, and the training of women as doctors.

Active in Glasgow were Edward Caird (1835–1908), Professor of Moral Philosophy in the university, and Principal Thomas M. Lindsay (b. 1843) of the Free Church College. Together, they worked to have women elected to the new School Boards, helped with the organisation of the suffrage society (including the considerable arrangements required for the Scottish National Demonstration of Women in 1882)[44] and were founder members of the Glasgow – later the Scottish – Council for Women's Trades, established in 1894. When in 1902 a new Glasgow and West of Scotland Society for Women's Suffrage was set up, Professor and Mrs Caird, although by then resident in Oxford, were invited to sit on the executive committee, as were Professor and Mrs Lindsay.

These three organisations – the Glasgow Suffrage Society of the 1870s and 1880s, the Scottish Council for Women's Trades, and the Glasgow and West of Scotland Society for Women's Suffrage – spanned a period of some forty years, and had other key people in common. The purpose of the Scottish Council for Women's Trades (1894–1939) was to 'take an interest in women's work, conduct special and systematic investigations into it, and endeavour to promote legislation in the interests of women and children' and was composed of 'well-known citizens of Glasgow, clergymen of various denominations, members of School Boards, Parish Councils, Town Councils, trades councils and labour societies, and other people who sit on representative bodies'.[45] There was a significant overlap of representatives, and the new suffrage society even met in the offices of the Council for Women's Trades at 58 Renfield Street until 1909. Each of these organisations was middle class in composition and outlook.

A common contemporary criticism of the women's suffrage movement, and one which has been upheld by misogynist historians, is that it was purely self-interested, with the narrow aim of obtaining the vote for women of property. Nothing could be further from the truth. Those agitating for the extension of the franchise saw it as the means to an end, the key to liberate women from low pay, poor working conditions, domestic violence and prostitution,[46] a beginning in the emancipation of the female sex, and a way of obtaining better education for women. According to Lady Frances Balfour, the issues for women were 'education, medicine and suffrage', and in that order.[47]

The education issue was one of the reasons for campaigning for the election of women to the School Boards. The first woman in Scotland to be elected was Mrs Jane Arthur, to the Paisley Board in 1873. The *Bailie* magazine, which specialised in biographical sketches of prominent men, welcomed her with the following caution:

> It has been whispered that the lady who is a 'Man You Know' shows sometimes an inclination to espouse the cause of the 'shrieking sisterhood' who rave about 'Women's rights' and 'Women's wrongs' until honest men are well nigh 'deaved wi' skirlin!' . . . It would be a misfortune that a gracious dame should, from a mistaken sense of duty, sink down to the level of agitators who sport their petticoats on platforms and contaminate themselves and outrage their sex.[48]

The woman candidates put forward for the Glasgow and Govan School Boards by Professors Caird and Linsday in 1885, had a less radical stance. Grace Patterson and Margaret Barlass were both teachers of domestic economy, 'departments of female education which in the past have been sadly neglected in Glasgow'.[49] Their candidature was to benefit girls who were not 'educated in the future for the part they had to play as wives and mothers' and who therefore might make unhappy marriages.[50] They stood as a pair, agreeing to stand down if one of them should fail to be elected for – according to Professor Lindsay – 'it was easy to understand that one lady could scarcely be asked to go on a board with fourteen gentlemen'.[51] In the event, both were elected. Grace Patterson served on the board for twenty-one years, retiring in 1906,[52] and with Margaret Barlass, served on the Scottish Council for Women's Trades and in the Glasgow and West of Scotland Suffrage Society.

Much of the agitation for women's suffrage in the decades 1870–1900 was of a genteel nature, with meetings taking place in church halls, and more commonly in the drawing rooms of the wealthy. Large public meetings, like the Scottish National Demonstration of Women of 3 November 1882, were the exception rather than the rule.

One way in which it was felt that women's franchise could improve women's lives was in relation to domestic violence. In the mid-1870s, wife-beating in Britain had reached epidemic proportions, and a parliamentary report on the state of the law relating to brutal assaults in 1875 recommended that offenders would be lashed. There was much debate and discussion on the proposal, which inevitably, because women had no representation in parliament, was quietly dropped.[53] As might be expected men and women took up different stances in this debate. For example, the men of Edinburgh Trades Council petitioned the Lord Advocate against lashing on the grounds

> That the effect of lashing the wife beater would not be to produce any beneficial influence on the delinquent. It would only further brutalise him. He is thereby reduced to the same treatment as is inflicted on the brute creation, and would seldom, if ever, recover his manhood.[54]

Some women were firmly of the opinion that retaliation was the only way. Marion Bernstein, a music teacher who wrote verses for the popular *Glasgow Weekly Mail*, advised her readers in 1875 that

> If beating can reform a wife
> It might reform a husband too
> Since such are the effects of strife
> My sisters, I advise that you
> Should try it with the fists – Oh no!
> For that would seem like some weak joker
> In husband curing let each blow
> Be given with the kitchen poker
>
> And if you cannot cure them, 'kill'
> As coolly teaches the Wife beater
> In widowhood, you no doubt will
> Find your existence somewhat sweeter.[55]

In another poem, she urged wives to 'exert your common sense/ And form a combination/ For mutual defence/ Against assassination'.[56]

Jessie Russell, a Partick carpenter's wife who also wrote verse, was not convinced by Marion Bernstein's call for women's suffrage as a cure for the problem, but in her poem 'Women's Rights versus Women's Wrongs' agreed that

> A life for a life, and the murderer's hung
> and we think not the law inhuman
> Then why not the lash for the man who kicks
> Or strikes a defenceless woman?[57]

Marion Bernstein's retaliation in print was swift, concise, and to the point:

> Pray in what way is wrong redressed
> But by conceding right?
> And Woman Suffrage is the best
> For which our sex can fight

> You'd give the lash to wifebeaters
> But surely you should know
> If women legislated, they'd
> Have had it long ago
>
> You speak of women's wages
> Being scandalously small
> Believe me, Woman Suffrage
> Soon would find a cure for all
>
> Our claims are oft misunderstood
> We would but share with man
> The human right of doing good
> In any way we can
>
> Why should we put our trust in men
> Who oft betray our cause?
> Let women vote away their wrongs
> And vote for righteous laws[58]

Jessie Russell was thus convinced, and responded with a two verse 'Recantation'.

While the word 'feminism', according to the Oxford English Dictionary, did not appear until 1894, both Jessie Russell and Marion Bernstein are immediately recognisable as feminists. In 1876, Marion Bernstein had a dream which is still to be realised:

> I dreamt that the nineteenth century
> Had entirely passed away
> And had given place to a more advanced
> And very much brighter day
>
> For Woman's Rights were established quite
> And man could the fact discern
> That he'd long been teaching his grandmama
> What she didn't require to learn
>
> There were female chiefs in the Cabinet
> (Much better than males I'm sure)
> And the Commons were three parts feminine
> While the Lords were seen no more!

THE NEW CENTURY

The twentieth century brought fresh hope for the enfranchisement of women when the Pankhursts established the Women's Social and Political Union (WSPU) in 1903, and turned the request for Women's suffrage into a demand which was neatly verbalised for the first time as 'Votes for Women'. One of their staunchest male supporters in Scotland was Tom Johnston (1881–1965), the young editor of *Forward*, the radical newspaper established in 1906. When asked to do a public lecture estimating the possible effects of women's franchise on society, he was at his prophetic best, improving on Marion Bernstein's dream. He remarked of woman that:

> yesterday she was battering at a university door, today she cries for a voice in the laws which govern her, tomorrow she will demand economic equality with man . . . She will demand payment for maternity, recognising that child rearing is as valuable a service to the state as the carrying of sandwich boards or the hammering of nails. If unmarried, she will demand equal wages and equal advantages for work she can do as skilfully as a man. She will break down senseless conventions. She will invade Parliament via the ballot box She will teach from pulpits, sway the world from Downing Street, edit the *Times*, judge women's cases from the bench and plead them from the Bar, become occasionally Provostess of Glasgow, design the newest flying machine, discover the latest bacteria. . . Women being economically independent, marriages will lose their present suspicion of servant purchase. Marriage will be a bargain between equals and will partake of a greater spirit of comradeship than it does at present. No woman will be driven to Sauchiehall Street or Trongate to earn a living.[60]

He went on to say that women voters would be pre-occupied with obtaining old-age pensions – as they had done in New Zealand – slum clearance, housing and town planning legislation, and drastic temperance reform. He also prophesied wages for housework, payable by the husband's employer, and co-operative housekeeping between families. He fondly imagined that cosmetics and jewellery would disappear, and that tenements would be supplanted by cottages.[61]

Some of the early success of the WSPU in Scotland can be attributed to the support of Johnston and *Forward*. Apart from regular weekly coverage on the suffrage question, all of the theoretical issues were tackled there, and several pamphlets on the subject came from the *Forward* Press, including Johnston's own, *The Case for Women's Suffrage and Objections answered*.[62]

The WSPU offered a totally new approach to agitating for women's suffrage. For the first time since the 1840s, feminism was at the top of the agenda. WSPU headquarters were established in London in 1906; by this time, there were unions in Glasgow and Edinburgh and speakers were engaged in the process of 'opening up' Scotland. Usually, the unions were independent of headquarters, though united to it by sympathy and loyalty. Flora Drummond (1879–1949), an Arran woman who joined the WSPU in Manchester and followed Mrs Pankhurst to London, was the secretary for the local unions, providing them with speakers on request and dispensing advice.

Flora Drummond had great personal charisma. A small woman, she was disqualified from becoming a postmistress because she failed to make the regulation height of 5 feet 2 inches. Her talent as an organiser, her bravery, and her capacity for challenging cabinet ministers marked her out as a leader.[63] Very conscious of her Scots nationality, and being given the job of organising the great WSPU processions in London, she gave them a Scottish stamp. She was well-liked by the London crowds, who nicknamed her 'Bluebell' since she was Scottish and 'more than a match' for cabinet ministers. She was better known as 'The General' who marshalled the suffragette army, and a military outfitter supplied her with a uniform[64] (the sash of which was embroidered 'General') and which she wore with pride when she headed the demonstrations on horseback.

Like many other Scots who joined the WSPU in the early days, Flora Drummond was a member of the Independent Labour Party. She described herself as 'a married woman and a socialist in a hurry'.[65] Her son, born in 1909, was named Keir Hardie Drummond. In Scotland, the WSPU was an organisation of the left, and the older Glasgow and West of Scotland Society for Women's Suffrage mistook it as an ILP organisation.[66]

Thanks to the organisational talents of Theresa Billington-Greig (b. 1877), the intellectual young Manchester teacher who married a Scot, and Helen Fraser (b. 1881), the Glasgow artist who gave up her work for the cause, a national network had been built up by the time the Scottish Headquarters were opened at 141 Bath Street in January 1908. Dr Marion Gilchrist (1863–1952), the first woman to graduate in medicine from Glasgow University, and who was consistantly involved in the struggle to obtain higher education for women, was the person chosen to perform the opening ceremony. She resigned from the GWSSWS in November 1907 to lend her support to the militant cause, declaring that she

> at one time thought it a great pity that the militant suffragist should create rows at Westminster, but she had been brought round to another view. She saw clearly now that nobody had done more for the cause than those militant suffragists. She thought that they had been most heroic, and deserved the highest praise. They had brought the question to the public notice, and that was what the advocates of women suffrage who carried on the work quietly for sixty years had failed to do. The old school had managed to get over 400 members of Parliament to pledge themselves in favour of the cause, but had they got the vote yet?[67]

MEMBERSHIP OF SCOTTISH WOMEN'S SUFFRAGE SOCIETIES

For the most part, those who were accustomed to petitioning for women's suffrage from the sedate drawing rooms of Scotland were not tempted to join the WSPU. As mentioned previously, the GWSSWS was the child of the Scottish Council for Women's Trades. These two bodies shared two key people who were disliked intensely in the radical circles from which the WSPU membership came. The first was the secretary, Margaret Irwin. At a Glasgow Conference on working women and the Insurance Act, she told the audience that twenty years' experience had taught her that working women had not enough intelligence to look after their own affairs. A furious correspondent in *Forward* commented that 'for sheer impertinence and patronising insult, the meeting was one of the worst . . . it will be little short of a public scandal if employers' wives, daughters and sisters are going to be hoisted into positions to control the working of this Insurance Act'.

The second was her colleague, Andrew Ballantyne, who served as chairman of the GWSSWS from its inception until after the First World War. He worked for the Railway Servants' Union and the Scottish Trades Union Congress. His presence must have ensured the unpopularity of the suffrage society with socialists. In 1905 he also became manager of the Glasgow Public House Trust, which did not endear him to the temperance parties. Worse still, he was accused of reducing wages, lengthening hours, ordering slops to be served up (although not in the middle-class Sauchiehall Street public house) and employing one old woman in a state of near slavery. For weeks, the *Forward* castigated him to no effect.[69]

The older Suffrage Society was curiously unco-operative with other people and other bodies. Although the society had not many members when first formed, it took fright when the Co-operative Women's Guild branches started to apply *en masse* for membership.[70] When Susan B. Anthony wrote asking them to request her book on the history of women's suffrage through the local public libraries to ensure a circulation, they voted to take no action, as they felt that the society could not do this.[71] The committee almost had apoplexy when they read the pamphlet addressed 'To the Working Women of England' by Esther Roper of the Manchester Society.[72] In Manchester, the Suffrage Society was by contrast largely composed of women textile workers.

As no records of the WSPU in Scotland have survived, it is difficult to obtain an accurate picture of the membership. Although by general admission the membership was middle class, any working woman with an interest in enfranchisement would join either the WSPU or the Women's Freedom League.

While campaigning in the Kincardineshire by-election of 1908, WSPU speaker Mary Phillips was

> struck by the intelligence and warmth of the working women. Even in quite small places, they have grasped before we tell them of the meaning of our fight, and welcome us with kindly greeting that do our hearts good. They have in them all the makings of a vigorous movement in the north.[73]

In Glasgow, Celia Russell (1898–1984), who laughingly described herself as a 'double-breasted orphan', and who managed to obtain work as a pawnbroker's assistant even although her employer was looking for a boy, joined the WSPU and was one of Mrs Pankhurst's 'enforcers' in the St Andrew's Hall riot of 1914. Seventy years later, she still harboured a dislike for Walter Freer, the manager of Glasgow Corporation Halls, who allowed the police to baton charge the crowd.[74]

A working-class woman of some note who participated in WSPU militant action was Jessie Stephen, organiser of the Domestic Workers' Union in Glasgow.[75] In February 1913 there was a co-ordinated attack on Glasgow pillar boxes, when envelopes containing bottles of acid, partially stopped with cotton wool, were posted to destroy the mail.

> I was able to drop acid into the postal pillar boxes without being suspected, because I walked down from where I was employed in my cap, muslin apron and black frock . . . nobody would ever suspect me of dropping acid through the box.[76]

Working-class women were not encouraged to take part in militant action, because of the treatment meted out to them; Lady Constance Lytton proved the difference conclusively in 1910, when her health was permanently damaged by prison officials who did not know her identity. Helen Crawfurd (1877–1954), daughter of a Glasgow master baker and wife of a minister, realised that the prison wardresses were intimidated by their middle-class charges. One working-class woman, whom she remembered as Kirsty from Dumbarton, and who was in prison at the same time as herself, was probably the woman prosecuted under the name of Mary McAlpine. Mary was totally overawed in court. The magistrate could not understand her accent and the prosecutor and court official acted as temporary interpreters.[77] 'I jist broke ane . . . I'm sayin' am kind o' vexed noo that I did it, but I'll pay for the damage if ye like'.[78]

Her demeanour was in sharp contrast to that of sisters Frances and Margaret McPhun, daughters of Bailie John McPhun JP, timber merchant. They were jailed at the same time as Helen Crawfurd and Kirsty. Frances was furious at her sentence. In a letter to Miss Underwood, the organising secretary in Glasgow, she declared that Helen Crawfurd

> had the satisfaction of doing 10/- worth of damage while I only did $^1/_4$ of 9/-! I wish I had smashed the whole place and Mr Curtis Bennet's head into the bargain![79]

Frances and Margaret were highly distinguished graduates of Glasgow University, Frances in political economy and Margaret in psychology. They were in the university suffrage union, and joined the WSPU in 1910, after helping to organise the Edinburgh pageant of 1909. Both were imprisoned and force-fed in Holloway between 5 March and 29 April 1912. Their younger sister Nessie also joined the WSPU and their father, a distinguished east-end councillor who helped enlarge Glasgow Green and build the People's Palace, was immensely proud of them. Helen Crawfurd in her autobiography pays tribute to their organisational capacity. They regularly spoke for the WSPU on *Clarion* and socialist platforms.[80]

Janet Barrowman (1879–1955), another of the group of Scots imprisoned in 1912, was a middle-class woman who worked in a Glasgow
office. According to Helen Crawfurd, she lost her job on account of her
imprisonment.[81] She was not involved in politics in later life, but was
instrumental in putting together the collection of suffrage memorabilia
which came to the People's Palace in 1949.

Janie Allan, whose family ran the Allan Shipping line and whose
brother James was known as 'the millionaire socialist', put a lot of her
own money at the disposal of both the WSPU and the ILP. She was also
vice-president of the Women's Labour League.[82] During the great distress
of 1908–9, the ILP opened a shelter for women and children in a four-
room-and-kitchen house in Gibson Street, Calton, largely thanks to Janie
Allan's help and money. [83] By March 1909, it had been established for
nineteen weeks, and some 197,569 meals had been served.[84] Janie Allan
arranged for some of the women to be trained as cooks, and helped others
to emigrate to Canada.[85] In 1914, Janie Allan was one of the main Scottish
organisers involved in the St Andrew's Hall meeting in the March of that
year and its aftermath, gathering evidence to bring legal action against
the Glasgow police for brutality.[86]

THE GROWTH OF SUPPORT FOR THE WSPU

Through ceaseless work on the part of the organisers, a network of
Scottish groups was built up. Helen Fraser's schedule for 1907, leading up
to the opening of the Scottish headquarters in January 1908, gives an
insight into the frenetic activity involved. In September, she was speaking
at meetings in Kilmarnock, Dunfermline, Lochgelly, Dundee and
Springburn, and making arrangements for the great demonstration
which was to take place in Edinburgh on 5 October. She was also planning the establishment of new branches at Hillhead and Langside in
Glasgow. On 24 October, she held a meeting in Motherwell, followed by
one at Langside the next day. On 31 October she was addressing Cathcart
Parliamentary Association. On 18 November she was the main speaker at
a meeting in Inverness Town Hall, which, with the Provost in the chair
and the presence and support of most of the city fathers, was almost a
civic reception for the suffrage movement. The following day, she was
addressing a meeting at Aberdeen with Lady Ramsay. Further meetings
were held in Lenzie and Kirkintilloch, Tom Johnston chairing the latter,
and plans were laid for an impending visit from Mrs Pankhurst. On 19
December, she was back in Aberdeen again with Mrs Pankhurst, to
attend a public meeting held by H. H. Asquith. This culminated in a anti-
suffrage riot when a minister of religion attempted to move an amendment in favour of women's suffrage. Throughout December, she was
preparing for the formal opening of the WSPU headquarters at 141 Bath
Street, due to take place on 11 January.[87]

Given the opportunity however, the WSPU preferred to campaign at by-elections, persuading the voters to 'Keep the Liberal out' with the ultimate intention of destroying the government over the suffrage question. In March, April and May 1908 the golden opportunity presented itself four-fold in Scotland, with the deaths of Liberal MPs in Kincardineshire, Dundee, Montrose Burghs and Stirling Burghs. Liberal loyalties in Scotland were strong – each of the four seats were regarded as 'safe' – but the WSPU immediately took up the challenge. Political tactics were worked out in detail, campaign headquarters hired and forces drafted in from London. Mrs Pankhurst and her daughters came in person. The campaigns added spice and excitement to what otherwise would have been predictable elections with predictable results.

The chief interest was in the constituency of Dundee, where Winston Churchill had been a target for the WSPU since 1905; being limited in funds and unable to fight every election at that time, they had concentrated their efforts on him. The suffragettes had been largely responsible for his defeat in north-west Manchester. The Dundee by-election was tackled by the WSPU with vigour, if not glee. Mrs Pankhurst hired the Gaiety Theatre, the Kinnaird Hall and the Drill Hall for mass meetings; dozens of smaller meetings took place in halls and schools around the city; impromptu meetings were held at the gates of factories and football grounds. The suffragettes made their presence felt everywhere. They raided the Stock Exchange and invaded the offices of the *Dundee Courier* to address a meeting of the night staff. The local press as a whole were very favourable; the suffrage campaign was conducted and accepted in good humour. Churchill was not defeated, but the Liberal majority was reduced by 2,000, and Dundee was left with a strong WSPU organisation.[88]

Other constituencies looked forward to the arrival of the suffragettes. The Arbroath correspondent of the *Dundee Evening Telegraph* complained that the suffragettes had not come to Arbroath.[89] When the Dundee results were declared however, the WSPU campaign swung sharply to that part of the Montrose Burghs which included Arbroath, Brechin and Forfar.[90] The Arbroath fishermen extended an invitation to the WSPU to hold a meeting. The suffragettes were surprised and delighted at the arrangements. 'We were much astonished to find on our arrival not only the expected crowd of fishermen against a background of tarred boats and blue sea, to whom we had expected to speak from our wagonettes, but a spotless lorry arranged for us, covered with a new sail and wonderful strip of new green carpet. Standing in this was a table draped with a red cover and on it two bowls of primroses and a vase of daffodils, a very large glass of water and a tumbler! There were three cushioned chairs, and waving on this, a flag and a banner . . .'[91] The WSPU did not manage to unseat any of the four Liberal candidates in these 'conservatively radical' constituencies, but the Liberal majority was satisfactorily reduced, and the foundations of the militant suffrage movement consolidated.

In May 1909, a Scottish *Votes for Women* paper was launched. It was perhaps only a news-sheet, for no copies have survived. It was priced at a penny, while its English counterpart sold for threepence. The only material survivor of the paper is a hessian satchel, stencilled with thistles, the name of the paper, and the price.[92] In April 1910, the St Andrew's Hall in Glasgow was hired for a Grand Suffrage Bazaar and Exhibition. Part of the exhibition was a reconstruction of a second division cell, with WSPU members present in their prison dress explaining the conditions.[93] WSPU china with its purple and green motifs, to which the Scottish thistle had been added, was ordered for this occasion.[94]

Purple, green and white were the WSPU colours from May 1908, purple for dignity, green for hope and white for purity. Helen Crawfurd remembered them as Green White and Violet – Give Women Votes – [95] and because of the suitable colour match, the thistle was extensively used in Scottish WSPU imagery. When the suffragettes were counselled to be 'patient, gentle, womanly and flower-like', Mary Phillips pledged herself as 'a great big prickly Scots thistle'.[96] The Paisley soap manufacturers, Isdale and McCallum, had acquired a large sculpture at the 1888 International Exhibition, the title of which was 'You maunna tramp on the Scots thistle, laddie!' It had become a household slogan, but the suffragettes took it up as a war cry. Flora Drummond had it emblazoned on a banner as a 'Message to Mr Asquith' when she led a tartan-clad deputation to greet Mary Phillips on her release from Holloway in September 1908. The very finials of the banner poles were thistle-shaped.[97]

PANKHURST CONTROL AND THE WOMEN'S FREEDOM LEAGUE

Some women regarded Emmeline and Christabel Pankhurst as dictators; they in return regarded the dissenters as 'wreckers' of the movement, and in September 1907, the wreckers seceded to form the Women's Freedom League. Led by Theresa Billington-Greig, the Freedom League had strong representation in Scotland. Active women like Anna Munro, Eunice Murray, and actresses Maggie Moffat and Kate Evans who had previously worked with the WSPU, preferred the more democratic organisation of the Freedom League.

By 1909, the League had prominent Suffrage Centre premises in Edinburgh, at 33 Forrest Road, and in Glasgow, at 302 Sauchiehall Street. The latter had both a tearoom and bookshop, and even more spacious premises were acquired in George's Road in 1912.[98]

Whilst the WSPU indulged in active campaigning against Liberal candidates and cabinet ministers, the WFL preferred passive resistance in matters such as the payment of taxes, in order to create political capital and public sympathy.

Dr Grace Cadell of Leith for example, refused to pay inhabited house duty on one of her properties in Edinburgh. When her furniture was seized and sold by public roup at the Mercat Cross, she and her friends came along in a wagon and turned the occasion into a suffrage meeting.

Janet Bunten, secretary of the Glasgow branch of the WFL, took the same action during similar punishment for her refusal to pay for a dog licence.[99] The principle of 'no taxation without representation' was upheld and extended to cover matters such as the census of 1911, in which members of the Freedom League refused to participate, staying away from home all night to achieve their aims.

In their ordinary work for the cause however, the WFL was similar to the WSPU. Meetings were held, literature sold, lecture tours arranged and fund-raising bazaars and jumble sales were held. When Glaswegians went 'Doon the Watter' for their holidays at the Clyde coastal resorts, the Freedom League followed. Summer headquarters were established in Rothesay (advertised in their newspaper *The Vote* as 'the Naples of the North') and a holiday campaign was conducted, meetings being held in Dunoon, Kirn and Largs.[100]

The WFL had a summer centre at Dunoon as early as 1908. The work there was reported as strenuous:

> If we are not seen with a banner and bag of literature at the pier head in the morning, chalking the streets at tea time, and drawing crowds to the Castle Hill at night, the canny Scot would consider the collection penny ill-spent. In return, we have our privileges – stalwart policemen turn their backs discreetly when we produce our pipe clay and the music hall artiste makes a public apology before the inevitable reference is introduced. Yes, I think Dunoon is converted and everywhere 'doon the watter'. Those who come to scoff buy badges and postcards of the speaker, in which we do a roaring trade.[101]

In the autumn of 1912, the summer campaign was followed by a leisurely Edinburgh to London march, culminating in a deputation to the Prime Minister.[102]

Like every other suffrage organisation, the Women's Freedom League saw the vote as the means to an end, a key which would open the floodgate of legislation to alleviate the misery of women's oppression. They campaigned for justice, and published weekly in their newspaper a list of court cases, showing 'How Men Protect Women'. The injustices of the legal system, and the inconsistencies of man-made justice, were shown to be glaring, as for example, when Sheriff J. M. Gray at Dundee Sheriff Court sentenced one man to forty days' imprisonment for stealing two pounds of sugar, and another to fourteen days for sexually assaulting a little girl.[103]

The Freedom League members were deeply interested in women's pay and working conditions. They applauded the 1912 resolution of the Glasgow Branch of the Scottish Teachers' Association demanding equal pay for equal work,[104] and the forward progress of the Scottish Shop Assistants' Union.[105] Margaret Irwin, secretary of the Scottish Council for Women's Trades, advertised in *The Vote* a loan collection of clothing and embroideries from the Exhibition of Sweated Industries, as shown in Glasgow, Edinburgh and Dundee in 1913. 'The exhibits are very striking, and especially helpful for suffrage propaganda. They number over 400 and include garments made by women at 1d. or less per hour'.[106]

The Freedom League had a powerful speaker and propagandist in Eunice Murray of Cardross, who took the responsibility of organising members who lived outside the main towns in Scotland, the 'Scottish Scattered' as they were known. She produced many penny pamphlets on behalf of the WFL, such as 'The Illogical Sex', 'Prejudices Old and New' and 'Liberal Cant'. Her work for the Women's Freedom League continued into the 1930s.

The WSPU considered itself to be independent and self-governing within Scotland. It had a Scottish council, composed of a delegate from each of the Scottish branches, which was responsible for raising and administering funds for organising in new districts.[107] This was fine for as long as no one disagreed with the Pankhurst strategies, and after the purge from which the Woman's Freedom League was created, they commanded unquestioning loyalty. There was sometimes discontent, however. On 26 May 1914, Christabel Pankhurst wrote to 'My dear Miss Allan' from Paris to the effect that the Edinburgh branch should accept Miss Mary Allen as organiser, and not the Scotswoman they had chosen.

> As to the question of English organisers working in Scotland, when Englishwomen say they object to being organised by Scotswomen, it will be time for Scotswomen to say they object to being organised by Englishwomen. . . Some desire the appointment of Miss Lambie . . . the very idea is preposterous and on no account would we agree.[108]

This was apparently accepted. The entire membership of the Scottish WSPU were stunned when some months later, Janie Allan, their chief organiser and financier, was herself sacked by the Pankhursts, for bargaining with the Glasgow Lord Provost. She had promised no militancy during a royal visit if the prisoners in Perth were not forcibly fed. Helen Crawfurd and Dr Mabel Jones were sent to sort out the matter with the Pankhursts. Helen Crawfurd later wrote:

> While Chrystabel [sic] presented her case as the legal woman, it was to Mrs Pankhurst that the credit must be given for convincing us that the action taken was right. Mrs Pankhurst presented her case like this. You are all attached to Miss Allan because she is such a fine person, so are we. Not only that, but Miss Allan is a generous contributor to our funds. Do you think that this action has been taken without serious thought? The position is this, that the only thing that can stop militancy is the granting of the Vote to Women. We cannot bargain with the enemy. If Scottish women are prepared to bargain on any other terms, then English women are not.
>
> We felt humiliated that we could have made such an error. We

returned fully convinced that both Miss Allan and ourselves had allowed our hearts to run away with our heads. The majority of the Glasgow members accepted the decision, as did Miss Allan. Chrystabel's legal reasoning did not convince; it was Mrs Pankhurst's plain commonsense presentation. She could be very firm, but she was also an approachable human being, with charm and sound reasoning powers.[109]

WOMEN'S TORTURE IN PRISON

'Women Tortured in Prison – IS IT NOTHING TO YOU?' was stitched onto a Scottish suffrage penant in 1914. The torture was shocking, and it was Janie Allan's concern to end it that led to her dismissal. She had first-hand personal experience of force feeding, and her remaining papers contain evidence she was gathering on the drugging of women in prison.

Even when militancy was at the symbolic window-smashing stage, before the arson and terror campaign was adopted, women were being force fed. Frances McPhun wrote a graphic account from prison in 1912:

I started a letter to you on the third day of the fast but when I was in the middle of it the doctor and nurse and helpers rushed in, a sheet was thrown round me, I was held down in a chair and 2 pints of milk were poured down my throat. Don't gasp with horror, it was only the feeding cup they used. I didn't feel equal to the nasal tube. They give you the choice 'will you take the feeding cup or must we force it thro' the nose' they say. I took the cup. I had made up my mind to hunger strike but I wasn't prepared to risk being forcibly fed thro' nose. Margaret took the cup too – I made her promise to take it. Miss Allan had a feeding cup too – she made a brave fight – she barricaded her cell and it took 3 men with iron bars 3/4 hour to break it in! Miss Hudson I hear, nearly lamed the wardresses – she (fiery spirit!) scorned the feeding cup – using her head as a battering ram she kept them at bay for some time and when she was fed at last it was under difficulties – the fat nurse reposed on her tummy, a wardress on each foot, the doctor supporting her head between his knees! Even then with the tube in her nose she managed to tell them 'it was wonderful what dirty work a doctor would do for £500 a year'! Next day she was none the worse, out in the yard as happy as a lark – says she could not keep from laughing when the tube was in her nose! it didn't hurt her at all. One girl was hurt – her nose bled and she was unconscious for some minutes – wasn't it dreadful? Miss Parker had a tube also – she turned sick after it (poor thing) was taken to hospital, however she is all right now.[110]

The hunger strike medals of the McPhun sisters survive as a testimony, but none of the horror is evident in the morale-boosting little book of verse, *Holloway Jingles*, which the Glasgow group published after their release from prison.

Helen Crawfurd was also jailed on many occasions, under the Cat and Mouse Act. She was jailed during the royal visit to Perth in 1914 simply because she was there. While at home under the Cat and Mouse Act in Glasgow, she was arrested after the suffrage bombing of the Botanic Gardens, although she had nothing to do with it. Confined in Duke Street prison, she had a painful session fighting wardens who tried to hold her down for finger printing.

While she seems to have had no part in the 'outrages' herself, believing that some of the arson attempts were blamed on the suffragettes so that owners could collect the insurance on unwanted property, she did have the experience of unwittingly carrying parcels of bombs for an English suffragette visiting Glasgow. She also had the unpleasant task of trying to justify on a public platform the attempted bombing of Burns cottage for which Frances Parker, a niece of Lord Kitchener, had been arrested.[111] The burning of the mediaeval White Kirk in East Lothian, where £10,000 of damage was done (26 February 1914) was also difficult to justify.

Perth was one of the worst prisons as far as the torture of women was concerned. Hunger strikers committed elsewhere in Scotland were sent to Perth for forcible feeding because, according to the Secretary of State for Scotland, 'We have there medical officers who are accustomed to perform the operation in the criminal lunatic department there.'

Frances Parker was transferred from Ayr prison and received the worst Perth had to offer. She was fed by violence, and afterwards held down for two hours. On the third day of force feeding she lost consciousness, and instead of being subjected to the nasal tube again, three wardresses attempted to feed her by the rectum. This is her account:

Thursday 16 July The three wardresses appeared again. One of them said that if I did not resist she would send the others away and do as gently and as decently as possible. I consented. This was another attempt to feed me by the rectum, and was done in a cruel way, causing great pain.

She returned some time later and said she had 'something else' to do. I took it to be another attempt to feed me in the same way, it proved to be a grosser and more indecent outrage, which could have no other purpose than to torture.[112]

Frances Gordon, arrested for attempted arson, received the same treatment in Perth, and on her release, had the appearance of a famine victim, according to her doctor.[113]

Janie Allan did not manage to strike her bargain, and the royal visit of July 1914 had many little surprises for the royal party. At Dalmuir, the window of a cottage opposite the royal stand was thrown open and a banner with 'Votes for Women' and 'No Forcible Feeding' was flown, while a woman with a megaphone made a speech. Three days later (10 July) in Perth, 27-year-old Rhoda Fleming jumped on the bonnet of the King's motor and tried to smash the window. Typed petitions against forcible feeding were found. In another street, a placard was hung from a window with the inscription 'Visit Your Majesty's Torture Chamber in Perth Prison'.[114]

It is difficult to quantify and assess the total damage to property achieved on behalf of the women's suffrage movement in Scotland. Sometimes, even although no damage was effected, the publicity, because of the women and properties involved, was good. The arrest of Dr Elizabeth Dorothea Chalmers Smith, medical doctor, mother of six and wife of the Reverend Chalmers Smith of Calton Parish Church, Glasgow, whilst trying to burn down an empty house at 6 Park Gardens in the west end, caused a sensation. She and the artist Ethel Moorhead were caught red-handed.[115] Shortly before the trial, there had been a raid on a house of ill-fame in Pitt Street, and because quite a number of prominent Glasgow citizens were involved, the case was hushed up, and a trivial sentence of two weeks passed on the owners of it. By contrast, Dr Chalmers Smith and Miss Moorhead were sentenced to eight months.

When the sentence was pronounced, the women rose from all parts of the court and protested, crying out 'Pitt Street, Pitt Street' while others started to pelt the judge and council with small apples . . .

The contrast in sentences where human life and property were at stake was so great, that the women were filled with wrath and indignation at this outrageous travesty of justice.[116]

Ethel Moorhead was clumsily force fed thereafter and contracted pneumonia, the food having been poured into her lungs.[117]

The damage campaign in Scotland began with the pillar box attacks and the cutting and bombing of telephone links in 1912. A natural history case in the Royal Scottish Museum was smashed, and the King's portrait in the National Gallery in Edinburgh was damaged.[118] In 1913, the Western Meeting Club at Ayr was burned to the ground with a total damage of £3,500.[119] An attempt was made to set fire to Kelso raceground stand.[120]

In May 1913, the mansion house of Farrington Hall, Dundee, was bombed and burnt, £10,000 damage being caused.[121] Large unoccupied houses were a favourite target for the militants; it was hoped that the insurance companies would have to bring pressure to bear on the government to grant the vote, for their own financial protection.

The militants who had been caught in the act of attempting arson at Kelso, were sentenced at Jedburgh Sheriff Court. The ringleader, an Edinburgh teacher called Arabella Scott, described it as 'a mere attempt to burn a low gambling shed'. She and two others received nine months' imprisonment. A further two accomplices, the Misses Thomson – elderly Edinburgh ladies, who formerly been missionaries in India – received lighter sentences.[122]

On account of this 'Jeddart Justice', the Royal Observatory in Edinburgh was bombed and £100 of damage was caused.[123] This was followed by an unsuccessful attempt to set fire to the waiting rooms on both

platforms of Shields Road Station, Glasgow.[124] The Gatty Marine Labora-
tory of St Andrew's University was severely damaged by fire in June
1913,[125] and the following week, Leuchars Station was burnt to the
ground.[126]

Militancy was unabated. In August 1913 two women hid on the golf
course at Lossiemouth, and physically assaulted the Prime Minister.[127]
There were fires at Fettes College and Morelands House, Edinburgh.[128] In
December 1913, there was a spectacular fire at Kelly House, Wemyss Bay,
and the £30,000 mansion built by Alexander Stephen was left ruins.[129]
Another attempt was made on a similar mansion at Shandon, only three
days later.[130]

In the early spring of 1914, Mrs Pankhurst visited Glasgow to address
a mass meeting in the St Andrew's Halls. Her presence was only half-
expected, as she was subject to re-arrest under the Cat and Mouse Act.
The Glasgow WSPU were well prepared: the flower-screened platform
hid several strands of barbed wire, and the platform party was armed
with Indian clubs. Mrs Pankhurst was smuggled in in a laundry basket,
and to the surprise and delight of the audience, she was able to appear.
She had no sooner started her speech however, than the police rushed the
platform in great numbers. Rioting ensued, the police making free use of
their batons 'in a hysterical and brutal fashion',[131] the platform party
retaliating with flower pots and clubs. Mrs Pankhurst was re-arrested,
and police behaviour was such that the Glasgow WSPU spent the following months attempting to take legal action against them.[132] Unsuccessful
in their attempts – the police had seized more than enough evidence to
justify their actions – further destruction of property followed.

Until the outbreak of the First World War, the suffragettes were in the
news every other day, and were putting their lives in danger so that
women could have a future. Many historians have ignored this, and
others have had the cheek to say that the militancy alienated the government and inhibited the women's cause. Women might still be waiting for
the right to vote if it had been left to the men.

Elspeth King's contribution to this volume was written before the
publication of *A Guid Cause* by Leah Leneman, and we therefore felt
it appropriate that we should let her comments on the neglect of the
Scottish Women's Suffrage Movement stand. Furthermore, the publication of one book on the subject does not in itself fully remedy this
neglect, but only advances the process of historical investigation of a
rich and complex area which deserves study and debate from a
variety of perspectives. – *Editors*.

NOTES

1 Helen Crawford's autobiography is a typescript of 403 pages
    (90,000 words) and is in the Marx Memorial Library, London. A
    copy is kept in the Willie Gallacher Library, at the Scottish
    Trades Union Congress, 16 Woodlands Terrace, Glasgow.
2 Elspeth King, *Scottish Women's Suffrage Movement* (People's

Palace Museum, 1978, reprinted 1985). Rosalind K. Marshall, *Virgins and Viragos*, (Collins, London, 1983) pp. 283–293. It is no accident that both of us are museum curators and not academics. In 1980 Elspeth King also provided an introduction for a microfilm edition of the *Papers of the Glasgow and West of Scotland Association for Women's Suffrage 1902–1933*, the original of which is in the Glasgow Room of the Mitchell Library, with the intention of making this important original source more widely available.

3 *Glasgow Sentinel*, 6 December 1856.

4 See Lisa Tickner, *The Spectacle of Women, Imagery of the Suffrage Campaign 1907–14* (Chatto & Windus, London, 1987) for a list of surviving banners.

5 Listed in King, *Scottish Women's Suffrage Movement*, p. 29–30.

6 Crawfurd, *Autobiography*, p. 92.

7 *Forward*, 30 May, 6 June 1908.

8 Pamphlets by Eunice Murray include *The Power of Women in the Church* (n/d), *Women's Place in the Early Church* (1928) *Women and the Church* (n/d c. 1914) and *Women in the Ministry* (Govan, 1923).

9 Ellen Ross 'Women's History in the USA' in Raphael Samuel (ed.) *People's History and Socialist Theory* (Routledge, London 1981). pp. 182–8.

10 The ring was sent back to Scotland after Skirving's death and is in the People's Palace collection (PP, 1987, 36.1)

11 *Glasgow Courier*, 10 August 1819.

12 *Glasgow Chronicle*, 4 November 1819.

13 *Glasgow Chronicle*, 28 October 1819.

14 *Glasgow Courier*, 1 November 1819.

15 *Glasgow Chronicle*, 11 November 1819.

16 *Glasgow Courier*, 2 November 1819.

17 Scottish Record Office *ex* AD/14/20/174.

18 The above references, 10–17, were supplied by my colleague Michael Donnelly. In order that this female reform pageantry would not remain buried in newspaper references, he also supplied them to Ken Currie, who depicted it in Panel 2 of the Glasgow History Mural in the People's Palace, 1987.

19 *Scottish Patriot*, 2 November 1839.

20 *Scottish Patriot*, 9 May 1840.

21 *True Scotsman*, 22 December 1838.

22 *Scottish Patriot*, 10 August 1839.

23 *Scottish Patriot*, 27 July 1839

24 *Scottish Patriot*, 14 March 1840.

25 *Scottish Patriot*, 21 December 1839.

26 *Scottish Patriot*, 2 May 1840.

27 *Glasgow Constitutional*, 20 November 1839; *Scottish Patriot*, 30 November 1839.

28 *Scottish Patriot*, 14 and 21 December 1839; 11 and 27 January, 2 May, 1840.

29 *Scottish Patriot*, 14 December 1839; 9 November 1840.

30 King, *Scottish Women's Suffrage Movement*, pp. 9–10.

31 Barbara Taylor, *Eve and the New Jerusalem: Socialism and Feminism in the 19th century*, (Virago, London, 1983).

32 *Glasgow Constitutional*, 12 October 1839.

33 See advertisements in the *Glasgow Courier*, 14 January, 16 March, 6 May 1843, and a mention of a lecture by her in 1856, in W. H.

Marwick's pamphlet *Alexander Campbell*, p. 14–15.

34   *Glasgow Free Press*, 16 April 1834.

35   Taylor, *Eve and the New Jerusalem*, pp. 152–155.

36   Her Scottish tour was reported in depth, in *New Moral World*, 21 December 1844, 11, 18, 25 January, 8 February, 1 March, 12 April, 31 May 1845.

37   *New Moral World*, 26 July 1845.

38   *The Reasoner*, 23 February 1848.

39   Taylor, *Eve and the New Jerusalem*, pp. 65–70.

40   *The Movement*, 9 October 1844.

41   Report of the Eighth Annual Meeting of the Edinburgh National Society for Women's Suffrage (Edinburgh, 1876) p. 7.

42   Ibid.

43   Report of the Eleventh Annual Meeting of the Edinburgh National Society for Women's Suffrage (Edinburgh, 1879) p. 5.

44   See reports of support meetings in the *Glasgow Weekly Herald*, 7 and 28 October 1882.

45   Women Shop Assistants: How they live and work. Evidence given by Miss Irwin before the Select Committee of the House of Lords on the Early Closing of Shops. (Glasgow, 29 April 1901).

46   A popular postcard *c.* 1909 was issued on this theme.

47   *Ne Obliviscaris – Dinnae Forget*, A Memoir of Lady Frances Balfour (1930) vol. 2 p. 120.

48   *The Bailie*, 25 June 1873.

49   *The Bailie*, 15 April 1885.

50   *Glasgow Herald*, 9 April 1885.

51   *Glasgow Herald*, 16 April 1885.

52   *Glasgow Herald*, 28 June 1906.

53   Frances Power Cobbe, 'Wife torture in England' in the *Contemporary Review*, April 1878, pp. 55–87.

54   Quoted by James D. Young *Women and Popular Struggles* (Mainstream, Edinburgh, 1985) p. 94.

55   Marion Bernstein, *Mirien's Musings, A collection of songs and poems* (Glasgow, 1876) p. 42.

56   Ibid., p. 89.

57   Jessie Russell, *The Blinkin' o' the Fire and Other Poems* (Glasgow, 1877) pp. 29–31.

58   Bernstein, *Mirien's Musings*, p. 81.

59   Bernstein, *Mirien's Musings*, p. 101.

60   *Forward*, 12 November 1910. See also 5 November 1910.

61   *Forward* ,19 November 1910.

62   Tom Johnston *The Case for Women's Suffrage and Objections Answered* (Forward Publishing Company, Glasgow, n.d.) 16pp.

63   For an assessment of Flora Drummond see Sylvia Pankhurst, *The Suffragette Movement* (1931, republished Virago, London 1977) pp. 191–194, p. 266 and *Votes for Women*, 7 May 1908 p. 144.

64   See *Votes for Women*, 7 May, 18 June 1908.

65   *Forward*, 8 June 1907.

66   Executive Committee Minutes, Glasgow and West of Scotland Association for Women's Suffrage, 11 December 1906. (Hereafter abbreviated ECM, GWSSWS).

67   *Glasgow Herald*, 12 January 1908.

68   *Forward*, 16 March 1912.

69   *Forward*, 16 and 23 March, 13 April 1907.

70   ECM, GWSSWS, 18 December 1902.

71   Ibid., 27 October 1903.
72   Ibid., 15 September 1904.
73   *Forward*, 18 April 1908.
74   Tape recording made by Celia Russell, 1978.
75   See letters in *Forward* 6 and 13 April, 11 May 1912.
76   *Spare Rib*, no. 32 (1975) pp. 10–13.
77   Crawfurd, *Autobiography*, pp. 88–91.
78   *Glasgow Herald*, 11 March 1912.
79   Letter, private collection. Copy in People's Palace.
80   Crawfurd, *Autobiography*, pp 91–95.
81   Ibid., p. 92.
82   *Forward*, 4 July 1908.
83   *Forward*, 12 December 1908.
84   *Forward*, 20 March 1909.
85   *Forward*, 4 September 1909.
86   Janie Allan's Papers. Acc 4498, National Library of Scotland.
87   See reports in *Votes for Women*, September 1907–January 1908.
88   *Votes for Women*, 7 May 1908 pp. 152–4.
89   *Votes for Women*, 30 April 1908.
90   *Votes for Women*, 14 May 1980.
91   *Votes for Women*, 21, 28 May 1908.
92   People's Palace collections. See also *Votes for Women*, 21 May 1908.
93   *Scots Pictorial*, 7 May 1910.
94   Catalogue of the Grand Suffrage Bazaar and Exhibition, St Andrew's Halls, Glasgow 1910.
95   Crawfurd, *Autobiography* op. cit. p. 104.
96   *Forward*, 22 June 1907.
97   A photograph album with a number of 10"x 8" prints illustrating these points was found by a Glasgow cleansing department worker in a bucket in 1977. They were copied on 35 mm negatives for the People's Palace collection.
98   *The Vote*, 4 May 1912.
99   *The Vote*, 12, 19 October 1912.
100 *The Vote*, 6, 11 July, 10 August, 14 September 1912.
101 *Forward*, 29 August 1908.
102 *The Vote*, 5 October 1912.
103 *The Vote*, 14 November 1913.
104 *The Vote*,16 November 1912.
105 *The Vote*, 7 November 1913
106 *The Vote*, 7 November 1913.
107 *Forward*, 22 June, 28 September 1907.
108 Janie Allan's Papers, Acc 4498, National Library of Scotland.
109 Crawfurd, *Autobiography*, op. cit., pp. 110–1.
110 Private collection. Copy in the People's Palace.
111 Crawfurd, *Autobiography*, op. cit., pp. 86–113.
112 Sylvia Pankhurst, *The Suffragette Movement* (1931, republished Virago, London 1977) pp. 580–1. *Votes for Women*, 10 and 24 July 1914.
113 *Votes for Women*, 10 July 1914.
114 Newscutting *Glasgow Herald* (?) 11 July 1914 in Janie Allan's papers, Acc 4498, National Library of Scotland.
115 *Glasgow Herald*, 16 October 1913.
116 Crawfurd, *Autobiography*, op. cit., p. 109.
117 Pankhurst, *The Suffragette Movement*, p. 580.

118   *Glasgow Herald*, 11 February 1913.
119   *Glasgow Herald*, 25 May 1914.
120   *Glasgow Herald* 7 April 1913.
121   *Glasgow Herald*, 10 May 1913.
122   *Glasgow Herald*, 22 May 1913.
123   *Glasgow Herald*, 22 May 1913.
124   *Glasgow Herald*, 2 June 1913.
125   *Glasgow Herald*, 23 June 1913.
126   *Glasgow Herald*, 1 July 1913.
127   *Glasgow Herald*, 29 August 1913
128   *Glasgow Herald*, 23 August 1913.
129   *Glasgow Herald*, 6 December 1913.
130   *Glasgow Herald*, 9 December 1913.
131   See the evidence collected against the police from individuals in Janie Allan's Suffrage papers, Acc 4498, National Library of Scotland.
132   For a full account, see Graham Moffat, *Join Me In Remembering – the life and times of the author of 'Bunty Pulls the Strings'* (Camps Bay: Winifred L. Moffatt, 1955); *Glasgow Herald*, 10 March 1914; Walter Freer, *My Life and Work* (Glasgow, 1929).

SELECT BIBLIOGRAPHY

Elspeth King, *The Scottish Women's Suffrage Movement*, (People's Palace Museum, Glasgow, 1978).

Rosalind K. Marshall, *Virgins and Viragos*, (Collins, London, 1983).

Barbara Taylor, *Eve and the New Jerusalem*, (Virago, London, 1983).

Sylvia Pankhurst, *The Suffragette Movement*, (Virago, London, 1977).

7

THE LONG SLOW MARCH:
SCOTTISH WOMEN MPs, 1918–45

CATRIONA BURNESS

In 1918 Westminster was at last opened to women. The vote was extended to most women at 30 and to all men at 21. A Bill allowing women to stand as parliamentary candidates at the age of 21 was hustled through Parliament to become law three weeks before polling day. At the 1918 election women made up 39.6 per cent of the British electorate; after the extension of the franchise to women at 21 in 1928 women accounted for over 52 per cent of the electorate.[1]

The parties immediately turned themselves to the key concern of winning women's votes. Providing electors with women to vote *for* scarcely figured on the agendas of the political parties in a period of intense inter-party conflict. The outcome of this conflict saw the beginning of the long-term decline of the Liberal Party and the rise of the Labour Party. The Conservatives (fighting as Unionists in Scotland) reaped the benefit of the party struggle as the dominant party of the inter-war period. Women party activists were caught up in this struggle. The fervour of the Unionist women's anti-Bolshevik, anti-socialist message found its mirror image in the determination of Labour women to ward off any attempt to capture the women's votes for reaction. Yet very few women were to play a part in this conflict either as parliamentary candidates or as MPs. In all only eight individual women were returned as MPs for Scottish seats over the period from 1918 to 1945 while thirty-three stood as candidates.

The low levels of women's representation are perhaps not so surprising given the deep antipathy to women moving outside the domestic sphere demonstrated by the opposition to the demand for votes for women. The ten-year delay in giving women the vote on equal terms with men is an indicator of residual hostility to women moving into the political sphere. The barriers which faced women with the temerity to want to play the 'men's game' of party politics were formidable. At a time when women rarely asked questions at political meetings, let alone addressed them, the prospects of a woman becoming a parliamentary candidate were slim. This chapter will explore how the political parties came to terms with women as voters and party members and briefly study the experiences of Scottish women MPs and candidates. In doing so the chapter makes a preliminary foray into the neglected area of women in post-1918 Scottish party politics.

THE PARTIES AND THE 'WOMAN QUESTION'

The extension of the suffrage to women in 1918 had implications both for party structures and electoral appeals. Prior to 1918, while individual Liberal and Unionist women were involved in the suffrage campaign the party organisations avoided commitment on the question of votes for women. Women's suffrage was not be made a test question. By 1914 the Scottish Women's Liberal Federation (SWLF), while attacking 'the violent and criminal acts' of the militant suffragettes, had committed itself to support women's suffrage by 'all constitutional methods'.[2] However, of the political parties the Labour Party gave the greatest support to women's suffrage before 1918. Elspeth King has commented that in Glasgow the links between the Women's Social and Political Union (WSPU) and the ILP were so strong that 'the [WSPU] office-bearers had difficulty in convincing the more conservative ladies of the non-militant Association for Women's Suffrage that the WSPU was not in fact an ILP organisation'.[3] Yet as Elspeth King and Eleanor Gordon have pointed out, it would be a mistake to assume that all socialists and socialist organisations supported women's suffrage.[4] Nonetheless, the Labour Party might have been expected to be the party most likely to promote women candidates and women's issues. Yet Labour did not establish a lead in this area. Over time the Labour Party was to return more Scottish women MPs than the Liberal or Unionist parties, but between 1918–45 the Unionists were to prove as likely as Labour to put up women candidates in Scotland. Meanwhile, following party reorganisation in 1918, both the Liberal and Unionist parties were to create party structures within which women were far more visible than in the Labour Party.

THE LIBERAL PARTY

Prior to 1918 separate organisations of men and women had been a feature of both the Conservative and the Liberal parties. After 1918, both of these parties merged their male and female organisations. The new Liberal organisation was to be known as the Scottish Liberal Federation (SLF), fusing the Scottish Liberal Association and the Scottish Women's Liberal Federation. Striking commitment to equality of the sexes was shown in the new Rules which set out that representation on the SLF should be 'equally divided between men and women'.[5] Constituencies were thus required to nominate one man and one woman for places on the Federation; in 1920 when two constituencies nominated two men, Webster, the Liberal Scottish Secretary, returned the papers so that a man and a woman might be nominated, 'or failing a woman, only one man'.[6]

This was a wonderful start, acknowledged in the last meeting of the SWLF which decided that 'after the manner in which the women have been treated by the men, having been given equal rights in every way, a women's committee would be out of place'.[7] However, while the operation of the equal representation rule was not further discussed within the Federation between 1918–45, there are some indications that it was not fully applied. In 1930 Mrs Stuart indicated that she would rather not chair the Eastern Finance Committee, not that she was unwilling to help but she thought that a man ought to be in the position'.[8] Whatever had happened to equal representation within the Federation and its committees? She was the only woman among six men at the meeting.

Despite the initial feeling that women's committees were 'unnecessary', within a few years such committees were in place at both Federation and constituency level. Following the 1922 election the Federation consulted local associations on how best to ensure that 'greater interest would be taken by the women', and subsequently recommended that local Liberal parties should set up Women's Sections where they did not already exist.[9] By 1925 the Federation itself had formed a women's committee.[10] Although it was to be heavily pre-occupied with running bazaars to rescue Liberalism from its dire cash crisis, the Women's Educational and Social Council could at least send resolutions and have representation at the annual conference.[11]

The Liberals apparently found it difficult to draw women into the party, and in particular, to involve women on equal terms with men. A sense of purpose behind the commitment to equality was clearest at all levels, including the parliamentary level, over 1918–22. In 1918 within the UK the Labour and Liberal parties each put up four women, the Unionists, only one; in 1922 the Liberals put up more women candidates – sixteen – than Labour with ten and the Conservatives with five, added together. Two of the three women candidates to stand in Scotland in 1922 were Liberal, Mrs Alderton in Edinburgh South, and Mrs Smith, better known as the novelist, Annie S. Swann, in the Maryhill division of Glasgow. The other woman candidate, Helen Fraser, 'an educationalist',[12] stood as a National Liberal in Govan. From 1923 at a UK level Labour was to put up more women candidates than either of the other parties. Despite a promising start only eight of the thirty-three Scottish women candidates from 1918–45 were Liberals. The explanation for the failure to select women may be linked to the party's decline over the period but must also lie with the local associations given the prevailing candidate selection procedures.

In Scotland, the Liberal Federation had a key role to play in placing candidates, partly due to the increasing difficulty of getting candidates as the Liberal Party faced disintegration and decline. The placing of candidates, however, was negotiated between the Liberal Whip, Webster as Scottish Secretary, and local deputations 'in some cases ten strong'.[13] At the 1923 election the Federation rushed as many as twenty-two candidates into the field within eight days, and Webster commented that 'the candidates available were unfortunately limited. . .or another five or six could easily have been placed'.[14] Yet no Liberal women candidates stood in Scotland in 1923. Difficulties in finding candidates worsened and in 1928 Webster reported that 'the difficulty was to get proper adjustment between constituencies and individual candidates'.[15] It is not clear from the Federation minutes whether there were Scottish Liberal women who would have liked to have been parliamentary candidates, but who were turned down by the local deputations. However, no Liberal women stood for Scottish seats at either the 1929 or 1931 elections. Two Liberal women stood in 1935 and in 1945 Lady Glen-Coats, the only Liberal woman candidate, suffered the humiliation of becoming the first Liberal candidate to lose their deposit in Paisley, a former Liberal stronghold. No special shame on her – although three National Liberals were returned – as the Liberals lost every single one of their Scottish seats in 1945. No Scottish Liberal woman MP was to be returned over 1918–45 and indeed none until 1987. However, given the party structures which they had created for themselves, it remains surprising that more female candidates did not emerge.

THE UNIONISTS

The Unionists directed themselves towards winning women's votes with the purpose that might have been expected of the party which had created the Primrose League. Founded in 1883, the League had brought socialising into politics, and in its wake, a mainly female mass membership of over one million. A Scottish branch was formed in October 1885 and soon made a major contribution to League membership; as late as 1908 a Scottish membership of 100,476 was claimed.[16] However, some scepticism on the figures seems in order; by 1908 the League's minutes were dominated by references to the hostility of Conservative parliamentary candidates, attempts to revive Habitations (as local Primrose League branches were called), the difficulty of collecting Tributes (membership fees), and the encroachment of Women's Unionist Associations. From within the Unionist Party the Women's Unionist Associations lanced the *raison d'etre* of the Primrose League.[17] By 1918 the League's role had been overtaken by the Women's Unionist Associations and post-war reorganisation included winding up the League in Scotland ahead of its demise in England.[18] The League, however, had a significant history of drawing women into Conservative and Unionist politics. The lines of future Unionist organisation were set down in February 1918:

> The Council decided that women should be admitted to all Associations on the same footing as men; that they should be eligible to sit on committees, and hold office, the sole test of election being efficiency. . .should any Association desire to do so they might appoint

a Women's committee to deal with any question or questions in which women might be specially interested. The Council was unanimous in agreeing that the fusion between men and wo-men's Associations should be absolute and that the organisations should on no account remain separate.[19] In February 1918 local associations were informed that 'it was necessary to ensure that women, who make up roughly three voters to every five men in the new electorate, should have their proper share of representation'.[20] By 1919 the Scottish Unionist Association (SUA) Rules and Constitution had been revised to ensure that women took up at least one-third of the places on national and regional party councils. Each constituency was allowed to send three representatives,'at least one of whom shall be a woman'.[21] As with the Labour Party, women members of the Unionist Councils formed themselves into Women's Committees, although in the east of Scotland the women did not meet regularly as a committee, but only as they felt it necessary. Despite initial complaints that some constituencies had not sent women representatives to regional councils the rules ensured that women would be noticeable in the Unionist Party.[22]

While in England and Wales the formation of women's branches proceeded rapidly,[23] in Scotland the question of forming women's committees at a local level proved unpopular. Lady Glenarthur, convener of the West of Scotland Women's Committee, commented in 1919 that 'the formation of Women's Committees would be gradual, and it was not desirable that the matter should be forced in any way'.[24] Any tendency towards separate organisation aroused suspicion lest this perhaps encouraged the formation of a women's grouping in politics (in or out of the Unionist Party). Two women organisers were appointed in 1919 in the west and east of Scotland. They were not appointed 'for the sole purpose of organising women' in case this added to 'the danger of separate male and female organisations emerging.'[25]

Yet there was no doubting the determination of Unionists to draw women into the party. They embarked on organising women's meetings and in January 1920 Lady Baxter stressed that 'it was better that such meetings should be addressed by bad speakers than that they should not be held at all' and that, in particular, 'women should be fully informed of the horrors of Bolshevism . . . it was neither wise nor kind to protect them from such knowledge however unpleasant'.[26] Indeed women were deemed to be particularly at risk from socialism. A Unionist election leaflet in 1922 claimed that Labour, if elected, would nationalise women (*sic*).[27] Unionist women were quite at one with Unionist men in running up the Bolshevik bogey. In 1922 the Western Women's Committee blamed 'Socialist teaching in Socialist Sunday Schools and in Schools generally' for Labour's parliamentary breakthrough in Scotland.[28] Although a few months later the committee had to concede that they could not find specific instances of socialist propaganda in schools,[29] the fervour of the anti-socialist, anti-Bolshevik message went undiminished. Anti-socialism remained the key Unionist theme over 1918–45 despite the dominance of the National Government in the 1930s. As party stalwarts women were involved in every Unionist campaign. Protectionism, for instance, was promoted with the aid of displays of Empire food to encourage housewives to 'buy imperially'.[30] The vital contribution of women party workers at every election was acknowledged and in 1929 it was recommended that 'in view of the importance of the women's vote, at all future large meetings, a woman should be on the speaking list'.[31]

Women as party candidates were another matter. The view of leading Scottish Unionist women such as the Duchess of Atholl and Lady Baxter was that, having earned the vote, women would have to earn the right to be political representatives via a lengthy apprenticeship. Lady Baxter identified local government as 'a congenial sphere for women's work in politics',[32] while the Duchess referred to it as 'Women's Kingdom'.[33] Women were not to stray too far from home. The Unionist appeal was very much directed towards women as housewives as in Mrs Stanley Baldwin's (*sic*) eve of poll appeals to housewives.[34] Unionist women did not join Labour and Co-op women in raising contentious issues such as birth control, nurseries, unemployment benefit for women or pensions, and were prepared to wait for Baldwin to implement equal voting rights for men and women. Nonetheless, women amounted to a 'massive presence' within the Unionist Party, albeit one that subordinated women's concerns to the demands of party renewal.[35]

THE LABOUR PARTY

Labour had turned itself to the question of how best to organise to win women's votes as early as 1916. The Women's Labour League then successfully appealed to the second Scottish Labour Party Conference for help 'in anticipation of the competition of the organisations which will be set up by the middle classes to capture the women's vote for reaction'. The help sought was wide-ranging. It included the appointment of a Women's Organiser, the setting up of branches of the League in every constituency, and assistance such as local donations, free room hire, the provision of speakers, help in distributing literature and persuading women of their own families to join the nearest branch of the Women's Labour League. Conference was warned that failure to provide assistance would mean that 'Autocracy may reap where Democracy has sown'.[36]

By 1919, Agnes Hardie, later MP for Springburn, had been appointed as Scottish Women's Organiser, while it was reported that twenty-four Women's Sections had been formed. Also in 1919 the Scottish Executive convened and subsidised a Scottish Labour Women's Conference. This was to become an annual event although its status as such was not confirmed until 1926.[37] By 1919 too, better representation of women on the party's Scottish Executive had been secured by increasing the number of seats reserved for Women's Sections from one to four.[38] The reform of the Labour Party's constitution in 1918 had produced a party structure which accommodated the various categories of members – women, constituency parties (which for the first time had individual members), unions and socialist societies such as the Fabian Society and the ILP. Like the National Executive of the party, the Scottish Executive reflected these sections and was elected by the annual conference in which the trade unions had the major say. The Labour Party thus had a structure which was very different from that of the Liberal and Unionist parties, whose executives reflected geographic not sectional representation.

The key role of male-dominated trade unions in this structure combined with a low female membership, left women less visible in the Labour Party than in either the Liberal or Unionist parties. In 1919 Clarice McNab Shaw, a leading Labour woman activist of the inter-war years, became the first woman to chair the Scottish Labour Party Conference, or indeed any Scottish party conference. Her chair's address singled out the indifference of the men in the party to the necessity and value of securing the co-operation of women in building up the labour movement:

> Women are the chief victims of our wretched social conditions . . . it is of extreme importance, then, to arouse women to a sense of the political weapon which they now wield by means of the vote. In many districts the requirement of the Constitution for the development of the women's sections had not been complied with, and in very few instances are facilities given to the women to proceed with the necessary educational work.[39]

In 1919, at a point when Labour membership, especially that of the ILP, was rising quickly, 85 per cent of Glasgow's ILP members were men.[40] In 1920 Agnes Hardie commented that 'the support which is given to the Labour Party by women cannot be measured by the membership as it is difficult for women to attend meetings'.[41] Difficulty in attending meetings was certainly most likely to particularly affect the working-class women to whom Labour was especially directing its appeal. In an effort to reach these women Labour arranged 'kitchen' meetings as part of the street activity of the time. This activity was to cause anxiety in Unionist ranks disproportionate to its success in recruiting members. 'We must go into the backyards, and into the little alleys where people live, often in the greatest hardship and distress, and where nobody goes but the socialists',[42] Mrs Neville Chamberlain (*sic*) told a Unionist women's meeting in 1924.

In 1923 Agnes Hardie reported that 'there are forty-two women's sections in Scotland . . . a big increase has taken place in the membership of the sections which varies from about thirty to over 200'.[43] This would have given a female membership of the Labour Party in Scotland of between 1,266 and 8,400, and this soon after the ILP's 'Great Push' membership campaign during which the party considered it had broken new ground among women.[44] Yet, in general, the Labour Party and the ILP were never mass membership parties in Scotland. Labour membership was certainly far lower than that of the Unionists over the period. Although the Unionists did not set a membership fee, which must have inflated their membership figures, estimates of a peak of Scottish ILP membership of 8,030 in 1925 pale alongside Unionist membership of 21,689 in 1925 in Glasgow alone.[45] In 1929 Herbert Morrison pointed out that 'while all over the individual membership was bad . . . Scotland was even more backward'.[46] Michael Savage has shown that in Preston the growth of Labour ward organisation was closely linked to the development of women's sections and that the party's rise in electoral popularity in the late 1920s was linked to the growth of women's involvement in the party.[47] In Scotland Labour's breakthrough did not go hand in hand with notable success in drawing women into the party. If anything, Savage's observations on the connection between involving women and electoral success apply more clearly to the Unionists than to Labour. In 1931 (before the resignation of the Labour government), the then Scottish Labour Women's Organiser, Mary Sutherland, acknowledged that, 'as a rule, progress in women's organisation depends upon the general state of the party machinery in a constituency, and in certain constituencies any advance in women's organisation will have to wait upon improved general organisation'.[48] Thus the shockwaves of the formation of the National Government and the breakaway of the ILP in 1932 scarcely improved prospects for Labour's work among women.

Labour women were critical of what was seen as indifference towards winning women's votes and involving women in the party, and Scotland was perceived as a poor area for women's organisation. However, although the low representation of women in Scottish local government was discussed and concern expressed at there being only four women county councillors in 1936,[49] the absence of Scottish Labour women MPs went unraised. It seems as though there must have been low expectations of how many women MPs would be returned, and in the context of Labour's struggle to establish itself as a party of government in the 1920s and to recover from electoral catastrophe in the 1930s, improving women's parliamentary representation was not an issue let alone a priority.

A WOMEN'S PARTY

Welcoming the end of a fifty-year struggle for the vote for women the suffragette historian, Ray Strachey, noted that the men did not know just what to expect but that a Women's Party was dreaded:

> In 1918 the politicians had not realised that women would not vote in a solid block, as women; they feared that perhaps a Women's Party might be formed; and consequently they did not know what to be at. They wanted very naturally, to secure the women's vote for themselves but they did not know how this was to be done.[50]

The 1918 election offered the first test of how this might be done. Only seventeen women stood for parliament in 1918, eight as Independents. Christabel Pankhurst was selected as the standard-bearer of the Women's Party which had emerged from the WSPU. She was invited to stand in several constituencies before deciding on Smethwick. Given the suspicion of political parties held by many of the suffrage campaigners it is rather surprising that she was the only woman candidate to received the 'coupon', that is, the endorsement of the continuing Lloyd George wartime Liberal–Tory coalition – all the more surprising given the Women's Party's pledge to continue militant feminism. However, as a candidate she was unsuccessful and as an organisation the Women's Party was short-lived. The Countess Markievicz was the only woman MP elected in 1918 but like other Sinn Fein MPs she did not take up her seat.

Only one woman candidate appeared in Scotland in 1918. Eunice Murray, described as 'the daughter of a well-known Glasgow lawyer', stood as an Independent in Glasgow Bridgeton, 'barring even the Women's Party'.[51] As a propagandist and speaker for the Women's Freedom League, a non-militant suffrage organisation with a keen interest in women's pay and working conditions, she was a seasoned campaigner. Her programme focused on the need for social reform, especially in housing, and for the need for women's representation on the reconstruction committees. Her vote of 900 was 'indifferent' and she lost her deposit.[52] As an Independent candidate she was not typical of the Scottish women candidates; thirty of the thirty-three women candidates over 1918–45 were party candidates.

The 1918 election offered considerable reassurance to the parties on women's likely voting behaviour. *The Scotsman* noted with relief:

There is no appearance of anything like a tendency towards a block vote. There is no dominant issue which is capable at the moment of aggregating the women voters in one camp; it is, indeed, doubtful if any such issue is ever likely to arise and it is to be hoped that it never will. All candidates are appealing to women electors on the assumption that the political divisions among them run on the same lines as among men; but conscious of the numerical strength of this body of voters, and recognising that certain questions appeal specially to women, candidates everywhere have made arrangements for addressing meetings confined to women electors. This is a tribute to the power of the feminine vote.[53]

Much indeed was being made of women's new-found influence; Ray Strachey optimistically wrote that the absence of women at Westminster in 1918 'was much less important than it had been before, for every member there knew that he owed his election to the votes of women as well as men, so that the whole atmosphere of parliament was changed'.[54] There was an assumption that one or two women would be elected soon and so it proved. In a 1919 by-election Nancy Astor replaced her husband

TABLE 7.1 Women elected – general elections, 1918–45

	UK		SCOTLAND	
Election	Total elected	% of total MPs	Total elected	% of total MPs*
1918	1	0.1	nil	nil
1922	2	0.3	nil	nil
1923	8	1.3	1	1.35
1924	4	0.7	1	1.35
1929	14	2.3	2	2.7
1931	15	2.4	3	4.05
1935	9	1.5	2	2.7
1945	24	3.8	3	4.05

*Note: Over 1918–45 the Scottish total is taken as 74 including the 3 Scottish University seats. From 1950–79 there was a total of 71 Scottish MPs; and since 1983 a total of 72 Scottish MPs.

as Conservative MP for Plymouth Sutton, on his elevation to the peerage, while in 1921 the Liberal Mrs Wintringham followed her husband as MP for Louth, Lincolnshire, on his death. As Elizabeth Vallance has pointed out, it is unlikely to be coincidental that the first women MPs inherited seats from their husbands. Their role as MPs was an acceptable extension of their role as wives.[55]

Not all women candidates won such acceptance. By 1922 the Women's Party no longer existed. As an issue, however, it dominated the election campaign in Edinburgh South. The controversy arose when the Edinburgh branch of the Women's Citizens' Association (WCA) decided to back the Liberal candidate, Mrs Alderton. A national organisation, across Britain the WCA supported a broad programme on women's rights, ranging over the equal franchise, working conditions, women's access to careers in the police and the civil service, and childcare. The decision to back Mrs Alderton divided the association and several members resigned in protest. The correspondence columns of *The Scotsman* heaved with complaints that it was unconstitutional for a non-party organisation such as the Edinburgh WCA to support a party candidate. *The Scotsman* joined the attack:

> The association alleges nothing against Sir Samuel Chapman . . . nor is he being opposed because he is a member of the Unionist Party   . . . but because he is not a woman . . . the action of the Association is equivalent to creating a 'Women's Party'.[56]

Mrs Alderton attempted to defuse the situation saying that while she wished to raise women's issues 'she was not standing as a woman

TABLE 7.2 Women candidates at general elections in Scotland, 1918–45

Year	Comm	Con &Un	Eco	Lab & ILP	Lib	N.Lib	SDP	SNP	Other	TOTAL	Elected
1918	–	–	–	–	–	–	–	–	1	1	–
1922	–	–	–	–	2	1	–	–	–	3	–
1923	–	2	–	–	1	–	–	–	–	3	1–1Un
1924	–	3	–	2	1	–	–	–	–	6	1–1Un
1929	2	3	–	4	–	–	–	–	–	9	2–1Un, 1 ILP
1931	1	4	–	4	–	–	–	1	–	10	3.3Un
1935	–	4	–	2	2	–	–	–	1	9	2.2Un
1945	–	3	–	3	1	–	–	–	1	8	3–3Lab

candidate but as a Liberal candidate'.[57] It was to no avail; the Unionists rallied to the defence of Sir Samuel Chapman whose share of the vote rose from 57.7 per cent in 1918 to 66.7 per cent. The furore, however, appeared to focus Unionist attention on the need to have at least one or two women candidates in Scotland. Thereafter the Unionists did field a few women candidates at each election; on the other hand the Liberals put up less women after 1922. Research for this chapter suggests while organisations such as the WCA and the Freedom League petitioned party candidates on women's rights at subsequent Scottish elections, they neither endorsed nor fielded candidates. This restraint contrasts with the position in England, where the WCA in some localities put up their own candidates, particularly at local elections. For instance, the WCA put up candidates for local elections in Preston; and when the local Labour Party refused to give a clear run to a WCA candidate the Association moved towards a local alliance with the Conservatives.[58] Nor was there any apparent Scottish parallel with the efforts of Norwegian and Swedish women in the late 1920s to improve women's representation by fielding women candidates. Instead, in 1923 *The Scotsman* called on the 'Women's Party' to celebrate the return of the anti-feminist Duchess of Atholl as Scotland's first woman MP.[59]

SCOTTISH WOMEN MPS AND CANDIDATES

There were very few British or Scottish women MPs elected over 1918–45. Table 7.1 shows that from 1924 the average percentages of women MPs and candidates were fractionally higher for Scotland than for the UK while Table 7.2 sets out the election of women MPs by party over 1918–45. An inter-war peak was marked in 1931 by the election of fifteen women

MPs; this figure included three Scottish women MPs, all of whom were Unionists. Twenty-four women MPs were returned in 1945, again including three Scottish women, this time for the Labour Party. In part the fluctuations in women's representation were linked with the fortunes of the political parties. It is not surprising that Unionist women did well in 1931 nor that Labour women did well in 1945.

Over 1918–45, however, Scotland presents a different party pattern of women's representation from that of the UK. At UK general elections, from 1923 Labour put up more women candidates than did the other parties, and at every general election put up between two and three times as many women as did the Unionists. In Scotland, however, the Unionists were as likely as Labour to put up female candidates. Only in 1929 did Labour's four women candidates outnumber a Unionist trio. The Unionists put up more women candidates than Labour in 1923, 1924 and 1935 and an equal number of candidates in 1931 and 1945. Nine individual women stood as Unionist candidates over 1918–45, with seven of the nine standing more than once. Three were elected as MPs; the Duchess of Atholl for Kinross and West Perthshire over 1923–38, Florence Horsbrugh for Dundee from 1931–45, and Helen Shaw for Bothwell over 1931–5.

The Duchess of Atholl became Scotland's first woman MP when, in 1923, she won the seat which her husband, then Lord Tullibardine, had held from January 1910 until his accession to the peerage in 1917. As with the Liberal Party, selection procedures within the Unionist Party were a matter of decision for a few key national or local figures. The Duchess of Atholl had been identified as a most suitable female candidate and was persuaded to stand by a powerful combination of leading Unionists. Apart from her aristocratic social and political connections, the Duchess had an extensive background of service on public bodies. In 1920, for instance, she sat on no less than twenty-five committees, and positions held 'ranged from Chairman of the Highlands and Islands Consultative Council of the Board of Health, to President of the Perthshire Federation of District Nursing Associations, to twelve Education Committees, to membership of the National Council of Women of Great Britain and Ireland – and more'.[60] She had also been active in Scottish Unionist circles and knew most of her party leaders personally. Taken together with her personal qualities as a conscientious and hard worker on behalf of her chosen causes the Duchess of Atholl must have seemed the obvious choice as the first Scottish Unionist MP.

In terms of forwarding women's representation, however, she was not the obvious choice. The irony that the first women MPs should not have been suffrage reformers has often been pointed out. So far as the Duchess of Atholl was concerned it was most marked, as she had spoken publicly against votes for women before 1918 and in 1924 was the only woman MP to vote against reducing the female voting age to 21 on the grounds that:

The proposal means that women will be in the majority on the parliamentary register . . . I cannot forget that the preponderance . . . will have been largely due to the fact that we lost 740,000 precious lives of men in the Great War . . . I feel that to propose a great extension of this kind looks like taking advantage of the heroic sacrifices of those men.[61]

During the franchise debate the Liberal MP, Mrs Wintringham, pointed out that the Duchess's contribution showed that 'women were not at all in agreement' and that there was no prospect of 'a women's party against a men's party'.[62] Sheila Hetherington, her biographer, commented on the irony of the Duchess of Atholl, of all people, 'the anti-feminist . . . breaking the mould so effectively – trail-blazing almost by accident certainly never by design'.[63]

While the Duchess continued to infuriate feminists, for instance by opposing equal pay in the civil service in the 1930s, her own career mapped out a series of firsts. Apart from being the first Scottish woman MP, in 1924 she became the first Conservative woman minister on her appointment as Parliamentary Under-Secretary at the Board of Education from 1924–9. The appointment was made to match Labour's appointment of Margaret Bondfield as a junior minister in 1923 and Katharine Atholl was preferred over Nancy Astor on account of her knowledge of education and Baldwin's feeling that she would be 'loyal and decorous'.[64] As a junior minister she had a difficult relationship with her chief, Sir Eustace Percy, who 'never favoured the idea of having a woman as his Parliamentary Secretary and made no attempt to hide his disdain'.[65]

After 1929, however, the Duchess's humanitarian concern for women and children contributed to her espousal of causes that set her at odds with her party. The first of these was opposition to the practice of female circumcision in Kenya, a campaign which met with blank incomprehension in the House of Commons. 'Die-hard' opposition to the Simon Report on the future government of India followed. Her reluctance to concede Indian Home Rule was linked to concern over the position of women and children in India without, as she saw it, the restraining influence of the British Raj. She campaigned for Randolph Churchill when he stood as a 'die-hard' Independent Conservative at the Liverpool Wavertree by-election in 1935. His intervention handed a safe Tory seat to Labour. The Duchess of Atholl faced growing criticism in her own constituency but it did not prevent her from resigning the Unionist Whip over the India Bill. Yet the West Perthshire Conservatives could live with the Duchess on India as *The Scotsman* reported: 'Her supporters . . . do not quarrel with her independent attitude, indeed, are more disposed to admire it'.[66] Opposition to the fascist rebels in Spain, concern for Spanish women and children, vocal opposition to appeasement, and a spate of publications such as the best-selling *Searchlight on Spain* were another matter and made her an increasing embarrassment to the Unionist Party.

Sheila Hetherington has pointed out that she became more marginalised than other anti-appeasers:

Firstly she was a woman; for most of the men, the trade of politics was still exclusively a male domain. Secondly she was viewed as being old and dowdy. This too was unfair, since many MPs were themselves much older and dowdier than she was ... Thirdly, Kitty – and to an extent Churchill too – were seen to have abandoned their fellow aristocrats at a time of crisis'.[67]

Most of the anti-appeasers, including Churchill, were able to hold the support of their local party but in May 1938 the West Perthshire Unionists decided to look for another candidate for the general election. The Duchess had been dumped. Now dubbed the 'Red Duchess' by angry Unionists, the attitude of her local and national party combined with a worsening international situation led her to resign and fight a by-election in December 1938 as an Independent. She expected to win. The Liberal candidate, Mrs Coll MacDonald, reluctantly stood down to give the Duchess a clear run against the official Unionist candidate. With the full weight of the Unionist machine flung into the constituency she lost by 1,333 votes. It was one of the last victories of appeasement and the end of the Duchess of Atholl's parliamentary career. It was the closing of a parliamentary career of British and Scottish importance. The Duchess had made a major contribution in parliamentary debate, ranking third in Brian Harrison's measurement of gross debating contributions of the inter-war women MPs, and in opposing the India Bill in 1935 she contributed 42 per cent of all that was said by women MPs that year.[68]

None of the other women candidates were either as lionised in the early days or as reviled latterly as the Duchess. Both Florence Horsbrugh and Helen Shaw were elected in the National Government landslide of 1931. This provided Helen Shaw, a soldier's widow, with her only session as an MP although she fought the Bothwell seat seven times between 1924 and 1945. Bothwell was unpromising territory for the Unionists; *The Scotsman* recognised 1931 as 'the best opportunity she [Helen Shaw] ever had of capturing a safe Socialist seat'.[69] A factor in the Bothwell contest in 1931 apart from the groundswell of support for the National Government was the appeal made by the Orange Order on her behalf. Brian Harrison categorised Helen Shaw as essentially a lobby-fodder loyalist, voting often but speaking little in debate and raising few parliamentary questions.[70] 1935 found her fighting a losing battle for survival as Labour pinned its hopes on the mining vote, estimated at nearly 75 per cent of the electorate, at a time of industrial unrest. On her defeat she later told the Western Unionist Women's Committee that 'one of the greatest difficulties had been the influence of the Co-operative Women's Guild'.[71] Mrs Shaw became active in local politics and remained a key figure locally until her death in 1966.

Florence Horsbrugh was perhaps the political survivor of the three.

Elected MP for Dundee in 1931, she topped the poll in 1935 but was defeated in the Labour victory of 1945. She was selected as Unionist candidate for Midlothian and Peebles in 1950 but was unsuccessful and was eventually returned as MP for Manchester Moss Side in a poll delayed by the death of the Conservative candidate. She held this seat until she retired in 1959 and was created a life peer. Her political career also involved some firsts; in 1936 she was selected to move the Address in Reply to the Speech from the Throne. She referred to her own first commenting that 'whatever else may be said about me in the future, from now henceforward, I am historic'.[72] Jean Mann commented of Florence Horsbrugh that at close quarters she was 'kind, warmhearted, unstuffy and genial' but that there was another side, 'a cold, stern appearance, formidable in controversy. Detached and inflexible – complete party politician'.[73] Her merits as a party politician were rewarded by a series of ministerial posts. She served as parliamentary secretary to the Ministry of Health from July 1939 to May 1945, and to the Ministry of Food from May to July 1945. On her return for Moss Side in the 1950s she was appointed Minister for Education from November 1951 with a seat in the Cabinet from September 1953 to October 1954.

It has been commented of the Unionist women candidates in general that 'they were . . . much stronger on titles than on scholarship'.[74] Of the nine Unionist women who stood for Scottish seats between 1918 and 1945, however, only two were titled. The titled ladies were the Duchess of Atholl, and Lady Grant of Monymusk who contested Aberdeen North unsuccessfully in 1945 and was later returned for Aberdeen South from 1946 to 1966 under her second married name of Lady Tweedsmuir. Given the proliferation of titled ladies active in Scottish Unionist circles it is surprising that a majority of the Unionist women candidates were professional women. Catherine Gavin was a doctor of literature while Laura Sandeman was a GP. Margaret Kidd, who fought the 1928 West Lothian by-election on the death of her father, the sitting MP, was Scotland's first woman advocate and became the first woman barrister in Britain to appear at the bar of the House of Lords.[75] Despite these achievements, throughout the by-election campaign she was mainly referred to as her father's daughter. Other candidates such as Violet Roberton and Helen Shaw had strong local connections and local government experience.

Although there were only three Unionist women MPs, Scotland was apparently the most fruitful territory for Unionist women candidates so far as the numbers went. Two factors may help to account for this. Perhaps the efforts made by the Unionists in Scotland to draw women into Unionist politics resulted in a higher tendency to put up women candidates. Such efforts were by no means confined to Scotland, however, and a stronger factor may have been the Unionist perception of Scotland as much less promising territory for the party. Not one of the Unionist women candidates was put up in a 'safe' seat. Only Margaret

Kidd was put up in a Unionist-held seat. She lost it, but according to *The Scotsman*, with no discredit:

> With three candidates in the field it was always doubtful whether she could win. In like circumstances the late Mr Kidd was twice defeated, and his daughter has improved on both of his unsuccessful polls.[76]

Most of the Scottish Unionist women, even when unsuccessful, polled around 30 per cent of the vote. This indicates that they were not being put up in the most hopeless seats, although generally they had actually improved their party performance. All three of the Unionist women MPs took the seat from another party to enter Westminster. There was clearly nothing to lose in fielding a woman candidate but equally clearly winning women's votes took a much higher priority than providing the electorate with women to vote for.

Five Labour women were returned for Scottish seats over the 1918–45 period, of whom three were elected for the first time in 1945: Clarice McNab Shaw for Kilmarnock; Jean Mann for Coatbridge, and Margaret (Peggy) Herbison for North Lanark. Only two Labour women were returned to the House before 1945. Jennie Lee held North Lanark from the by-election of March 1929 until her defeat in 1931 while Agnes Hardie represented Springburn from her election in 1937 on the death of her husband, the sitting MP, until she retired in 1945. Eleven individual women stood as ILP or Labour candidates over the period, with seven standing more than once. Clarice McNab Shaw and Jean Mann were among those who served a lengthy political apprenticeship as unsuccessful candidates before being selected for seats which Labour expected to win in 1945. In this sense their return was a different matter from the return of Helen Shaw and Florence Horsbrugh in 1931. Neither Bothwell nor Dundee were good long-term prospects for Unionism – Florence Horsbrugh did exceptionally well to top the poll in the two-member seat in 1935 – but in 1945 Labour women were returned for seats which they held until retiring. Sadly, in the case of Clarice McNab Shaw, this was due to illness in 1946. She was never able to relish the achievement of a parliamentary ambition which she had pursued in 1929 and 1931.

Would-be Labour candidates faced a far more competitive selection procedure than either Liberal or Unionist women as 'in the Labour Party there had always been an attempt to consult the constituency party members in drawing up the shortlist and agreeing the prospective candidate'.[77] Further research would be required, however, to investigate whether there was much of a record of women losing selection contests. A key factor in the selection was the ability to offer sponsorship, to bring a dowry. Over the 1920s 'the ILP was the fulcrum of Labour Party activity in Scotland'; in 1929 of sixty-eight Labour candidates, sixty-seven were ILP members and thirty were ILP-sponsored.[78] In 1931 three of the four Labour women had ILP backing. After the break with the ILP, union backing became crucial. Given the important part played by male-dominated unions such as the National Union of Mineworkers, women were at a disadvantage in securing sponsorship.

There were other barriers. At a time when women rarely asked questions at political meetings, let alone addressed them, how were women going to emerge as suitable candidates? The ILP took the view that a woman speaker always attracted crowds and tried hard but apparently found it difficult to recruit women for their speakers' panel. Jean Mann recalled being outmanoeuvred in her objections to going on to the panel as she couldn't possibly leave her five children, by the discovery that her husband had already agreed to babysit:[79]

> I was pushed into it. No woman setting out to have six of a family is planning a parliamentary career. It just happened – pushed into it by men.[80]

Promoted particularly by Labour, outdoor meetings were a feature of inter-war political propaganda and women speakers were rare. Jennie Lee was among the exceptions, but, for all her eloquence, she thought that other factors won her the North Lanark selection in 1928 over the miners' nominee in a mining seat:

> They were just as much impressed by my university degree as by my oratory. And just as important, I came out of the right stable. I was Michael Lee's grand-daughter [of the Fife & Clackmannan Miners' Union].[81]

The North Lanark by-election of March 1929 returned Jennie Lee to become Scotland's first Labour woman MP at the age of only 24. Apart from the help poured in by Labour Party members she had the unexpected support of British bookies. Furious at the introduction of a bookmakers' levy by Winston Churchill, then Chancellor, bookies turned up from all over the country to help make sure that the Unionists lost the seat. *The Scotsman* commented that the 6,578 majority won by Jennie Lee exceeded 'even her own expectations', and went on:

> During the campaign . . . it was stated that the Roman Catholics had been advised to vote for the Liberals because of the uncertainty of Miss Lee's attitude on the question of birth control, but it is now apparent that the advice was not accepted.[82]

At the 1929 general election Jennie Lee held the seat but with a reduced majority. In 1931, however, she lost, confronted by a tide of support for a National Government, the emerging hostility of right-wing miners' union leaders, and above all, the fury of the Catholic church. Fellow ILP-ers, Maxton, McGovern and Campbell Steven, had tried to persuade her of the need to support the Scurr amendment for increased provision for Catholic schools. 'I was livid with contempt . . . All they cared about was saving their seats. They succeeded. I went under'.[83] Despite being furious with Maxton, and critical of his leadership of the ILP, Jennie Lee could not bear to leave the ILP on the break with Labour – an attitude which led her future husband, Nye Bevan, to call her 'my Salvation Army lassie'.[84] She fought North Lanark again in 1935 but as an ILP candidate against a Unionist and an official Labour candidate. The official Labour intervention ensured a Unionist win. Jennie Lee did not stand again in Scotland although she was returned as Labour MP for Cannock in Staffordshire in 1945. Scotland thus lost one of its most charismatic if controversial female representatives.

Charisma aside, youth was Jennie Lee's marked characteristic as a Scottish woman MP. Her election at the age of 24 was exceptional in the period 1918–45. Among the Unionist women, the Duchess of Atholl was 49 when she first entered parliament, Helen Shaw was 52 and Florence Horsbrugh, 42; among the Labour women, Peggy Herbison was 38, Jean Mann, 56, Clarice McNab Shaw, 62, and Agnes Hardie, 63. Most of the women were married but childless.[85] It is not surprising that the unmarried women, Florence Horsbrugh and Peggy Herbison, who each entered Parliament at around 40, should in time have the longest ministerial careers. Jean Mann was exceptional among the women in entering into political activity while her five children were young. Maxton teased her that she was 'known all over Scotland as "haud the wean" Jean, and that all over . . . the comrades had to decide who would take the chair, who would lift the collection, and who would "hold her bairn"'.[86]

The Scottish Labour women MPs typically had long involvement in the party behind them. Clarice McNab Shaw and Agnes Hardie provided striking instances of this. Although Agnes Hardie's selection as Labour candidate for Springburn was attributed to her marital connections, in her own life she had pioneered a path for women. A former shop worker, she was a founder member of the Shop Assistants' Union and its first female organiser. She also became the first Women's Organiser of the Labour Party in Scotland, and Glasgow's first woman MP. She became known as the 'Housewife's MP' on account of her voluble attacks on the price of meat or shortage of potatoes.[87] These attacks certainly aroused anxiety among Unionist women, prompting them to react with leaflets setting out the 'true facts'.[88] After 1945 Jean Mann was to take on the mantle of the 'Housewife MP' although there was also to be a reaction against this 'housewife's focus' among younger women – not that Jean Mann or Agnes Hardie had been typical housewives anyway! Yet of all of the Scottish women MPs of the period 1918–45, Agnes Hardie and Jean Mann showed the greatest inclination to identify themselves with women's issues.

However, while Jean Mann expressed concern over the lack of women at Westminster, she made a string of objections to George Bernard Shaw's suggestion of the 'Coupled Vote'. This was the suggestion that every constituency should have two representatives, a man and a woman:

> Is a housing, or rent question concerning children, peculiar to one
> sex? Would conflict not arise as to who should handle which? And

would there by a dominant partner? As to the House of Commons, much overcrowded with 630 members, what would it be like with 1,260? . . . think of the voters at a general election. The issue might be man or woman. Spoiled papers enormous.[89]

Jennie Lee described her friend, Rebecca Sieff, chair of Women for Westminster, as 'born before her time, with every fibre of her being she resented the restrictions imposed upon her because of her sex'.[90] Jennie Lee continually refused to join Women for Westminster saying, 'No, Becky, I shall always vote on policy issues, not on the sex of the candidate'.[91] None of the early women MPs were likely to disagree with her.

CONCLUSION

Obviously very few women stood for Parliament or were elected as MPs over 1918–45. All of the early women MPs made a breakthrough for women simply by virtue of being among the first women at Westminster while Katharine Atholl and Florence Horsbrugh served as junior ministers over the period. After 1923 the Scottish pattern of women's representation was marginally better than the UK average. Over the period Labour returned the highest number of women MPs while the Unionists fielded the highest number of women candidates. Labour was slightly less likely to put up women in Scotland than at the British level, perhaps because of poorer local organisation and women's involvement in the party. The converse may explain the higher number of Unionist women along with Scotland being perceived as a weaker area for Unionism in which women were given more opportunities to fight seats. After a promising start in terms of candidate numbers the Liberal women fell away. This falling off seems likely, at least in part, to be linked to the crisis of survival faced by Scottish Liberalism over the period. In general there were links with party fortunes in explaining which party would send a woman or two to Westminster.

The lack of women at Westminster does not seem to have been a burning issue over the period. The great triumph was the winning of votes for women. The post-1918 reform of party structures was intended to equip the parties to meet the challenge of an enlarged electorate and to accommodate women inside the party structures. Despite apparent equality arriving with the vote the parties found it difficult to involve women.

The women who became MPs tended to share advantages of family connections with politics and a higher than average level of education. The exception to this pattern was Jean Mann who claimed that she never wanted to be an MP anyway! Jean Mann was also exceptional among the women MPs in becoming active in politics as 'haud the wean' Jean, mother of five. Most of the women who became MPs were married, childless, and over 40. The barriers faced by would-be women candidates were numerous and included low expectations of women in public life, lack of encouragement, hostility to women moving into the political sphere, difficulty in gaining political experience and in being identified as a potential candidate – over and above the pressures bearing down on women to remain within the domestic sphere and the difficulties of combining the pursuit of political ambitions with other responsibilities. Women were, nonetheless, the political novelty of the 1920s as new voters. However, the welcome discovery that women voted on party lines as men did made it likely that the novelty would wear off as the women's vote assumed manageable dimensions for party managers. In addition, as Deirdre Beddoe has commented, 'Larger events, including the economic crisis at home, the rise of fascism in Europe and the growing threat of war . . . crowded women off the stage of history.[92]

Reviewed in 1945, however, an appraisal of women's parliamentary debut would undoubtedly have been more optimistic than one made in 1992. In 1945 with women's representation at the then record levels of 3.8 per cent in the UK and 4 per cent in Scotland there was still room for hope that women's representation would rise gradually, inexorably and of itself. The vantage of 1992 underlines the reality that having won the vote in 1918 and the equal franchise in 1928, women faced and continue to face a long, slow march to equal involvement in Parliament.

NOTES

Abbreviations

LPSC   Labour Party Scottish Council
SACLP Scottish Advisory Council of the Labour Party
SLA   Scottish Liberal Association
SLF   Scottish Liberal Federation
SUA   Scottish Unionist Association
SWLF   Scottish Women's Liberal Federation

1 All election statistics are drawn from F. W. S. Craig, *British Electoral Facts, 1832–1987*, (Parliamentary Research Services, Aldershot, 1989), and *The Yearbook for Scotland, 1966*, (Scottish Conservative and Unionist Central Office, Edinburgh, 1966).
2 Scottish Women's Liberal Federation (SWLF), Minute Book 9, 12 March 1914.
3 Elspeth King, *The Scottish Women's Suffrage Movement*, (People's Palace, Glasgow, 1978), p. 15.
4 E. King, *Scottish Women's Suffrage Movement*, pp. 15–6; Eleanor Gordon, 'Women and Working Class Politics in Scotland, 1900–14', *passim*, in L. Jamieson and H. Corr (eds), *State, Private Life and Political Change*, (Macmillan, London, 1990).
5 Scottish Liberal Association (SLA), vol. 1, Meeting of Special Rules Committee from Joint Executives of SLA and SWLF, 2 October 1918.
6 Ibid, Eastern Finance Committee, 27 April 1920.
7 SWLF, vol. 9, 20 November 1918.
8 SLF, vol. 3, Eastern Finance Committee, 27 May 1930.
9 SLF, vol. 2, 13 July 1923.
10 SLF, Executive Committee, 25 March and 24 April 1925.
11 SLF, 31 March 1926.
12 *The Scotsman*, 11 November 1922.

13 SLF, vol. 2, Report for the Executive by Mr Webster on 1923 election, 19 December 1923.
14 Ibid.
15 SLF, vol. 2, Central Organising Committee, 7 December 1928.
16 Primrose League, Scottish Branch, Minute Book 2, 13 November 1908.
17 Ibid, *passim.*
18 Ibid, 3 February 1920.
19 Scottish Unionist Association (SUA), Minute Book 1, 15 February 1918.
20 SUA, Memo on Representation of the People Act 1918, February 1918.
21 SUA, Executive Council, 3 February 1919.
22 SUA, Women's Committee, 15 October 1921.
23 Arthur Fawcett, *Conservative Agent,* (National Society of Conservative and Unionist Agents, Driffield, Yorkshire, 1967), p. 24.
24 SUA Central Council, Minute Book 1, 3 December 1919.
25 SUA Eastern Office, Minute Book 1, 25 June 1919.
26 Ibid, 21 January 1920.
27 Gordon Brown, *Maxton,* (Fontana, Glasgow, 1988), p. 11.
28 SUA Western Office, Minute Book 2, Women's Committee, 6 December 1922.
29 Ibid., 2 May 1923.
30 Ibid., 3 September 1924.
31 SUA Western Office, Minute Book 3, Women's Committee, 1 May 1929.
32 SUA Eastern Council, 26 July 1920.
33 Sheila Hetherington, *Katharine Atholl 1874–1960: Against the Tide,* (Aberdeen University Press, Aberdeen, 1989), pp. 120–1.
34 *The Scotsman,* 23 October 1924.
35 Bea Campbell, *The Iron Ladies: Why do women vote Tory?,* (Virago, London, 1983), p. 63.
36 SACLP, Report of 2nd Annual Conference, 23 September 1916, pp. 6–7 and pp. 36–7.
37 LPSC, Report of Executive 1918–9, pp. 22–3; Report of Eleventh Annual Conference, 13 March, 1926, p. 17.
38 Ibid, Report of Fifth Annual Conference, 20 Sept 1919, pp. 43–4.
39 Ibid, p. 31.
40 Gordon Brown, 'The Labour Party and Political Change in Scotland, 1918–29: The Politics of Five Elections', Ph.D. Edinburgh University, 1982.
41 LPSC, Report of Sixth Annual Conference, 25 September 1920, p. 20.
42 B. Campbell, *The Iron Ladies,* p. 58.
43 LPSC, Report of Eighth Annual Conference, 24 February 1923.
44 G. Brown, *Maxton* (Fontana, Glasgow, 1988), p. 117.
45 G. Brown, Ph.D. pp 165, 400 & 183.
46 LPSC, Report of Fourteenth Annual Conference, 6 April 1929, p. 38.
47 Michael Savage, 'Urban Politics and the Rise of the Labour Party, 1919–39', pp. 213–5, in L. Jamieson and H. Corr (eds.) *State, Private Life and Political Change.*
48 LPSC, Report of Tenth Annual Conference, 2 May 1931, p. 19.
49 LPSC, Report of Twenty-first Annual Conference, 9 May 1936, p. 6.

50 Ray Strachey, *The Cause,* (Virago, London, repr. 1979), p. 366.
51 *The Scotsman,* 3 December 1918.
52 *The Scotsman,* 9 and 30 December 1918.
53 *The Scotsman,* 10 December 1918.
54 R. Strachey, *The Cause,* pp. 368–9.
55 Elizabeth Vallance, *Women in the House, A Study of Women Members of Parliament,* (Athlone Press, London, 1979), p. 27.
56 *The Scotsman,* 13 November 1922.
57 *The Scotsman,* 11 November 1922.
58 M. Savage, 'Urban Politics', p. 212.
59 *The Scotsman,* 8 December 1923.
60 S. Hetherington, *Katharine Atholl,* p. 93.
61 S. Hetherington, *Katharine Atholl,* p. 65.
62 E. Vallance, *Women in the House,* p. 121.
63 S. Hetherington, *Katharine Atholl,* pp. 120–1.
64 S. Hetherington, *Katharine Atholl,* p. 108.
65 S. Hetherington, *Katharine Atholl, p. 109.*
66 *The Scotsman,* 11 November 1935.
67 S. Hetherington, *Katharine Atholl,* p. 182.
68 Brian Harrison, 'Women in a Men's House: The Women MPs, 1919–45', in *Historical Journal,* 29, 3 (1986), p. 632.
69 *The Scotsman,* 29 October, 1931.
70 B. Harrison, 'Women in a Men's House'.
71 SUA Western Office, Minute Book, 5, Women's Committee, 4 December 1935.
72 *Hansard,* 3 November 1936, vol. 317, col. 14, *cit* E. Vallance, *Women in the House.*
73 Jean Mann, *Woman in Parliament,* (Odhams, London, 1962), p. 24.
74 E. Vallance, *Women in the House,* p. 64.
75 Deirdre Beddoe, *Back to Home and Duty,* (Pandora, London, 1989), p. 31.
76 *The Scotsman,* 6 April 1928.
77 E. Vallance, *Women in the House,* p. 27.
78 G. Brown, Ph.D. p. 400.
79 J. Mann, *Woman in Parliament,* pp. 118–9.
80 Ibid., p. 10.
81 Jennie Lee, *My Life with Nye,* (Penguin, Harmondsworth, 1981), p. 71.
82 *The Scotsman,* 23 November 1919.
83 J. Lee, *My Life with Nye,* p. 94.
84 G. Brown, *Maxton,* p. 310.
85 *Who's Who of British MPs, Vol. 111, 1919–45,* (Harvester Press, Hassocks, 1979), *passim.*
86 J. Mann, *Woman in Parliament,* p. 120.
87 E. Vallance, *Women in the House,* p. 85.
88 SUA, Western Office, Minute Book 5, Women's Committee, 4 May 1938.
89 J. Mann, *Woman in Parliament,* p. 42.
90 J. Lee, *My Life with Nye,* p. 168.
91 Ibid.
92 D. Beddoe, *Back to Home and Duty,* p. 132.

SELECT BIBLIOGRAPHY

L. Abdela, *Women With X Appeal*, (Macdonald Optima, London, 1989).

D. Beddoe, *Back to Home and Duty: Women between the Wars, 1918–1939*. (Pandora, London, 1989).

P. Brookes, *Women at Westminster*, (Peter Davies, London, 1967).

B. Campbell, *Iron Ladies – Why do Women Vote Tory?* (Virago, London, 1981).

S. J. Hetherington, *Katharine Atholl 1874–1960, Against the Tide*, (Aberdeen University Press, Aberdeen, 1989).

J. Lee, *My Life with Nye*, (Penguin, Harmondsworth, 1981).

I. Lovenduski and J. Hills, *The Politics of the Second Electorate: Women and Public Participation*, (Routledge, London, 1981).

J. Mann, *Woman in Parliament*, (Odhams, London, 1962).

M. Phillips, *The Divided House: Women at Westminster*, (Sidgwick and Jackson, London, 1980).

R. Strachey, *The Cause*, (Virago, London, 1979 (reprint)).

E. Vallance, *Women in the House*, (Athlone Press, London, 1979).

E. Wilkinson, *Peeps at Politicians*, (Allan and Co., London, 1931).

8

RENTS, PEACE, VOTES: WORKING-CLASS WOMEN AND POLITICAL ACTIVITY IN THE FIRST WORLD WAR

JAMES J. SMYTH

'This was pre-eminently a strike for a poor woman and . . . poor
women should undertake it.'
John Wheatley, reported in *Forward*, 19 June 1915.

'But the rent strikes had a much more enduring effect. In the most
literal sense, they were to change the face of Britain, and nowhere
more than Glasgow.'
I. S. McLean, *The Legend of Red Clydeside*

As the bones of 'Red Clydeside' are picked over and the extent and
significance of Glasgow's wartime militancy is questioned, revised and
reasserted, the rent strike of 1915 remains undiminished.[1] If there have
been doubts cast on such heroic events as the Forty Hours' Strike of
January 1919 and the subsequent riot in George Square, there can be few
such doubts about the rent strike. This was no glorious failure. On the
contrary it may well have been the most successful example of direct
action ever undertaken by the Scottish working class.

Any discussion of popular political activity in Scotland in the twentieth century, therefore, must make direct reference to the rent strike.
Furthermore, the role played by women is crucial. Indeed it is because
of women's involvement and leading role that the rent strike is so important.

The success of the rent strike lay in provoking a near overnight U-turn
by the government and the introduction of a major piece of legislation
restricting increases in rents, and on terms more or less dictated by the
strikers. It may well have been that this immediate impact was possible
only due to the pressures of wartime and a total war economy, that the
threat of the non-payment of rent increases was not of significance in
itself but that the likelihood of unrest spreading to the munitions factories
and shipyards on the Clyde was of critical import to the government. But
it must constantly be remembered that it was the women who forced the
issue, and it was their determination to oppose rent increases and con-
front not only their factors and landlords but also the wider authorities
that made this action possible.

The rent strike is part of the collective memory of Glasgow. Images of the rent strike are powerful and familiar: armies of women barricading tenements; factors fleeing from home-made bombs of flour and peasemeal; women and children on demonstrations with placards such as, 'While my father is a prisoner in Germany the landlord is attacking our home.' In his memoirs *Revolt on the Clyde*, Willie Gallacher provides a vivid description.[2] 'Notices printed by the thousands and put up in the windows; wherever you went you could see them. In street after street, scarcely a window without one: WE ARE NOT PAYING INCREASED RENT. These notices represented a spirit among the women which could not be broken.'

In addition to what might be termed the 'old romantic' accounts such as Gallacher's – which have the value of being produced by eyewitnesses and participants in the events – there are the more detailed and scholarly accounts such as those by Damer and Melling and in particular the latter's book, *Rent Strikes*.[3] Both types of account share a common framework which locates the greater significance of the rent strikes as being part and parcel of the growth of Labour as a political force on Clydeside.

Where there is a difference between historians is in the relation the rent strike bore to the workplace struggles of the First World War. While Mclean makes a sharp distinction between housing and industrial struggles, and sees the former as contributing solely to Labour's eventual electoral growth, Foster argues that housing and industrial issues should be seen as part of the same, broader movement of class conflict.[4] However, there appears to be no disagreement that the rent strike was both a product of the development of political labour on Clydeside and in turn boosted Labour's political and organisational strength.

The most detailed examination of the rent strike phenomenon is that provided by Melling, who concludes his study with the observation that:[5]

> It was the ability of the ILP and Labour Party to harness this creative upsurge in organisational growth, channelling it in a broad framework of demands and aspirations, that accounts for the remarkable success of [the] strikes. In doing so the Labour leadership was able to translate in a very practical way what the alternative political economy of the working class represented.

There is no denying the fact and significance of this process. Yet it seems to me that in doing so we also diminish the role of the women who fought the rent strike and other campaigns. The rent strike and the broader issue of women's political activity become too easily incorporated into the 'forward march of labour'. It is all a bit too unproblematic. It is not just a question of identifying women with Labour but a submersion whereby the dynamic of women's own activity and the discord which existed between women and the labour movement are too easily overlooked. This chapter attempts to look at this relationship and process from another angle, by trying to identify the continuities of women's political experiences during this period. And in so doing to point out some of the ambivalences in Labour's appeal to women.

LABOUR AND HOUSING

By 1914 housing had become the major political issue in Glasgow municipal politics. This was due to the campaigning activity of Labour which saw housing as offering the best means of building electoral support. John Wheatley's scheme for 'Workmen's Cottages' had become the focal demand though Labour's concern with housing had long predated this policy.

An identifiable Labour presence was gradually established on Glasgow Town Council in the early and mid-1890s. This was partly due to the growth of the Independent Labour Party (ILP) and the increased interest of the Trades Council in local politics, but the leadership was provided by John Ferguson of the United Irish League (UIL). Ferguson was elected to the Town Council in 1893 on a programme which included a call for, 'comfortable healthy homes.'[6] In 1896 the Workers' Election Committee (WEC) was formed with the explicit aim of getting 'Labour' councillors returned. This committee was a relatively loose coalition of ILP, Trades Council, Irish Nationalists and Co-operators and was the organisational force behind that group of ILP and other councillors who, collectively, became known as the 'Stalwarts'.[7] In its original programme the WEC included demands for legally fixed maximum rents and direct building of houses by the corporation. Two years later it developed this into a more precise call for the 'erection of artisan dwellings', through the City Improvement Trust, 'to be let at rents sufficient to cover the cost of construction and maintenance.'[8]

The housing question occasionally dominated local elections, as in 1902, but, generally, it tended to be overshadowed by other issues, for example, the campaign for municipal control of the tramways in the 1890s and calls for the eight-hour day and a minimum wage for corporation employees. The difficulty for Labour partly lay in the terms of the debate. The housing 'problem' was regarded as one affecting the 'poorest classes' only. Melling has commented how the Glasgow Municipal Commission on Housing, set up in 1902, 'combined statistical analysis with sweeping generalisation on the minority of vicious loafers and criminals amongst those inhabiting ticketed dwellings.'[9]

Such attitudes were not exclusive to bourgeois or propertied interests. George Carson, secretary of the Trades Council and a member of the ILP, stated in his evidence to the commission, that the Trades Council supported the corporation building houses but was opposed to these houses being, 'restricted to . . . the criminal and vicious classes only.' He went on, 'If the corporation are to build houses at all, it must be for the thrifty, industrious and sober working classes.'[10] This was the perspective of Labour which was combined with a new view of the type of housing which should be built. Joseph Burgess, an ILP councillor, argued in his submission to the Municipal Commission for the construction of 'cottage'-type houses rather than more tenements.[11] It was this route – that of garden cities of low-rise housing – which Glasgow Corporation eventually decided it should attempt to follow, a decision reached in 1912.[12]

Therefore, Wheatley's proposal, of workmen's cottages to be constructed out of the tramway surplus and let at yearly rents of £8, did have very definite precedents. However, this new policy made much more of an impact due to the combination of a number of other factors: apart from the attractive simplicity with which Wheatley presented the case there was the extension of the city boundaries in 1911, the concomitant increase in Labour's representation on the town council, and the development of Labour's own organisational strength in the years preceding the outbreak of war.

WOMEN AND POLITICAL ORGANISATIONS

Another difference in the immediate pre-1914 period was the quite markedly greater involvement of women both in Labour organisations and in the agitation over housing. While the extent of this involvement should not be exaggerated it was still significant.

Branches of the first socialist societies, the Social Democratic Federation (SDF) and the Socialist League (SL), were established in Glasgow in the 1880s. Both had women members but only one or two at most. In the 1890s a more distinctive organisation was set up in Glasgow – a Women's Labour Party. This was effectively a branch of the Scottish Labour Party (SLP) which had a very autonomous type of branch structure. When the SLP joined up with the National ILP, however, the Women's Labour Party retained its distinct identity; it was not a women's section attached to another branch but a separate branch in its own right. Unfortunately, we know very little about the Women's Labour Party, either its membership or its activity. It lasted until 1898 and had, at its high point in 1896, a paying membership of fifty women. Like most branches it had difficulties in raising money which was undoubtedly exacerbated by women's general lack of earning power; at one point its secretary appealed to 'monied people in the country' to help keep the Glasgow women afloat.[13]

Of all the socialist organisations it was the ILP which had the greatest proportion of female members. Women who rose to prominence in the ILP, though, tended to do so as propagandists and not as leaders of the party. Of the published lists of branch secretaries of the ILP in Glasgow from 1893 up to 1914 (and not including the Women's Labour Party) only one was a woman.[14] Concentration on formal structures, however, may well under-estimate the true extent of women's involvement. According to the late Annie and Ada Maxton, sisters of James Maxton, each branch of the ILP – in the Glasgow area at any rate – had its own women's group. These would meet separately one night a week for discussion, usually with a speaker. Their meetings were not directly concerned with feminism so much as with what they saw as the 'broader' issues of socialism. Annie Maxton, who joined Barrhead ILP in 1909, remembers of the women's groups that 'local gossip was their main topic' but also, and more seriously, that 'there were, of course, many women who knew what they were talking about – knew their socialism.'[15]

The Women's Labour League (WLL), which operated as the women's section of the Labour Party had been formed in 1906 and established its first branch in Glasgow, in 1908.[16] Within the year it had a membership of 130 and by the end of 1914 it had three branches in Glasgow.[17] In 1913 the Glasgow Labour Party, only recently formed itself, established a distinct Housing Committee. The moving spirit behind this body was Andrew McBride, a close colleague of John Wheatley's, and the Labour Party Housing Committee took up the cause of the latter's cottages scheme.[18] In turn this committee was instrumental in setting up a Glasgow Women's Housing Association (GWHA) just prior to the outbreak of war. Also behind this body was the WLL, a number of whose members became prominent leaders and activists in the new organisation.[19] The rationale behind this development was the explicit intention of drawing women into the housing agitation and in this it was very successful. The GWHA very quickly established associations throughout the city and with its non-party political basis broadened the movement beyond Labour's own supporters. It was the GWHA which became the organising focus of the rent strike in 1915.

THE RENT STRIKE

Andrew McBride described the immediate pre-war situation with regard to housing availability in Glasgow as being near to a 'famine'.[20] With the outbreak of war in 1914 this already drastic position deteriorated further with a flood of labour into the city to work in the rapidly expanding munitions industry. In addition landlords were seen to be quick to take advantage by imposing sharp increases in rents. Evictions of tenants for arrears, particularly those involving the dependents of men under arms, hardened attitudes even more and provided flashpoints for the expression of outrage and hostility. For example, in Shettleston in June 1915, a crowd gathered at the eviction of a soldier's family and John Wheatley had to dissuade them from attacking the landlord's home. *Forward* reported that: 'The women particularly were greatly and indignantly excited. Wheatley said this was pre-eminently a strike for a poor woman and that poor women should undertake it. At the end of the meeting, some 500 women went to the ILP rooms and handed in their names as pickets.'[21]

This sort of crass action by landlords combined with general increases in rent provided a moral imperative to the rent strike, especially in a situation where the whole country was being exhorted to make sacrifices.

This was ruthlessly exploited by Labour propagandists who compared landlords to 'spies' or 'the Hun at home'. *Forward*, in the very first week of the war, challenged the government to extend its moratorium on business debts to include rents and declared, 'No Highland Clearances Trick this time'.[22]

It was Govan which was the initial storm centre of the strike in the spring of 1915 and which remained the major bulwark of the struggle. Throughout the summer the rent strike continued, flaring up in one area after another but eventually by the autumn becoming a more cohesive and threatening campaign. During October and November the situation really boiled over. The rent strikes continued to make progress, not only in Glasgow but further afield as well. New rent rises were imposed and eviction notices issued. Tenants resisted evictions physically with mass pickets and fought the landlords in the courts as well. In fact it was in the unlikely setting of the Glasgow small debts court that the issue came to a head.

The decision by a Partick factor to prosecute eighteen tenants for non-payment of a rent increase meant that 17 November 1915 became D-day. The attempts by the landlords and factors to impose their legal rights to set the level of rents they wished was met by the mass protests of tenants and the explicit threat of industrial action. The tenants summoned to court were mostly shipyard workers. Prior to the case being heard, the issue had been raised at mass demonstrations and workplace meetings. On the day of the proceedings there were strikes in support of the defendants and a number of deputations sent to the court. Huge numbers of women, children and men assembled in George Square. Inside the court the defendants refused to accept an adjournment but resolved to force the issue. Eventually the prosecution capitulated and the cases were dismissed. Before Christmas a Bill had been introduced and passed through Parliament; the Rent Restriction Act covered the whole country and all rents under £30 per annum.

This movement of activity between home and workplace and the involvement of the shipyard workers indicates that the industrial and housing issues were not separate and watertight compartments. Beyond the shipyards other workers indicated their concern. From Parkhead Forge emanated an implicit threat of industrial action in a letter from the shop stewards to the City Corporation: 'the men here wish to make it perfectly clear that they would regard this as an attack on the working class . . . which might have the most disastrous consequences.'[23] Furthermore, the women on rent strike were married or otherwise related to the men working in the shipyards and munitions factories, and it was the men whose names were on the rent books. Melling is surely right to comment that:[24]

> The salient feature of the Clyde rent strikes was not their distance
> from workplace unrest, but precisely the way in which the industrial

and housing protests combined to challenge the authority of landlords and the state.

Nevertheless it is important to emphasise that this was – at heart – a women's campaign. More than this it was a housewives' campaign. Crucially, and especially in wartime, defence of the home fell upon the wife and mother; and the nature of tenement life meant that any defence was almost bound to become a collective act. It would be extremely difficult to isolate individual tenants in a tenement since each house or flat was part of the collective 'stair' or 'close'. The sharing of communal facilities such as the wash-house and toilets made contact and communication between tenants a constant feature. This is not to romanticise tenement life but to recognise the structures it imposed upon tenants and particularly women. And, crucially in the rent strike, tenement closes could be made secure against intruders quickly and effectively.

Much of the organisation of the strike effectively took place at home. Close committees were formed by women and kitchen meetings held to discuss their immediate situation and organise their defence. Homes were made secure by maintaining mass pickets against intended evictions and, when necessary, forcibly driving away factors and sheriff officers.[25] There had to be another level of organisation, however, which went beyond the close, the street or the ward and which made the strike a movement rather than a series of disparate events. It is widely accepted that the role played by the Glasgow Women's Housing Association in this process was 'critical and . . . decisive.'[26]

As well as acting as a co-ordinator for the various local tenants' groups the GWHA organised large-scale public meetings and demonstrations. One of the most important of these took place a few days before the 17 November court case. The demonstrators were mainly from the areas north of the Clyde and gathered on Thornwood Hill overlooking the shipyards.[27] Clearly the GWHA was deliberately broadcasting its message on rents into the workplace. This could take very direct forms, as one occasion in Govan when a woman had been tricked into paying the increase after the factor told her the other tenants had paid. Mary Barbour went straight to the shipyard and got a large body of men to accompany her to the factor's office where the money was returned.[28]

Mary Barbour was a member of a distinctive group of women leaders. This included prominent Labour women like Helen Crawfurd and Agnes Dollan and also local figures like Barbour, Mary Laird and Mrs Ferguson. They, like the vast majority of women on strike, were working-class housewives and their methods of organisation were geared to their own situation. Building on the 'spontaneous' organisation of the kitchen and close the GWHA held regular public meetings in halls and theatres on weekday afternoons to discuss and co-ordinate general activity.[29] The timing of these meetings is significant – they were usually held at 3pm – since it was a time which made it impossible for workers of either sex to attend. However, it was eminently suitable for housewives who could attend and still get back home to make dinner. Apparently simple matters like this were important both in developing new political techniques and in extending political involvement. This form of organisation and this local leadership did not disappear with the conclusion of the rent strike but continued into a number of other campaigns, most notably in the anti-war movement

THE WOMEN'S PEACE CRUSADE

The advent of war saw the suffrage movement fracture as women divided fundamentally over what their response should be. The militant Pankhurst-led Women's Social and Political Union (WSPU) is most famous for its full-blooded support for the military and jingoistic stunts such as handing white feathers to young men in civilian clothes. Even the constitutional National Union of Women's Suffrage Societies (NUWSS) was split on the issue. Both the WSPU and the NUWSS dropped their agitation for the vote, the better to assist in promoting the war effort, and the latter turned itself into a 'Women's Active Service Corps'.[30]

This was not the response of all suffragists, however, and in the spring of 1915 an International Women's Congress was held at The Hague in defiance of the belligerent nations. Out of this Congress developed the Women's International League (WIL), the British section of which was organised by those who had left the NUWSS and other suffragist women.[31] In Glasgow a branch of the WIL was established by women across a wide political spectrum. President of the branch was Mrs Crosthwaite, a member of the Liberal Party and non-militant suffragist, and the secretary was Helen Crawfurd, a well-known ILP-er and ex-member of the WSPU.[32] The twin platforms of the WIL were opposition to the war and to conscription. To this end the Glasgow members organised conferences, demonstrations and public meetings. Among the prominent speakers brought to Glasgow under WIL auspices were Ethel Snowden, Helena Swanwick and Muriel Matthews, the WSPU member who had chained herself to the grid in the Ladies' Gallery of the House of Commons.[33]

There was an incipient division within the Glasgow WIL, however, between the predominantly middle-class and apolitical membership and a smaller group of socialist and more militantly pacifist women. Helen Crawfurd identified herself, Agnes Dollan, Miss Walker, Mrs Barbour and Mrs Ferguson as the 'local propagandists' of the WIL and it was this same group, subsequently, which went on to found the Women's Peace Crusade (WPC).[34] Crawfurd explained the thinking behind this development:[35]

> The Women's International League was very constitutional but did some good educational work. Its members were, however, women who were merely anti-war and not socialist. Some of the more

active spirits in Glasgow who were socialists decided that we would hold a conference and take greater risks in our literature and propaganda methods in a 'Women's Peace Crusade'.

This did not represent a split since these women did not resign from the WIL but ran the WPC parallel to it. Helen Crawfurd resigned from the secretaryship though she remained a member and the British executive appointed her a delegate to the WIL conference in Zurich in 1919.[36] Also the Women's Peace Crusade was not a revolutionary body – its principal demand was for an immediate, negotiated settlement and it was sometimes referred to as the Women's Peace Negotiation Crusade.

The Glasgow branch of the WIL was established in November 1915 when the rent strike activity was at its height. The WPC was launched at a conference in Glasgow on 10 June 1916. Over 200 women delegates attended representing sixteen separate organisations, including the WIL, the Women's Humanity League, the Workers' Suffrage Federation, the WLL and the ILP.[37] Following on from this conference the WPC organised a 'campaign' of street meetings during July and then again in September. This would seem to mark the great difference between the WPC and the WIL. While the latter concentrated on holding regular monthly meetings in public halls with regular speakers and on issues dealing not only with the war, the former concentrated solely on the war and in taking that message onto the streets and into working-class communities. The first meetings of the Crusade were in Maryhill and Springburn.[38] Commenting on the early campaign, *Forward* commented:[39]

> Large crowds have attended the meetings, and collections and literature sales have been excellent. At most of the meetings the resolution calling for the government to 'institute negotiations for peace' was carried unanimously, and in the whole campaign only a few dissented.

After running these campaigns the WPC's activity seems to have gone into abeyance, although the same women remained active in other organisations; as well as the continuing role of the WIL, the ILP and the WSF kept up a 'street' presence. There was a second launch of the WPC in Glasgow in the summer of 1917. On this occasion, however, it was being promoted as a national movement and activity was maintained until the end of the war. Other towns followed Glasgow's example, in particular in the industrial north of England, such as Manchester, Bradford and Leeds, and one author claims that over 100 branches were established.[40] Gauging the influence of bodies such as the WPC is difficult but Willie Gallacher, for one, considered that, 'it played an increasingly important part in the struggle against the war.'[41]

Women's Peace Crusade activities included organising street meetings, public meetings, marches, demonstrations, selling badges and distributing literature. Much of their propaganda used very explicit emotional and religious appeal. WPC badges depicted the 'Angel of

Peace' protecting children and hymns were sung at demonstrations. However, such tactics did not save them from attacks by the press and even on occasion physical attacks, sometimes led by clergymen.[42] At one demonstration outside the City Chambers Helen Crawfurd and Agnes Dollan managed to break into the building and showered leaflets onto the heads of the assembled councillors. On another occasion both they and Mrs Ferguson were charged with obstruction for holding a meeting in George Square. Offered their freedom if they agreed not to hold any more meetings, they refused and were eventually admonished.[43] The WPC was by now able to hold big public meetings under its own auspices with national speakers such as Sylvia Pankhurst and Charlotte Despard. However, its main activity and contribution to the anti-war struggle remained the work done at grass-roots level. A typical example of their efforts can be seen by the number of street meetings held by the WPC over a three-week period in June and July 1917. In this time WPC members spoke at: Partick, Maryhill, Bridgeton, Parkhead, Govan, Govanhill, Shettleston, Barrhead, Springburn, Possilpark, Bellahouston, Rutherglen, Paisley, Overnewton, Cambuslang, Clydebank, Renfrew, Kirkintilloch, Dumbarton, Whiteinch, Blantyre, Alloa, Cowdenbeath, Drongan, Drumpark, Douglas Water, Lanark and Edinburgh.[44]

Parallels and continuities between the Women's Peace Crusade, the rent strike and the GWHA are very apparent. Once again, the WPC seems to have been a housewives' movement. The leadership of both campaigns was much the same group of women. As with the rent strike there was a great emphasis on the family; on demonstrations women, children and men marched in separate contingents; children carried banners with slogans such as, 'I want my daddy'; contributions for funds came from women who had lost husbands and sons in the war. Like the GWHA, the WPC was an autonomous women's body both in leadership and membership. Similarly, the methods of organisation were geared to reaching and involving working-class housewives. Most meetings were at street level directed at women in or as near to the home as possible. Regular organisational and other meetings, as with the GWHA, were held in local halls in the afternoon and were closed to men. The continuities with the rent strike were apparent from an advert in *Forward* in February 1918. This was a WPC meeting for women only, to be held on Tuesday 19th at 3pm, in the Picture House, Helen Street, Govan. Speakers: Mrs Kaye and Mrs Dollan; Chair: Mrs Barbour, the latter two having been prominent in the rent strike.[45]

Other campaigns were led or supported by this group of women during the war, for example, against food shortages and in defence of the living standards of the dependents of soldiers and sailors. At the same time this group also took on more prominent roles within the labour and socialist movements. On May Day 1917, among the platform speakers on Glasgow Green were Mrs Barbour, Mrs Dollan, Mrs Ferguson and Mrs

Laird – all activists in the rent strike and in the peace campaign.[46] We shall refer to the future careers of these women below but the important point to emphasise here is their method of political organisation; women-led, direct action, based in working-class communities and involving housewives.

THE SCOTTISH CO-OPERATIVE WOMEN'S GUILD – THE HOUSEWIVES' CHOICE

The most significant organisation as far as working-class women were concerned and the one which dwarfed all others in terms of membership was the Scottish Co-operative Women's Guild (SCWG). Established in 1892 with twenty-two branches and a membership of 1,500, by 1913 it had grown to 157 branches and 12,420 members.[47] It was the Guild which provided most women with their initial experience of organisation and nearly all the labour women activists of this period appear to have been Guild members.

While the English Women's guild had been formed in 1883, in Scotland there were only unofficial women's groups run through Co-op Educational Committees. Influenced by the English example and with the encouragement of a few sympathetic men, a group of women from the Kinning Park Society took the lead in setting up their own Guild and then the Scottish body. In an echo of the rent strike the initial assembly was a kitchen meeting.[48] The founding document of the SCWG stated that:[49] 'The Women's Guild is an Association of the Women of the Co-operative Movement. Its object is to assist in the propaganda of Co-operation, and to draw a closer bond of union between the wives, mothers and daughters of Co-operators, by mutual aid and social intercourse.'

Most of the work of the Guilds was in fund raising for Co-operative causes such as the convalescent homes established at Seamill and Abbotsinch, and most of their 'social intercourse' revolved around cookery and dressmaking lessons and discussions. As such the Guild reinforced women's domestic role and was seen in this light by male co-operators, an attitude of, 'The Guild should be to the movement what the wife and mother is to the home.'[50] Despite such a limited perspective being offered to the Guild, nonetheless its own role was crucial in two inter-related areas: in breaking down the institutional barriers to women's active involvement in the broader labour movement, and in developing the abilities of individual women. The task confronting women in both respects was considerable.

In addition to expectations that married women would not seek paid employment outside the home, there was a conscious hostility to women playing an active role in the organisations of the labour movement. Patrick Dollan, in his history of Kinning Park Co-operative Society, remarks that it was 'not considered good form for women to appear on the platform at Co-operative or other working-class meetings.'[51] This was clearly shown at the laying of the memorial stone of the Society's new buildings in 1891 when not a single woman was permitted to attend. Snubs like this may have been a motivating factor behind the women organising themselves. At any rate the following year, after the creation of the SCWG and through its pressure, women were present at the opening of Kinning Park's new buildings, 'the first time' women had attended 'a public occasion in the life of the Society'.[52] Kinning Park seems to have been one of the most progressive societies and certainly it was a pioneer of the Women's Guild, yet it was not until 1916 that it elected its first woman director.[53]

The influence of the Guild may have been slow and gradual in making itself felt but it was real nevertheless. It was through the work of the Guild that women began to take up positions within the co-operative societies and the Guild itself became recognised by the labour movement as a significant entity in its own right, with the right to delegate representation on local Labour Parties.[54] Furthermore, there can be little doubt that the Guild was of major significance in the self-development of many working-class women, particularly housewives, whose isolation within the home should not be under-estimated. As the SCWG president and historian argued, the Guild was important in teaching women how to organise, and[55] 'the real attraction, no doubt, lay in being brought out of their own little narrow groove, and so becoming acquainted with what other women had to contend with in life and through combination trying to make life sweeter for many women workers.'

The space provided by the weekly Guild meeting, free of any male domination, was crucial in allowing the members to 'be their natural selves, and freely express their ideas and opinions.'[56] Within such an atmosphere women could more easily learn the mechanics of organisation and gain the confidence to chair meetings and speak in front of an audience. What was learned within the Guild could then be applied elsewhere. This was done to most dramatic effect in the rent strike when members of the Women's Guild took on leading roles. Dollan claims that the rent strike was 'an agitation instigated and conducted by Kinning Park members' in South Govan.[57] This was the area where the strike originated and which was covered by the Kinning Park Society. Among its members who played prominent parts in the rent strike were Agnes Dollan and Mary Barbour.[58]

As well as such internal activity, the Women's Guild also debated and took positions on important political issues of the day. The SCWG was an early advocate of women's suffrage, petitioning the government on the issue in 1893 and in 1905 it rejected the Labour Party's position on adult suffrage.[59] The Guild did not ally itself to the 'militant party'[60] but was affiliated to the 'constitutional' NUWSS through the West of Scotland Suffrage Society, the only working-class women's organisation in the west of Scotland to do so.[61]

WOMEN, SUFFRAGE AND ELECTIONS

The campaign for the vote was the most significant political issue involving women in the decade prior to the war. While the history of the movement has been dominated by the suffragettes, the Pankhursts and the WSPU, more recent work in this field has emphasised the role of the non-militant suffrage societies and the involvement of working-class women in the north of England.[62] The position taken by the Women's Guild in Scotland, however, does not indicate a significant working-class involvement in the suffrage campaign similar to that in Lancashire and Cheshire. Working-class women who were active in the suffrage movement did so on a very individual basis. Jessie Stephen was a young activist in the Maryhill Branch of the ILP who joined the WSPU when only 16. Her father, a tailor, was also in the ILP and Jessie worked as a domestic servant and was active in the Domestic Workers' Federation. She left the WSPU after the outbreak of war and was invited to London by Sylvia Pankhurst where she continued her activity in the WSF and the ILP.[63] Individuals like Jessie Stephen, however, were thin on the ground; no suffrage societies branches were established in working-class communities. The movement, in personnel and leadership, was overwhelmingly middle class. As Helen Crawfurd remarks, 'The women who became most prominent in the WSPU were middle-class women to whom the best paid professions were closed because of their sex.'[64]

Nevertheless, links between the suffrage and socialist movements in Glasgow were close, in particular between the WSPU and the ILP. This is not surprising given the origins of the WSPU, for the Pankhursts were a Manchester family and all were active members of the ILP. However, as the WSPU grew in size and notoriety, so increasingly it became detached from its links with the labour movement. The shift towards a more socially exclusive constituency was expressed geographically when the Pankhursts moved the WSPU from Manchester to London.[65] Despite the growing national hostility between the Labour Party and the WSPU, in Glasgow the suffragettes retained a close relationship with the ILP. This was based largely on *Forward* and its editor Tom Johnston who gave the WSPU case sympathetic coverage and even provided it with a regular column. Johnston also provided practical aid such as arranging protection for Mrs Pankhurst when she spoke in Glasgow. Hearing that a group of students from Glasgow University intended to disrupt her meeting, Johnston mobilised a group of dockers and navvies; when the students began their ructions they were bodily ejected.[66] As a reaction to WSPU militancy the government suppressed its newspaper *The Suffragette*. When it did so, both *Forward* and the *Socialist*, organ of the Socialist Labour Party and also published in Glasgow, offered to print it.[67]

Like Keir Hardie, Johnston fully supported women's demand for votes on the same terms as men. In the second issue of *Forward*, he described the campaign as 'another Chartist revival.'[68] Yet, just as the

Chartists stopped short of calling for universal suffrage (by failing to include women in their demand), so the women's suffrage movement did not challenge the restrictive, property-based franchise. The demand was for votes on the same terms as men, as it was or may be given to men. But, as things stood, not all men had the vote. By 1911 it is estimated that about 60 per cent of adult males had the vote nationally,[69] while in a city like Glasgow that figure was significantly lower at around 54 per cent. Even this figure disguised considerable discrepancies within the city with much lower levels of enfranchisement in poorer working-class areas.[70]

Thus the demand for votes for women could be seen as a demand for votes for some women. Within the Labour Party the official policy of adult suffrage was adopted more as a blocking manoeuvre against women's suffrage than as a firmly held belief.[71] Despite this, many Labour women held true to the principle of universal suffrage. Certainly for the radical suffragists of Lancashire there was a constant tension between the two rival positions, between the notions of class and sex loyalty, and women did change their allegiances from one side to the other; Liddington and Norris have shown how much of an 'agonising dilemma' the choice between adult and women's suffrage could be.[72] In Glasgow the adult suffrage position was defended by women like Agnes Pettigrew, secretary of the Shop Assistants' Union and member of the ILP and WLL. Pettigrew argued that 'votes for women' was essentially a middle-class measure which would work to the electoral advantage of the Conservative Party and subsequently weaken the Labour Party.[73]

This argument was bolstered by the prevalent view that the existing female, municipal electorate was anti-Labour. To counter this view suffragist supporters undertook a number of surveys of the local female electorate which showed that most women voters were working class. However, the selective nature of the areas surveyed and the fact that the surveys were conducted by interested parties (including the ILP) meant that the findings did not carry much weight in the suffrage debate.[74] Insofar as the property qualification for the franchise remained, then extending the vote to women would have left the vast majority of working-class women unaffected, and, indeed, most middle-class women because they were not householders in their own right. Certainly the housewives of the Women's Guild still would not have had the vote. Perhaps this explains why there was so little working-class involvement in the suffrage movement in Glasgow, even where, as with the SCWG, there was formal support and sympathy.

It is tempting to see a direct line of continuity between the pre-war militant suffrage campaign and the militancy of the rent strikes, but this cannot be substantiated. A link does exist in the person of Helen Crawfurd who played an important, indeed crucial, role in many of the movements and organisations of this period but she remains a unique figure. None of the other rent strike leaders appear to have been active in the suffrage movement. On the other hand there were ex-suffrage colleagues of Crawfurd's whose political development went in a diametrically opposite direction. Helen Fraser was secretary of the Scottish WSPU and had been at least partly responsible for recruiting Helen Crawfurd, Fraser being the first woman suffrage speaker Crawfurd had heard.[75] On the outbreak of war Fraser remained with the WSPU and became an arch-patriot, touring the United States to help drum up support for American intervention. To further this cause she wrote a book, *Women and War Work*, glorifying the contribution women were making to the national effort.[76] After the war Fraser contested Govan as the National Liberal candidate, by which time her old colleague Helen Crawfurd was a leading figure in the Communist Party.

One of the arguments utilised by advocates of women's suffrage was to point out the anomaly whereby women were permitted the vote at the local, municipal level while being denied it at the national, parliamentary level. The municipal vote had been a right for women householders in England and Wales since 1867, though it had not been introduced to Scotland until 1882.[77] However, only single women or widows were allowed the vote, married women not being allowed to register.[78] This crucial qualification effectively curtailed the development of a significant local electorate. In Glasgow in 1901 the female municipal electorate numbered some 23,223 women who represented just over 17 per cent of the total municipal electorate of 112,322. The proportionate size of this female electorate varied by area; the smaller proportions were in artisan wards such as Cowlairs and Springburn (both under 10 per cent), while the greater proportions were in middle-class, residential areas such as Kelvinside and Park (both around 30 per cent).[79]

Tom Johnston, in a pamphlet in support of women's suffrage, argued that, 'no evil effects have followed' from women voting in local elections.[80] Yet, for many socialists it was the accepted wisdom that the existing female electorate was a reactionary force dominated by the churches. At times the perceived hostility of women voters to Labour could provoke a vitriolic response that not even the likes of Johnston was immune to. William Stewart the unsuccessful Labour candidate in the Dalmarnock Ward in 1904, explained away his defeat:[81]

> In reality we did win on the men's vote. There are twelve hundred women voters, mostly controlled by the churches, and the most of them voted against Labour, the result being that Mr Harvie joins his friend Mr Willock as the representative of the old women – of both sexes.

The following year, after a second defeat, Stewart's explanation remained the same, 'So we were beaten comrades by the old women of both sexes.'[82] Given that Labour lost by 358 votes and then by 750 votes, technically it was feasible that the 1,200 women voters could have swayed the result. However, by focusing on the women Stewart was ignoring a whole series of local factors operating against Labour and, more importantly, the fact that the coalition of forces behind Labour's municipal challenge at this time had collapsed.[83] In 1906 Stewart lost in Dalmarnock for the third consecutive year coming last of three candidates and more than 2,000 votes adrift; on this occasion he did not mention the 'old women'.[84] Tom Johnston, however, did. The municipal election of 1906 saw Labour do badly and in reaction Johnston fulminated against the 'Temperance Party' for its hypocritical opposition to Labour and characterised it as 'old women wearing trousers to pose as men.'[85]

Apparently throwaway remarks such as this at the very least indicate a tension between a formal belief in sex equality and more personal, deeply rooted antipathies towards women. Nevertheless, the purely negative attitude toward the female electorate did change, albeit gradually. After another poor showing in the 1909 municipal elections *Forward* complained that socialism was struggling because it had 'neglected the women'.[86] Prior to 1914 women could stand for election to town councils though Labour never selected a female candidate in Glasgow. However, by early 1915 with housing firmly established as the priority issue and the GWHA growing in popular support, a new perspective on women and elections was expressed. *Forward* urged that the president of the GWHA, Mrs Laird, be selected as a municipal candidate and connected this with Labour's housing policy and appealing to women voters:[87]

> Housing is, above all, a woman's question. Women have already enough votes and influence to turn the balance in favour of the Labour Party – which is the only housing party – in two-thirds of the wards in Glasgow.

If such a view could be outlined under the old, restrictive franchise system, the argument became even more germane after the mass mobilisation of women in the rent strike and the reform of 1918 which gave women the vote at last.

CONCLUSION

In her memoirs Helen Crawfurd writes of how, in the years prior to the First World War, working-class men in Scotland were becoming increasingly aware, organised and self-confident in demanding better conditions. But Crawfurd saw this as very much a one-sided development.[88]

> The women of Scotland, however, were still bound hand and foot to the church in its various forms, to Evangelical religion and even Spiritualism. The men failed to see the importance of educating their women folk and bringing them as intelligent fellow comrades into the struggle for human betterment.

Helen Crawfurd is an important witness, one who thought that her own strict, religious upbringing allowed her particular understanding of the difficulties facing working-class women. For all that, it may be that hers is too negative and bleak a picture. Recent historical work points to working-class women's involvement rather than quiescence.[89] We have seen how, in the immediate pre-war period, Labour began conscious efforts to appeal to women and to draw them into the movement. During the war women's own self-activity and organisation developed apace and a significant group of women leaders emerged out of this ferment. In this process the question of housing was crucial as was the rent strike. Housing was a fundamental issue affecting women in their daily lives, and to which they could contribute in an active way, not just passively on the sidelines. If housing was the issue, the rent strike was the key incident which provided the spur to mobilisation. Put at its simplest, as Helen Crawford writes: 'this struggle brought great masses of women together.'[90]

The successful conclusion of the rent strike did not mean the end of this activity. The continuing role of the GWHA, campaigns like the peace movement and the increasing prominence of leading women activists all show that women's political involvement now operated on a significantly higher plane than before. There remained one element missing however: the vote. Almost on the outbreak of war a member of the Glasgow WSPU wrote that the vote was not an end in itself but was a requisite first step in a continuing struggle:[91]

> But the vote, after all, is only a weapon, not a stronghold: a symbol, not a magic key. The possession of the weapon is necessary for the greater conflicts; and the symbol of political equality is necessary to the self-respect of women.

In 1918 women got the vote, almost though not quite on the same terms as men but, most significantly, there was no longer any property qualification.[92] All political parties, whether or not they had been hostile to women's suffrage, now had to make direct appeal to women. They had little choice; in Glasgow there were suddenly 220,000 women on the municipal voters' roll, 49 per cent of the total, and in eleven of the city's thirty-seven wards women constituted a clear majority of the electorate.[93]

Labour had good reason to expect to do well with the female electorate. Most obviously Labour was the tenants' champion over housing but as well as the policies, Labour also had the means to approach this new constituency. The methods of activity and propaganda utilised to effect in the rent strike and the peace campaign were quickly adopted to electioneering in the post-war world. This can be seen in the municipal election of 1919. The sitting Labour councillor in Woodside ward, George Smith, was regarded as being in a vulnerable position since he had been gaoled as a conscientious objector during the war. In the event he won by a comfortable margin of over 600 votes, a victory attributed in part to 'Councillor Smith's practice for months past of regularly holding meetings during the afternoons in the back courts, whence he addresses the housewives at their kitchen windows.'[94]

This example reflects on the broader question of how electoral politics would be conducted in the new age of a mass, democratic electorate. In turn this is related to the rise of Labour and the demise of the Liberal Party. One view is that while the Tories and Labour are seen as being better able to appeal to the new, ignorant electorate, the Liberals are seen as the party which relied above all upon an electorate with a high level of political awareness and intelligence.[95] Accounts which emphasise the role of a Labour Party 'machine' herding working-class electors into the polling booths tend to reinforce this image of a dumb, docile mass.[96] A more interesting perspective on the post-1918 electorate is offered by Hutchison who comments on how 'the very techniques of traditional political debate seemed ill-adjusted to new conditions.' However, 'Labour had developed techniques to reach voters in, so to speak, their natural habitat than in the artificial context of large meetings.'[97]

For women in particular, it could be argued, a large public meeting was likely to be a more intimidating and unenlightening experience than being addressed in the security of their everyday surroundings and amongst their neighbours. The strength of the organisation behind the rent strike and the peace campaign lay in this ability to speak to and involve women directly. Labour's victory in Woodside in 1919 showed that such techniques, born out of the exigencies of wartime direct action, had an important part to play in electoral politics.

The women who, in a sense, pioneered these techniques went on to play significant roles in the Labour and socialist movements. Helen Crawfurd was elected to the executive of the Scottish ILP in January 1919, polling more votes than anybody else apart from James Maxton.[98] Crawfurd became a leader of the 'ILP Left' and subsequently joined the Communist Party. Agnes Dollan became Labour's first woman municipal candidate, also in January 1919.[99] In the following year Labour got its first two women councillors elected, one of whom was Mary Barbour.[100]

Between 1917 and 1920 the Glasgow ILP underwent a rapid growth in membership with many women among its new recruits. However, women appear to have accounted for around 20 per cent of the membership only, and they comprised less than 10 per cent of delegates to the central Glasgow Federation. Furthermore, after 1920 the ILP began to lose members, chiefly among young workers and women.[101]

The intensity of political activity evident during the war and immediately after could not be sustained. The rent strike of 1920 was a pale reflection of 1915 and the return of mass unemployment after the initial post-war boom cast a long shadow over the labour movement. As the 1920s wore on working-class politics became increasingly defensive. It would appear that there was less scope for women's involvement and that some of Labour's ambivalence towards women reasserted itself, for instance over birth control. In July 1920 the American radical and birth control pioneer, Margaret Sanger, visited Glasgow and gave a lecture on the subject as part of the ILP's Sunday lectures series, with the anarchist,

Guy Aldred, acting as chairman. In her autobiography, Sanger quotes the startled reaction of one male socialist to the number of women in attendance: 'Look . . . The women have crowded the men out of this hall. I never saw so many wives of comrades before.'[102] However, this concern on the part of women received scant support from the official labour movement either in Parliament or in the city chambers. As Minister of Health in 1924, John Wheatley refused to change existing policy which forbade doctors or health visitors to give advice on contraception. [103] In 1927 a majority of Labour councillors in Glasgow voted against allowing the magazine, *Birth Control News*, being allowed into public libraries.[104]

It is clear that more research needs to be done on the 1920s and beyond. To give some examples, a collective biography of the rent strike leaders and their subsequent political careers is needed as well as work on women and electioneering; an examination of women's continuing involvement in ILP branches and in the Women's Guild are all possible routes of enquiry. Further work may reveal that the contrast between wartime and after is less pronounced than we think. As things stand there is an undoubted sense that post-1920 women's political activity went into near abeyance.

The achievements of the war years were not, however, lost completely. Through the vote women were now part of the political life of the country, working-class women had shown their capacity for activity and organisation, and there was a small but significant number of women in prominent positions within the labour movement and in public life.

It could be argued that this represents a continuity or the culmination of processes already in operation before the war. Yet, the combination of factors and the dramatic intensity of the wartime experience marks a sharp distinction in the situation prior to 1914. Such changes, limited in many respects as they might have been, need to be taken into consideration if we are to fully comprehend the impact of politics on women and women's role in influencing and shaping political change in the early decades of the twentieth century.

NOTES

1 For the most recent reflections on the period see, J. Melling, 'Whatever Happened to Red Clydeside? Industrial Conflict and the Politics of Skill in the First World War' and J. Foster, 'Strike Action and Working Class Politics on Clydeside 1914–1919', both in *International Review of Social History*, vol. xxxv, 1990, no. 1, pp. 3–32 and pp. 33–70.

2 W. Gallacher, *Revolt on the Clyde*, (Lawrence & Wishart,London, 1978) pp. 52–53.

3 S. Damer, 'State, Class and Housing: Glasgow 1885–1919', and J. Melling, 'Clydeside Housing and the Evolution of State Rent Control, 1900–1939', in J. Melling (ed), *Housing, Social Policy and the State*, (Croom Helm, London, 1980); J. Melling, *Rent Strikes: People's Struggle for Housing in West Scotland 1890–1916*, (Polygon, Edinburgh, 1983).

4 I. S. McLean, *The Legend of Red Clydeside*, (John Donald, Edinburgh, 1983) see especially chapters 2 and 13; Foster, 'Strike Action and Working Class Politics'.

5 Melling, *Rent Strikes*, p. 115.

6 *Labour Leader*, 22 October 1898, which reprinted Ferguson's programme.

7 J. Smyth, *Labour and Socialism in Glasgow 1880–1914: The Electoral Challenge prior to Democracy* (Unpublished PhD thesis, Edinburgh University, 1987) chapter 3.

8 *Labour Leader*, 27 August 1898.

9 Melling, *Rent Strikes*, p. 17.

10 Glasgow Municipal Commission on the Housing of the Poor (Glasgow, 1904) Evidence of George Carson, p. 550.

11 Ibid., Evidence of Joseph Burgess, p. 254.

12 J. McKee, 'Glasgow Working Class Housing Between the Wars, 1918–1939', (M. Litt, Strathclyde University, 1977), p. 3.

13 Smyth, *Labour and Socialism in Glasgow,* chapter 5.

14 Ibid.

15 Interview with Annie and Ada Maxton, 3 September 1979.

16 E.Gordon, *Women in the Labour Movement in Scotland 1850–1914* (Clarendon Press, Oxford, 1991) pp. 265–6.

17 Gordon, *Women in the Labour Movement; Forward,* 16 January 1915.

18 Melling, *Rent Strikes*, p. 40.

19 Ibid, pp. 32–33.

20 Ibid., p. 40.

21 *Forward*, 19 June 1915.

22 *Forward*, 8 August 1914.

23 *Forward*, 9 October 1915.

24 J. Melling, 'Work culture and politics on "Red Clydeside"' the ILP during the First World War', in A. McKinlay and R. J. Morris, *The ILP on Clydeside 1893–1932: from foundation to disintegration,* (Manchester University Press, Manchester, 1991) p. 107.

25 Comparison with the contemporary anti-poll tax campaign hardly needs to be stated.

26 Damer, 'State, Class and Housing' p. 104.

27 Melling, *Rent Strikes*, p. 92.

28 Helen Crawfurd, *Typescript autobiography*, n.d., pp. 145–6.

29 These meetings were advertised in *Forward* and there is evidence that some at least were barred to men.

30 S. Pankhurst, *The Suffragette Movement,* (Virago, London, 1977) p. 593.

31 Ibid; S. Rowbotham, *The Friends of Alice Wheeldon,* (Pluto, London, 1986) pp. 34, 117.

32 Crawfurd, *Typescript autobiography* p. 150.

33 Ibid.

34 Ibid.

35 Ibid, p. 154.

36 Ibid, p. 150.

37 *Forward,* 17 June 1916.

38 *Forward,* 8 July 1916.

39 *Forward,* 5 August 1916.

40 J. Liddington, 'The Women's Peace Crusade: The History of a Forgotten Campaign', in D. Thompson, *Over Our Dead Bodies: Women Against the Bomb,* (Virago, London, 1983) pp. 180–198;

D. Mitchell, *Women on the Warpath: the Story of the Women of the First World War,* (Case, London, 1966).

41 Gallacher, *Revolt on the Clyde,* p. 152.

42 Mitchell, *Women on the Warpath,* pp. 310–311.

43 *Forward,* 23 March 1918; Crawfurd, *Typescript autobiography,* p. 155.

44 *Forward* 16, 23, 30 June. WPC meetings were advertised regularly in *Forward.*

45 *Forward* , 16 February 1918.

46 *Forward* , 5, 12 May 1917.

47 A. Buchan, *History of the Scottish Cooperative Women's Guild,* (Scottish Co-operative Women's Guild, Glasgow) pp. 50, 112.

48 Ibid. See Chapters 1 and 2.

49 Ibid., p. 50.

50 Ibid., Preface by James Deans.

51 P. J. Dollan, *History of the Kinning Park Co-operative Society Ltd* (Kinning Park Co-operative Society, Glasgow 1923) p. 48.

52 Ibid., p. 47. See also Melling, Rent *Strikes,* p. 25.

53 Dollan, *History of the Kinning Park Co-operative Society,* p. 94.

54 The Maxton sisters regarded the Guild as, 'quite a power to be reckoned with'. Interview with Annie and Ada Maxton, 3 September 1979.

55 Buchan, *History of the Co-operative Women's Guild* p. 61.

56 Ibid., p. 10.

57 Dollan, *History of the Kinning Park Co-operative Society,* p. 93.

58 Ibid., p. 86.

59 Gordon, *Women in the Labour Movement* p. 269.

60 Buchan, *History of the Co-operative Women's Guild,* p. 68.

61 Gordon, *Women in the Labour Movement* , p. 268

62 In particular the seminal work by J. Liddington and J. Norris, *One Hand Tied Behind Us,* (Virago, London, 1978).

63 *Spare Rib,* no. 32, 1975.

64 Crawfurd, *Typescript Autobiography,* p. 87.

65 Liddington and Norris, *One Hand Tied Behind Us,* p. 200.

66 Crawfurd, *Typescript Autobiography,* p. 108.

67 Ibid; R. Challinor, *The Origins of British Bolshevism,* (Croom Helm, London, 1977) p. 153, who mentions the SLP offer only.

68 *Forward,* 20 October 1906.

69 N. Blewett, 'The Franchise in the United Kingdom 1885–1818', *Past and Present,* no. 32, 1965.

70 Smyth, *Labour and Socialism in Glagow?,* pp. 244–246, 250-256.

71 Liddington and Norris, *One Hand Tied Behind Us,* p. 232.

72 Ibid., pp. 231–238.

73 *Forward,* 16 February 1907.

74 M. Pugh, 'Labour and Women's Suffrage', in K. D. Brown (ed) *The First Labour Party, 1906–1914,* (Croom Helm, London, 1985) pp. 242–3.

75 Crawfurd, *Typescript Autobiography* p. 86.

76 H. Fraser, *Women and War Work,* (G. A. Shaw, New York 1918).

77 M. Ramelson, *The Petticoat Rebellion: A Century of Struggle Women's Rights,* (Lawrence & Wishart, London 1972) p. 82.

78 B. Keith-Lucas, *The English Local Government Franchise: A Short History* (London 1952) p. 74.

79 Smyth, *Labour and Socialism in Glasgow* p. 226.

80   T. Johnston, *The Case for Women' Suffrage and Objections Answered* (Glasgow, 1907) p. 10.
81   *Labour Leader*, 11 November 1904.
82   *Labour Leader*, 17 November 1905.
83   Smyth, *Labour and Socialism in Glasgow*, pp. 124–127, 228.
84   *Labour Leader*, 16 November 1906.
85   *Forward*, 17 November 1906.
86   Quoted in Gordon, *Women in the Labour Movement*, p. 274.
87   *Forward*, 16 January 1916.
88   Crawfurd, *Typescript autobiography*, pp. 48–49.
89   Gordon, *Women in the Labour Movement*, chapter 7; Brown and Stephenson, in this volume.
90   Crawfurd, *Typescript Autobiography*, p. 147.
91   *Forward*, 1 August 1914.
92   There was no property qualification at the parliamentary level but there was a residual property qualification at the municipal, with the result that the latter was somewhat more restrictive than the former.
93   Smyth, *Labour and Socialism in Glasgow*, p. 337.
94   *Forward*, 15 November 1919.
95   H. C. G. Matthew, R. I. McKibbon, J. A. Kay, 'The franchise factor in the rise of the Labour Party', *English Historical Review* (1976) pp. 747–749.
96   Mclean, *The Legend of Red Clydeside*, p. 163.
97   I. G. C. Hutchison, *A Political History of Scotland 1832–1924*, (Donald, Edinburgh 1986) p. 289.
98   *Forward*, 11 January 1919.
99   *Forward*, 11 January 1919.
100   *Glasgow Herald*, 3 November 1920.
101   A. McKinlay, 'Doubtful wisdom and uncertain promise': strategy, ideology and organisation, 1918–1922', in McKinlay and Morris, *The ILP on Clydeside*, pp. 138–139.
102   M. Sanger, *An Autobiography*, (Dover Publications, New York, 1971) p. 274.
103   In 1923 Guy Aldred and his partner Rose Witcop were prosecuted for publishing a pamphlet on birth control. I. S. Wood, *John Wheatley*, (Manchester University Press, Manchester 1990) pp. 145–6.
104   I. Mclean, *The Legend of Red Clydeside*, p. 224.

SELECT BIBLIOGRAPHY

A. Buchan Scottish Co-operative Women's Guild, (Scottish Co-operative Women's Guild, Glasgow, 1913).

W. Gallacher, *Revolt on the Clyde*, (Lawrence & Wishart, London, 1978).

E. Gordon, *Women in the Labour Movement in Scotland 1850–1914*, (Clarenden Press, Oxford, 1991).

I. G. C. Hutchison, *A Political History of Scotland 1832–1924*, (John Donald, Edinburgh, 1986).

J. Liddington, 'The Women's Peace Crusade: The History of a Forgotten Campaign', in D. Thompson, *Over our Dead Bodies: Women Against the Bomb*, (Virago, London, 1983).

McKinlay and R. J. Morris, *The ILP on Clydeside 1893–1932: from foundation to disintegration*, (Manchester University Press, Manchester, 1991).

I. S. Mclean, *The Legend of Red Clydeside*, (Donald, Edinburgh, 1983).

J. Melling, *Rent Strikes: People's Struggle for Housing in West Scotland 1890–1916*, (Polygon, Edinburgh, 1983).

D. Mitchell, *Women on the Warpath: the Story of the Women of the First World War*, (Cape, London, 1966).

S. Pankhurst, *The Suffragette Movement*, (Virago, London, 1977).

M. Pugh, 'Labour and Women's Suffrage', in *The First Labour Party, 1906–1914*, (London, 1985).

M. Ramelson, *The Petticoat Rebellion: a Century of Struggle Women's Rights*, (Lawrence & Wishart, London, 1972).

9

MOVING STORIES: WORKING-CLASS WOMEN

ANN McGUCKIN

INTRODUCTION

Only in recent years has the growth of historical sociology, the use of oral
and life history methods, allowed us to hear the voices of ordinary
women. Such research has been crucial in broadening and redefining the
analysis of women's roles in the past and has helped develop theoretical
understanding in the area of meaning and action. A surge of feminist
writing on the sexual division of labour, the family, the public and private
spheres, gender and the urban environment, the labour market and the
construction and control of knowledge has brought about a clearer understanding of the connections between theoretical analysis and political
practice.[1] This has allowed us to understand exploitation and class relations in a much more comprehensive way. Implicit in a feminist approach
has been the acceptance that there are different ways of knowing and
learning about the world by stressing subjectivity in the production and
validation of knowledge.[2] Analysis of women's experience, using both
social and self-knowledge has been put forward as the central tenet of a
feminist methodology.[3] However an over-emphasis on women's subordination has removed a sense of women as actors. This focus is the
product of the research process itself.

SEPARATE SPHERES

The restructuring of urban space and the physical separation of work and
home has been reflected at the analytical level.[4] The ideology of separate
realms of existence – public and private, work and community, male and
female[5] have characterised approaches to social research. These form part
of the 'social creation' of knowledge identified by Spender whereby a
particular way of viewing the world is encoded in knowledge and presented as truth.[6]

The conceptualisation of work and community as analytically discrete
categories rather than two sides of the same coin fails to encompass the
complexities of social relationships.[7] This false division between work
and community has defined separate places and contexts for conflict. By

and large conflicts in the community are accorded a different form of importance than those at the workplace. Historically the definition of and focus for class struggle has been strongly situated in the workplace. Community struggles are seen as elements of or appendages to the main struggles on the shop-floor. This dichotomous approach has led to the experience of class as a series of partial relationships.[8] Above all to make sense of consciousness and action there is a need, argues E. P. Thompson,[9] to understand the experience of class as it is lived and how people make sense of it in their everyday lives. Classes emerge through common struggle and these vary in time place and in context.

There are but few instances where community and work struggles coalesce. The Glasgow rent strikes of 1915 and 1922 are two examples. In general community struggles and workplace struggles were defined as separate and different forms of resistance. More commonly the true interface of class exploitation is seen as firmly embedded in issues of production. Yet increasingly there are struggles over issues of consumption – housing, education and health to name a few and women predominate in these at the local level. Cynthia Cockburn in her book on the local state argues for the recognition that 'alongside struggle at the point of production, in the mines and factories, there is a struggle at the point of consumption in schools, in housing estates, in the street and in the family.'[10]

Working-class women have had and continue to have first-hand experience of workplace confrontation. Historically they have also been in the frontline over the provision of services at a local level. It has been women who have dealt with landlords, who bargained with factors for fair rents, and negotiated paying arrears. Working-class women have traditionally harried housing officials for better accommodation and for homes for their daughters and sons. They have been responsible for paying the rent, keeping the family fed, clothed and out of the clutches of the 'social'. They have had and continue to have direct interface with pawnbrokers, petty money lenders and credit sharks. They negotiated 'tick' [credit] for themselves and their families with local grocers, butchers and coal merchants – the local petty bourgeoisie. They had primary contacts with schools, nurses and housing visitors. Although women's experiences vary across social, racial and ethnic groups and in different parts of the country, in essence these relationships form part of the totality of class relationships.

Early research into working-class life focused on the constraints of poverty. This led to an emphasis on the problems women encountered in their day to day lives. Analyses of working-class women have been affected more than most by this emphasis where the language of repression, exploitation and powerlessness has constrained debate. The early poverty studies by Mayhew and Booth[11] documented the living conditions of the poor and the heavy burdens that women had to bear. Some early feminist studies of mothers and wives in the home by Pember Reeves and Spring Rice[12] had a similar emphasis. The latter have proved invaluable for redefining the parameters of the research process – making women visible – but have left enduring images of working-class women as victims, weighed down by poverty, children and violent men, unable to exert any control over their daily lives.

More recent approaches by sociologists, social historians and human geographers have challenged these images. These have in common a well-thought-out theoretical framework which directs analysis towards the most pertinent questions – the roles that women performed and their experiences and responses to subordination. By redefining the analytical categories some writers have recorded the resistance and struggles of working-class women to gain some control over their lives.[13] What follows is an attempt to illustrate the forms that resistance took for a particular group of women.

The first part of this chapter deals with the historical construction of images of working-class women in the home. It then looks in detail at the everyday lived experience of class and domination through a group of working-class women in Glasgow during the 1930s. Through their confrontation with factors, school board officials and moneylenders these women define and interpret their own lives. The emphasis is on power, conflict and resistance not interdependence, support or altruism. Essentially the focus is on resistance – the way it was organised and the forms it took. This analysis seeks to achieve some sense of the values and attitudes of a group of working-class women and in so doing to reveal some misconceptions of working-class life. Within the confines of poverty this particular group of women exerted a fair degree of control over their lives and used the few resources available to them to organise and resist authority.

By using a combination of oral evidence and statistical data the chapter examines in detail the everyday lived experience of a group of women.

IMAGES OF WORKING-CLASS LIFE

Images of working-class life were graphically illustrated in the early studies of poverty.[14] Living conditions in the slums became a source of national concern and scandal during the 1880s. Clergymen, doctors and philanthropists alike vilified the slum landlords. When the census returns of 1831 revealed the staggering levels of overcrowding – 41 per cent of Glaswegian families lived in one room – 'the facts were so startling in their nature that they were barely believed' said J. B. Russell, Glasgow's medical officer of health in a public lecture in 1888.[15] Enid Gauldie singled out the constellations of interest supporting inaction:

> The British dislike of centralised authority, religious support for self-help, the political theory of *laissez-faire*, and the belief in the

sanctity of private property, united to form a middle-class creed of inviolable strength and vitality.[16]
However, some writers describe this interest as stemming more from a fear of the residuum than from humanitarian concern.[17] In addition, critics argue that the proliferation of narratives of the attitudes of the middle and upper classes towards the poor and the unemployed gave scant recognition to the values and attitudes of the poor themselves.[18] In essence 'the working classes were the "objects of study", in the same sense that reformers considered them as material ripe for education and tutelage.'[19]

'Typical' working-class families were reputed to be the subject of most of these studies but it was the women's control over the household budget that came under careful scrutiny. The 'proper' structure of family relations and women's responsibilities were effectively defined. As such, moralistic concerns underpinned enquiry and women were denigrated for gossiping, drinking, and generally being unkempt. Journalist George Simms wrote in horror about the weekly visits to the pawnbrokers by women who would later 'adjourn to the public house for a glass and gossip'.[20] Despite Booth's revelation that both men and women were over-worked and underpaid, the association of poverty in women with power-lessness and exploitation became firmly established in the public mind. A mother's ability to work or cope made the difference between life and death.[21] These early studies formed part of a process where, in the context of imperial rivalries, concerns about the health and welfare of the nation translated into a concern with, and a focus on, the role of women as mo-thers and attempts to 'improve' the quality of working-class motherhood.

WORKING-CLASS WOMEN

As the public health reformers gained momentum and national housing policies were implemented, early feminist studies concentrated on the living conditions of women in the slums. Inspired by the newly available census data, social observers regarded the breeding patterns of women, their standards of cleanliness and eating habits, as well as the manner in which they dressed, as legitimate areas of interest. The relationship between living conditions, poverty and health was somehow masked by these other concerns. In effect individual attributes become explanatory variables for subsequent behaviour patterns. Although the physical prob-lems of poverty were explored little was said about the experience, reaction and resistance to poverty by women.

Maud Pember Reeves' study of the daily lives of working-class wives in Lambeth in 1913 was provoked by national concern over women's health and reproductive capacity. The book reveals the contradictory nature of early feminist research. Essentially it is two books; the research-er's story and that of the women. Wives are described as 'slaves' who are muddleheaded by the time they reach 30. Yet the women are exact and precise as they account for their day, in half-hourly intervals to suit, we are told, 'the protection of the visitor'. The number and complexity of tasks that the women performed seemed staggering to the researchers. Nor is there any trace of such muddleheadedness in the co-ordinated efforts of one mother in managing eight children under 13.[22] All of which proved 'richly interesting and led to some absorbing anecdotes' for the observer. The rhetoric of the visitor emphasises the 'problems' faced by the woman whereas the words of the women themselves are active and decisive, displaying organisation and control.

The concern with women's health translates itself easily into analysis of breeding patterns. Prolonged periods of childbearing in bad housing conditions on extremely low incomes affected women's health considerably. However the way this aspect of their lives was examined had a Malthusian tinge to it. The 'problem', and possible solution, is clearly defined in the following passage:

Much had been written. . .on the question of the poor and large families. We wrangle as to whether their numerous children are an improvidence and insult to the community. . .or whether the poorer class is the only class that does its duty to the nation. One thing is quite certain. . .it would be as unthinkable as impossible to bring compulsion to bear on the poor because they are poor. But for those who deplore large families. . .it must bring comfort to remind us that as poverty decreases, so does the size of the family.[23]

Conquering the 'problem of poverty' went hand in hand with conquering the 'problem of excessively large families'. This 'problem' was reinforced by the general recalcitrance of mothers who refused to 'take advantage' of free meals and medical checkups.

A persistent part of the analysis of working-class people has focused on their washing habits or, more accurately, the lack of them. Criticisms of infrequent washing ('the coal in the bath type') were offset by the persistence and quest for cleanliness by some sections of the working class perceived by many as a desire for separation and respectability ('the lace-curtained type'). On the poor unwashed the rhetoric used by Reeves is instructive:

Mrs K with her 'casual' ways has a delicate mind and flushes deeply if the visitor alludes to anything which shocks her . . . Mr and Mrs K seem to sleep among a herd of boys and Mrs K's skirts look as if the rats have been at them and her blouse is never where it should be.

The animal-like behaviour of the woman elicits moral outrage in the middle-class observer. Cleanliness, thrift and moral rectitude were virtues which were demanded or imposed upon working-class women, and which it was supposed that they lacked. These are to become enduring themes in studies of working-class women, and opinion is often passed off as analysis.

The women, however, are not alone in being singled out for attention. What is perceived as the passivity of mothers is also translated to their children:

> They too readily accepted limitations and qualifications imposed on them. These children never rebel against disappointment. It is their lot. They more or less expect it.[24]

This method of approach confirmed and reinforced existing stereotypes. Working-class women seemed imprisoned within a definition of powerlessness and degradation that they themselves had little part in defining. Such images have been remarkably enduring.

One of the most forthright investigations into the condition of working-class women was carried out by Margery Spring Rice in 1939. In the detailed descriptions of the daily lives of mothers and children similar images emerged. Physical degeneration was a continuing theme: 'an attractive girl rapidly grows old and drab after a few years' marriage.' She 'loses her looks and ceases to take a pride in her appearance.' And yet again 'minor ailments are neglected, temper is frayed.' These women do not seem to talk, they 'gossip' on the 'doorstep, untidy and slatternly'. They find solace in the 'cinema' which brought 'mental peace and refreshment'. The observer reprimands the recalcitrance of such women who 'object to their children being removed for training' and simply refuse to attend hospital and antenatal clinics.

New approaches have not been completely successful in undermining these images. Elizabeth Roberts' oral history of women[25] is a fine example of an alternative approach and records the hidden lives of ordinary working-class women. Whole areas of women's lives are opened up as they discuss their everyday experiences. The author acknowledges the contradictory nature of research in this area yet still a few images of conformity and respectability persist: 'Working-class children learned the habit of obedience from a very early age. Their own wills and desires had to be subordinated to those of their parents.'[26]

Although there is some acceptance that 'lapses did occur', in general Roberts argues that 'working class children . . . followed both the implicit and explicit moral, social and ethical guidance which they received from their parents'.[27] There are, however, plenty of examples in the text to contradict this conclusion as individuals display independence of thought and action.

These few examples reveal how images of working-class women have been constructed through subjective assessments of living patterns. Through the research process itself moral judgements become explanatory concepts. The working-class woman seems forever cast in the role of victim – constrained and restrained by children, hard work and poverty. She is quite powerless, unable to change or control any aspect of her daily life. Such a perspective perpetuates the myth that all working-class women are poor and that all poor women are oppressed and powerless.

While this description was appropriate for some individuals, the emphasis on powerlessness negates a broader understanding of how working-class women make sense of their lives, how they react to exploitation and the manner in which they resist. Looking at the lived experience of women and accepting the definitions they place on their actions forms an essential part of feminist analyses and moves towards creating an arena where working-class women are seen as active participants.

THE WOMEN

The women here represent a 10 per cent random sample of the first tenants at Blackhill, a local authority rehousing scheme. The sample was taken over three time periods, 1935, 1937 and 1939, stratified by occupation, social class, previous dwelling, number of children, wage, old rent, new rent and previous area of residence. A variety of sources were used including valuation rolls, rental rolls, draft rolls, original housing application forms, the minutes of Glasgow Corporation meetings – in particular the Special Committee on Housing – and contemporary newspapers. Semi-structured, face to face interviews were carried out with sixty women, ex-factors and ex-housing officials.[28]

Blackhill tenants were predominantly unskilled. Of the 605 tenants, over two-thirds were 'labourers'. There was also a high number of 'widows' and single women. Of the sample around 50 per cent had moved from one apartment houses. One third of these had three or more children. Around 47 per cent moved from two-apartment houses and more than half of this group had four or more children.(See Table 9.1).

Income levels were low and irregular and new rents high. According to the draft roll, around 60 per cent of residents earned forty shillings per week or less and around 21 per cent of the sample earned twenty-five shillings per week. Average rents in Blackhill were eight shillings per week. Interviews with residents revealed very high levels of unemployment, so actual income levels may have been considerably lower than would first appear. Rent increased three- to four-fold when the tenants moved to Blackhill.

Around 60 per cent of Blackhill tenants came from the Garngad area in the north-east quadrant of Glasgow's inner city. All lived in slums rented from private landlords. Living conditions in the Garngad during the 1930s were appalling. It had a reputation as a rough neighbourhood, known locally as 'Little Ireland' because of the high proportion of Irish Catholics crammed into its vermin-infested housing. Describing the living conditions that existed during the 1860s in Glasgow, J. A. Handley described the 'Glasgow Central District as an incubator for contagious diseases and illnesses, particularly among the Irish immigrants who crowded into the cheaper slums.'[29] The Report of the Commission of Enquiry into the Garngad Road Clearance Area Compulsory Purchase Order of 1933 revealed little change.

TABLE 9.1 Size of family x previous house size: N = 57

Families by number of children	1–apt	2-apt	3-apt	Total
1	12	5	-	17
2	5	5	-	10
3	5	-	-	6
>4	7	13	4	24
Total:	30	23	4	57

Source: Blackhill Draft Roll.

In the area there was at present 297 persons per acre, compared with an average density for the city of 36 persons per acre. The death-rate was 29.99 per 1000 persons, as against 14.77 per 1000 in the city. The death-rate from respiratory diseases was 7.25 as compared with 3.54 in the city, and from pulmonary diseases it was 1.96 as against 0.88 in the city. The infant mortality was 178 per 1000 as against 106 per 1000 in the city.[30] Poverty was endemic. The biggest single concentration of applicants for public assistance in the early 1930s lived in the Garngad. Unemployment was extremely high among Catholics who faced systematic exclusion from the many engineering works in northern and eastern Glasgow – Springburn locomotive works and Beardsmore's Forge at Parkhead routinely refused to employ Catholics.[31]

Interwar housing policy during this period was closely linked to character management. Scottish local authorities had housed the better-off under 'general needs' provision during the 1920s when subsidies were high, then ditched both principle and populace following the shift in legislation during the 1930s. The result of this was the creation of a distinctive and second-class brand of housing where the socially undesirable would be housed.[32] Blackhill was the outcome of this policy.[33]

Built during the early 1930s the scheme had gained a city-wide reputation by the 1950s as a haven for thieves and criminals. Blackhill residents were defined by their local authority landlords and other sections of the working class as 'rabble', to be contained, controlled and policed at every opportunity. In common with many working-class housing estates, Blackhill, in the Springburn area of Glasgow, was stigmatised. Residents were (and still are) systematically blacklisted for credit by chain stores and by employment agencies, local authority services and taxi-drivers. The scheme has its 'own' police station (steel shuttered) and a complete tenement of social workers. Enclosed on three sides by motorways, physically distinct and socially segregated, it represents the failure of Scottish inter-war housing policy.

Blackhill residents were generally poor, unemployed and suffering from chronic ill health. Mechanisms for control were easily established through the corporation's housing management strategy. Resident factors were used to collect rents, arrange lettings, control arrears and carry out evictions. Many of those employed had already worked as factors in the private rented sector. Some were employed for their expert knowledge on 'court matters' and dealing with 'troublesome types'.[34] In effect they performed the same role as factors in the private sector. Many of the women interviewed confirmed this.

Families were therefore subordinated through the property relationships of landlord and tenant not unlike those operating during the late 1880s and early 1900s. Although the landlords were not also small shopkeepers who gave credit to their tenants, there was a stable set of property relations established. Although 'at the heart of this relationship was the chronic indebtedness of working-class families',[35] it was embedded in a form of subordination that was masked by the rhetoric of socialist housing policy. As McCrone and Elliot argue, high rents, combined with meagre wages for irregular work, and chronic ill health made being in debt a way of life. People were tied to districts through credit. Credit tied the tenant to the landlord and extending credit gave the landlord influence over a complex web of relationships – economic, social and even political. Many of these points hold true for the residents of Blackhill where women were the main negotiators and their roles were central to the nexus of property relations. However they had a more complex set of responses to credit and factors. Women were at the forefront of this battle. Making ends meet was their concern. Being evicted was their fault. Resisting at all levels was how they survived.[36]

POVERTY

Keeping or having a man in work provided only a slight protection against eviction or 'going on the parish'. The lives of the women in this study were hard and repetitive. Many had large families and a few had hard men. They did not rely on 'their man's' money because the men were often out of work, sick or 'drinking it'. Very few mention having a steady wage of any kind. The women went to enormous efforts to provide for their families in this separate world. Above all they aimed for dignity: 'there was poverty – but we weren't poor', as one respondent put it. Poverty is shameful, particularly for those who endure it. Even yet some cannot speak of it. Mrs L's reaction was typical: 'Oh! I couldn't talk about that. I just want to forget those times. Why do you want to bring back these memories?' Some simply refused to talk.

Along with the poverty went the supervision by 'concerned' agencies. Known collectively as the 'sanny folk' they ranged from housing visitors (nicknamed 'Panshine') to factors and an early type of health visitor. These groups could gain access at any time to the women's homes. Many of the women argued that the nature and frequency of supervision was in some sense worse than being evicted. 'At least in — Street you knew where you were, you paid your rent and that was it . . . but here you were never sure' (Mrs L). Beds were inspected for vermin, kitchens and bathrooms for 'cleanliness', and the floors, windows and walls for dust. Sometimes 'even the bairns' heads were looked at', though this was usually the preserve of school nurses who cut hair and shaved heads indiscriminately and painted young faces with 'bluestone' (gentian violet, a blue antiseptic dye) which was supposed to cover up impetigo but was in fact applied to any red blotch. The women felt ashamed at some stranger rummaging through their meagre possessions, fearful of whom they would tell. The little dignity they had evaporated as quickly as 'Panshine' could run her nimble fingers over the tops of the doors. But they worked out strategies to cope with such interventions.

The women recorded here described themselves as 'just ordinary working people, trying to get by as best we could'. Most felt they had 'nothing really to tell' about their lives. Fighting public battles in public arenas seems relatively easy compared to this private world of struggle and resistance.

WORKING COLLECTIVELY

The women worked collectively in all areas of their lives – from sharing food, 'making soup for the close', helping each other to pay the rent and warning each other of the coming of 'Panshine'. They shared extensively and unsentimentally. They spent time making nappies for new babies, saving through menages, baking and lending tablecovers and good dishes for weddings, birthdays and christenings as well as pawning collectively. Some knitted for the street or their close while others arranged savings clubs for the men coming back from the War. In general they looked out for each other. As Mrs G (born in 1914) put it: 'You had to because you never knew what was around the corner. It could be you next.' In times of crisis, during illness or childbirth, they looked after each others' children. Battered women were taken in overnight and very poor families were helped out continually.

MOVING

The women recorded here all moved from privately rented slum accommodation – one or two rooms without inside toilets or running water. Their new homes had two, three or four bedrooms, a bathroom, a separate living room and kitchen with a long lobby or hall. Some of them even had gardens to tend.

The joy of moving was tempered by the worry of paying the new rent – three times that of their old houses – and of furnishing their new homes. Rents had been paid weekly in their old properties and now had to be paid fortnightly or even monthly. The period of payment was negotiated with the factor. The furniture they possessed was sparse and consisted mainly of beds. Most of these were confiscated by the corporation because they were 'full of bugs'. This is how the women coped with moving in 1935. The reaction of Mrs C (b. 1926) is typical:

> When my mother first came up here there was no linoleum or anything except for the living room and the hall and a wee runner piece. The bathroom wasn't even covered. It [linoleum] was just brought up from the Barras and the rest wasn't covered, it was all just boards and newspapers that was put down. My mother had her bed in the living room and we had an old sideboard which cost £1, two smokers' chairs, that was all. In our room there was a big bed with brass knobs, an orange box and it was turned upside down and my dad made a wee shelf in it where we kept our shoes. She had an old box thing my dad made with a rod across it and that was where we hung our clothes. My mother and father slept in the living room. In the wee room there was absolutely nothing. In the scullery it was just stone floor.

Some women were able to plan ahead for the move. Mrs. F (b. 1929) remembers:

> The house that we were in was condemned property and had a lot of bugs in it – all the houses were the same then . . . rumours were going around, we were going to be rehoused, but nobody knew when. My mother stopped paying the rent and started to put money aside for the furniture. We had no flitting, she left everything that was in the house because she didn't want to bring any vermin to the new house. She went for a dining room suite and a bedroom suite and a couple of beds she bought later. She bought it all cash because she had been saving up. We thought we were the bees' knees compared to everyone else. Everyone was talking about us moving in without any furniture. Years later, just before the war finished she told me to buy furniture to start a house rather than putting the money in the bank, so I did.

Some remembered the excitement of the move:

> You could hear the click, click, click of the kids downstairs switching on and off the lights – it was gas we had [before] and this was a novelty having electricity. We were in a corner close, the rooms were enormous and we thought it was a mansion. We just did one room at a time, we liked living in one room anyway at the beginning, tho' the kids ran about switching the light switches on and off and opening and closing the doors.

For all of them having a separate scullery or kitchen and an inside bathroom was a novelty, and women commented that it was 'just out of this world . . . going into the bathroom was great, we were getting a bath twice a day! It was great to have constant hot water.'

Though for some their first bath was literally breathtaking:

We had been used to getting washed before – using the big basin like, but I had never sat in hot water before. And oh I just screamed and lost my breath, I thought I was going to drown. I couldn't sit down so I used to just stand up and wash until I got used to it. People don't seem to understand these things nowadays.

Along with the excitement came the shame, however:

We didn't have anything on the floor, except, well newspapers – for years until the boys were up and earning. We would keep the doors closed all the time in case anybody came. We told Panshine that we were just waiting on the linoleum coming, but we weren't.

Many of the women could barely bring themselves to talk about the new expectations of cleanliness that were now demanded of them:

I remember they [the corporation] took the beds away and got the mattresses. We didnae have interiors [interior sprung mattresses]. It was just the flock mattresses. Whatever they done to delouse them when they brought them back the flock was loose and the mattresses were open and tied with string and we had to sit and sew these mattresses. My mother went that white with anger.

The supervision by 'Panshine' increased anger and stress. Mrs K (b. 1913) recalls:

Well she [long pause] looked at the beds and cupboards and every-where, ran her fingers over the doors and everything. I mean we didn't have sheets, just blankets and we'd say they were being washed. She always went into the kitchen and the bathroom to see if we had towels and things – we didn't, only two and they were thin in the middle. I mean you couldn't afford these things, you just used what was there. I used to get so angry with the lassies after she went, and shout at my man when he came in. She made me feel . . . well dirty – and I wasn't!

Much of the women's anger was directed at the housing visitor. Housing policy was linked to character management. This involved close super-vision of sections of tenants. Character management was, however, con-centrated on the women. They resisted in a variety of ways – warning each other of Panshine's appearance in the scheme, standing as witnesses for neighbours who were charged with 'not washing the stairs', and taking direct action. Mrs C (b. 1926) recalls:

She [Panshine] would mark a wee cross, you wouldn't know where she would mark this wee cross, on the stair to see if you were washing the stairs. She would come on a Wednesday and then come back, you wouldn't see the cross. This time my mother was caught and the neighbours stood up for her [in the court]. But she was still fined. They could throw you out you know. A girl I knew, her man died, she was in the house with a wee baby and she wouldn't let Panshine in this day. They were shouting at her to let them in and eventually she did open the door and she had a basin of tattie peelings and she threw them all over Panshine. Well they threw her out, they wouldn't give her another house.

Faced with floors to cover, windows to curtain and beds to make up, the women used every kind of material they could lay their hands on. Like many working-class women they were adept at sewing because as Mrs L (b. 1909) said 'You just had to be. What money we had went on food and the rent, and sometimes not even that far.' Mrs C (b. 1926) remembers:

> Down at Riddrie there was a disinfectant place and you could go and buy bleach bottles for threepence and a great big bit of black soap on a muslin cloth. And they used to dollop it for about ninepence – that's what you got your bath with.

Q: Derback soap?

A: No, it was just black soap.

Q: Soft was it?

A: Soft it was, black soft soap, she used to lift it onto a ladle onto the muslin cloth. That was melted down to do the washing and put into sweetie jars. In fact the man used to keep us flour bags and they were put in the big sink for boiling. We could get four for a shilling and put them into the boiler and boil them until all the stiffness was out them. And she (her mother) used to wring them out on the old wringer – two rollers with a handle on it. It wasn't even a wringer and they were wrung into the big sink and that was put in with the bleach and let them lie until the name came off it. And that was our sheets and pillows and curtains. The man at Templeton's at Parliamentary Road used to keep her the muslin off the cheeses and that was all brought home and that was boiled, bleached and dyed. You put it in the big enamel bath tub and dyed all the curtains as well.

They also had children to clothe. Mrs M (b. 1923) remembers:

> We were not too badly off because my mother's brother was a cutter to trade, a tailor, and he used to get the cut-offs and my mum used to make clothes for us and my dad used to cobble the shoes. We never went bare-footed, we never went without a jersey or anything, she always used to knit even if she found just a wee bit of wool she would knit it and we had jumpers of all different colours. It was knitted round and round, no seams.

And on nappies:

> It was all nappies, there was none of this 'pampers' carry on. Old vests and things were never thrown out. My mother used to machine them to make an edge and they would be put in for babies' nappies. The nurse used to come. When she went away the nappy was taken off the baby and a vest or pillow slip was put on in its place, and when the nurse came back the good nappy was brought out again.

Despite such inventiveness and hard work many had to make do with

School Board clothes. Women in their 60s vividly remember the feelings
of shame that this created. Mrs K (b. 1922) recalls:

> Once we got to school my mother started hearing about these free
> clothes and things. The parish clothes were different from the
> School Board clothes. Well the parish clothes were of a finer mate-
> rial, but the School Board clothes were all stamped with 'educa-
> tional' on the tail or red marks on them. I used to tuck that bit in so
> that nobody would know it was a School Board jersey. We had big
> black hairy stockings and they were as itchy as anything and great
> big tackety shoes with a steel bit. I hated them and wouldn't wear
> them and I used to get called 'lady muck'. All the kids were like that
> except them in Robroyston in the miners' cottages.

These became one of the many badges of poverty worn by the children.
The way clothes were allocated increased their sense of shame. They were
made to feel 'terrible, just terrible . . . as though you didn't have any pride
or anything.' Mrs F recalls her first visit to get what she thought would be
new clothes:

> When we went to school we got a line for the clothes and you had to
> go away down to Martha Street way and you were stamped as you
> went in the door, you had to take this line. You weren't measured
> or anything, it was just thrown at you – 'there's the jersey, there's
> the socks, there's the knickers and there's shoes.' You had to take
> them whether they fitted or not.

Some resisted but were usually caught, like Mrs P (b. 1927): ·

> Once a year to get your shoes repaired you had to put a line in
> through the teacher which I would never do because I hated them.
> My mother would say 'Remember and get a line'. I would get a
> battering for not remembering to give the teacher a line. So my
> sister came up this day and she asked Mr Hunt for a line and he
> says, 'Is your sister not in this class?' and she says 'aye'. He called
> me out and says, 'How could you no ask?' I says 'Because I don't
> like them.' Everybody knew you had School Board clothes.

For the majority the struggle was too much on all fronts. Getting credit
or 'tick' was the only way to buy essentials. Many were excluded from
Co-operative Stores. Mrs L (b. 1909) recalls:

> No we never went to the co-op. Well we went once and they said
> come back when your man's in work. But I knew lots of people
> whose man was out a work and got their messages [shopping]
> there. It was just where we came from . . . we weren't good enough.
> So we just went to the wee shops. They were dearer but they didnae
> bother. Mind you when you run up your book in them [increased
> your credit more each week than you could pay off] you had tae be
> careful . . . but you would just send the lassies down and say it was
> for Mrs so and so. Och I'm sure they knew . . . but they kept you on
> and that was all that mattered.

Shopping was bought in small amounts daily and generally 'marked up' to be paid at the end of the week. Few women managed to pay this off completely but 'as long as you paid something towards it' you could carry on. When the amount outstanding became too great more credit was refused. Women went elsewhere. At the end of the day it was not uncommon to have credit in all of the local shops, with the coal merchant and any grocery vans that came around, as well as in other areas of the town where another member of the family worked or lived. Mothers, daughters and sisters negotiated credit for each other. In this sense credit was not always locally centred. Mrs L (b. 1909) recalls how for her sister's wedding: 'We "rigged out" [bought new clothes for] the children in my mother's name, and my man got his shoes in my sister's name.'

Mrs W (b. 1911) remembers the uncompromising attitude of some of the men.

My man said 'If you can't live on what you've got then do without'. But all I wanted was new shoes for the lassies and a couch and two kitchen chairs because there was five of us and we only had three [chairs]. He didn't like it when I got the couch.

Mrs P (b. 1927) remembers the friction between her mother and father over 'tick':

I think it was easier for women to get into debt in those days for there were lots of men coming round the doors selling things and for a woman who doesn't have very much she would say 'well it's only so much a week'. It's the easiest thing in the world to do. The men would open up their big cases and we would all crowd round looking at the nylons and shiny scarves and things. Many a time I used to fall out with my own man over the same thing.

The new houses brought added problems of cooking and cleaning. Friday night seemed the most common night for all the floors in the houses to be scrubbed for the week. Daughters were 'kept in' to help their mothers before taking off for 'the dancing'. All hot water was heated by the fire, a 'back-to-back', and fuel was a constant worry. None of the women burned coal. All used 'char' – coke from the local gas works. When coal was bought it was bought by the piece:

You could buy a lump of coal for about tuppence. But it was just to get the fire started. It was very hard to get it started with char and it took an awful lot of sticks, so my mother used to get paper and roll it tight instead and twirl it up to make paper sticks.

Char was considerably cheaper than coal:

Oh you got a great big bag like a coal bag. It was fourpence for a big double bag and tuppence for a half bag. My dad made a wee barrow and we put it in it and pulled it up the hill. My grannie used to give my mum a bag of coal for Christmas.

Sometimes other members of the family would raid the gas works and come round the doors selling the same coke at a penny less. When coke was unavailable 'anything' went on the fire including cardboard, old shoes and bits of furniture.

FEEDING THE FAMILY

Much criticism has been levelled at working-class women's inability to feed their families healthily. Only recently the then Junior Minister for Health, Edwina Currie, berated women for buying expensive, unhealthy foods and damaging the nation's health. Concern with managing the household budget is an enduring theme. In general, working-class women were criticised for their lack of a basic understanding of nutrition. They were seen as having little concern for 'balanced diets' and promoting 'unhealthy eating habits' in their children, spending money unwisely and failing to save for the future. This was seen to be in sharp contrast to the thrift, temperance and healthy eating habits (meat and two veg) of their contemporaries in the respectable working class. As controllers of the household budget it was their responsibility to spend their money 'wisely'. However women in this study walked for miles to save very small amounts of money. Mrs C (b. 1926) recalls:

My mother would go down to a place in Riddrie and get marmalade in a jar for about threepence. You would get a token stuck on it and you took it back and you got a refill for tuppence, if you lost that you would have to pay the full price of threepence. Also there was a man came round the street with a wee barrow and a wee motor thing selling skimmed milk. When you bought that it was cheaper, it was only a penny for a great big jug – and see if you missed that skimmed milk man! There was a man used to sell onions – Onion Johnny – he had lovely hard onions and you would get about twelve of the wee ones you would pickle for a penny or tuppence along with beetroot.

Vegetables were a common part of the diet. Again children and women walked some distance to buy the cheapest:

It was at Hogganfield Loch at Ruchazie Road where the miners' rows were, past the golf course, which went right away down to the Rex picture hall. Past that there was a wee farm and you used to go out there to buy cabbage, turnip, tomatoes and butter for about ninepence . . . eggs for one and sixpence. Your dad and mum got the eggs, we maybe got an egg between us, scrambled. We were all sat down at the table.

The women also gathered jam jars and sauce bottles 'till it came to half a crown'. Jam jars sold for a farthing at the local shops. They waited outside local bakeries to get stale bread and 'throw-outs'. Sometimes they bought a pennyworth of 'broken biscuits' or some 'spoiled fruit' for a halfpenny. Children bought 'misshapes' to eat at the local cinema. In general what little they had they shared. Making a dumpling which 'fed the stair' was common while others made soup. It seemed that everyone had a speciality and as one woman remembers 'you could get anything you wanted in the scheme . . . I mean anything.'

Rituals – baptisms, marriages and funerals – played an important part in the community, acting as symbols of continuity and cohesion. Women were the organisers and controllers of these events which brought together all family members on a regular basis. Such gatherings served as a forum for strengthening or establishing social networks. These were crucial for discovering where and when work was available outside the immediate area, or learning of the availability of housing (a constant concern for newly married couples). These events also provided opportunities to 'hand down clothes' from family to family and to discuss the care of older family members. It was common in this community for youngsters to live with a lone grandparent.

In general few men attended church and children went out of fear mostly, since their attendance was monitored by the school. They too stopped attending at the earliest opportunity. For this group of women the church functioned more as an early social service rather than an ideological weapon.

They lived in poverty and to some extent they could bear this but the shame that they experienced was crippling. Shame came with an outsider 'finding out'. When times were bad women often turned to the priest for help. This could be for food or clothes or to speak with the factor about the rent. Or it could be to comfort them when they had been beaten up, or their man had been 'put inside'. Mrs K recalls the time the priest was called after her father had spent all his wages on 'the drink' again:

> Well he used to get into bad company, he wasn't a bad man really. But there were seven of us and my mother was worried sick about the rent and she couldnae borrow anymore from the neighbours. They wouldnae give her any tick at the co-op so she had tae turn tae the priest. He came along on Saturday night with this box and it had jam and bread and a tin of meat in it and a big cabbage out of the church gardens and some potatoes as well. My mother was that relieved. We all had to go to church on Sunday that week.

Uppermost in most of the women's minds were food and money. Many of them combined these two in strategic job choice. The church was a coveted place for employment as a housekeeper or her assistant. Generally three women worked a rota at the local chapel. For many working-class women, finding a job where food was around was essential. At the end of the day they could take home left-overs and stale scones and bread. This was usually done secretively.

> We used to wait round the corner for my mum to see what she had tonight. She always went to work with her big message bag. Sometimes there would be bashed cakes or currant buns or those wee iced french cakes. We all used to fight over them.

Also they could 'acquire' some of the luxuries they were unable to buy,

like soap and the occasional towel, washing suds and the odd knife or
spoon, or sometimes a plate. Women who worked in kitchens and bakeries were a bit more organised and would bring boxes of bread and rolls
home with them to sell to neighbours.

The household budget was supplemented in other ways. Women
would buy cheap apples from the market and make toffee applies to sell.
Others made puff candy and sold it. Some bought cups and saucers and
'went round the doors'. Hawking was considered respectable as well as
necessary. Many sold their clothing coupons 'for five shillings a page'
and others borrowed money from small-time moneylenders in the
scheme – 'lending five shillings and getting back seven'. Pawning was
also done on a weekly basis. Rings, 'good' suits and blankets were
pawned at the beginning of the week and 'lifted' on the Friday.

PAYING THE RENT

Paying the rent, or rather avoiding eviction, was a constant worry for the
women. The rent was paid fortnightly or monthly to a resident factor.
There were four in the scheme. The factors had considerable power and
their control went far beyond the allocation of houses. Moving house was
dependent upon a 'note' from the factor, in effect a character reference, as
well as a clean rentbook. Intimate details on tenants were recorded and
were supplied to employers and local shopkeepers on request. As one
woman put it 'you didnae get on the wrong side of the factor'. Some of the
factors had worked for private landlords so they knew the previous
factors, and therefore histories, of many of the residents. The factor/
tenant relationship was a continuation of previous social relationships
founded on subordination and grounded in the debt-ridden lives of their
clients. In essence the emphasis was on control. The factors kept a high
public profile, walking around the scheme chiding children and tenants
alike about litter, gardens or general behaviour. Children were usually
sent to pay the rent since many of the mothers 'didn't want to face up to
him'. (Mrs C (b. 1926) remembers her visits and how she felt:

> He was a very strict disciplinarian, not only for looking after the
> area and making sure it was kept in good order, but rent wise as
> well, and many's a time I had to go round and say, 'Could you
> please excuse my mother and father but they will try and make it
> up the following month'. . . . He never actually knocked me back
> but he used to be very abrupt and say, 'Well tell them they better
> make sure they get it or else they will be out'. I didn't like going, I
> wasn't so much scared, I didn't like the embarrassment, you virtu-
> ally had to plead.

As in other areas women collectively helped each other. Mrs F (b. 1929)
recalls the response of her mother to a neighbour threatened with
eviction:

> Annie, she had a big family, about seven or eight of them – my

mother helped to rear the kids downstairs, and they didn't forget it when they grew up. After my dad died I went up and found a letter behind the door saying '28 days to leave the house.' She had given her rent to the folk down the stairs! This was to clear up her [the neighbour's] three months' rent. You see if she had paid a month's rent she got leave to pay up the other two months. But ye see if she didn't pay the three months she was put out. I asked her why she did it and she said she couldn't see all the wee weans getting put out.

SAVING FOR THE FUTURE

If women could save at all they did so through menages. These were organised savings clubs run by women. They were an attempt to keep the moneylenders at bay. A group of women, usually from the same close or corner of a street, would combine together, pay an agreed amount of money for a fixed period of time (usually ten weeks) and pay this out to each other. The amounts collected ranged from sixpence to five shillings per week. If there were ten women in the club then this was a substantial amount. The women drew lots to see which week they would receive their payment. With no interest charged this was an effective way of preparing for large outgoings at school time, Christmas or for a new baby. Women invariably belonged to one or two menages, one in the scheme and one at work. And priorities were clearcut, 'you would pay your menage before your tick' (Mrs L). In a menage you can only borrow once. It is a fixed amount and has to be repaid before another menage is started. These savings clubs formed an effective strategy against the crippling spiral of debt.

At another level the collective efforts of women savers were channelled into the Welcome Home Fund. This was a savings club organised again by groups of women for demobbed servicemen at the end of the Second World War. Mrs C (b. 1926) recalls the organisation and effort that went into this venture:

A Welcome Home Fund started during the war. We had whist drives in different houses. And whoever's house the whist was in supplied the tea. You didn't get any money for that, it was your donation to the Welcome Home Fund. It was five shillings for the ladies' prize and five shillings for the gents' prize and two-and-sixpence for the raffle and your night cost you one-and-sixpence for the whist and tea. We held dances and parties. Anything we thought would make money. My mother used to sell candy balls and table. I went round the doors every Sunday to collect a shilling from every house to go into the Fund. When the war finished, and the boys came back home again, they were given a bank book with £10 in it which was a lot of money.

Another woman remembered the 'clabbers' that were held to raise money for the Fund. Mrs P (b. 1927) explained:

A clabber was a get together in the back-court. You'd put up a washing line and hang old blankets over it, sort of like a stage. We all brought our chairs out and some would hing oot the windae and everybody would give us a song or a dance or something. Sometimes there would be a squeeze box, a penny whistle or a moothie. It was great.

RECALCITRANCE

Despite the control and organisation that these women displayed in running their daily lives they were consistently maligned for their persistent refusal to 'take advantage' of free school meals, health care and the like. Anyone who has experienced the degrading aspect of being singled out for 'free dinners' in front of their school friends will know it holds little 'advantage'. For some starving was better. Mrs C (b. 1926) remembers the feelings of shame this induced:'We were supposed to go over [to school] and get our dinners even when we were off. But we wouldnae go. It wisnae right what they made you do.'

Some women refused to subject their children to this experience:

My mum wouldnae let us have free dinners even though we qualified for them. We came home for our dinner and had a piece with chips on it. There wasnae much but my mum always managed to give us something.

Similar attitudes were expressed when referring to illness and childbirth. It cost between three and five guineas to have a doctor and nurse in attendance during labour. Even though many were covered by some sickness schemes there were other aspects to consider. Mrs J (b. 1909) tried to explain why she would not have a nurse attend her during labour:

You couldn't have a nurse in if you didn't have the proper things – I mean you needed to have proper underthings and towels and the like. Not that we were dirty you know . . . everybody was the same. I know the nurses were used to seeing it [poverty] but I didnae want anyone talking about what we had or didnae have – nobody was going tae talk about me!

One woman spoke of how she kept her children home from school on the days the nurse visited. They all had ringworm infections on their heads and this she thought would mean 'they would spray the place' and shave all their heads. Others spoke of the lengths they and their children went to to avoid any contact with nurses or doctors. Few had their children immunised unless they got 'caught' at the school. One women summed up the main feelings about such interventions: 'They put you in these houses and they think that they can do anything to you. But they can't.' This was a commonly held feeling amongst the women. Despite the hardship they endured they fought to maintain some self-respect. So they resisted by rejecting.

CONCLUSION

The women recorded here fought a constant battle against the poverty that engulfed and degraded them. The shame that poverty brought reached into every area of their lives. Each of the women could remember a single incident, whether as an adult or child, that separated them out from the rest, that had made them feel different. Whether it was the clothes they wore at school, the newspapers that covered their floors or the refusal of credit for food, they could still remember how they felt. No one, they argued, 'got used' to living on credit. When in debt the mechanisms of social control are explicit. The women felt the force of these through the factors and housing visitors. The tenant/factor relationship went well beyond rent collecting. The most intimate personal details of families' lives were recorded and their moral character assessed by these officials. Such information could be passed to employers, teachers and other factors on request. So a clean rentbook was more than a source of pride, it was a badge of approval, a buffer against control and a possible passport to better housing or employment. As one respondent put it: 'If your rentbook was clean that was it . . . they wouldn't ask any more questions'. Another was more explicit, 'A clean rentbook was an exit visa from this place.' This complex web of social relationships provoked resistance in the women. This took the form of collective self-help in all areas of their lives, from helping at childbirth, sharing food and clothes, to fending off factors and housing visitors. They worked almost independently of their men, drawing on the help and earnings of their children to supplement the family income. They were central figures in the shaping of this working-class community's response to poverty. They fended off the control exerted by factors and housing officials by developing forms of resistance which actively advocated rejection of outside help. In this way they retained their self-respect.

The experiences of these women should not be written off within any theory that equates poverty with powerlessness. That they were poor is true, that they were powerless is not. Within the constraints of poverty they organised and controlled their lives. Most of all they resisted.

NOTES

1 See, for example, Barrett, Michele, *Women's Oppression Today* (Verso, London, 1980); Spender, Dale, *Women of Ideas and What Men Have done to Them: from Aphra Benn to Adrienne Rich* (Routledge and Kegan Paul, London, 1982); Siltanen, J. and Stanworth, M., *The Politics of Private Woman and Public Man* in Siltanen, J. and Stanworth M. (eds.), *Women and the Public Sphere* (Hutchinson, London, 1984); Little, J. Peake, L., and Richardson, P. (eds.), *Women in Cities* (Virago, London, 1987).
2 Siltanen, J. and Stanworth, M. *The Politics of Private Woman and Public Man*; Spender, Dale, *Women of Ideas*.
3 Little, J. et al., *Women in Cities*.
4 Little, J. et al., *Women in Cities*.

5 Siltanen, J. and Stanworth, M., *The Politics of Private Woman and Public Man*.

6 Spender, Dale, *Women of Ideas*.

7 Little, J. et al. *Women in Cities*.

8 Katznelson, I. *City Trenches: Urban Politics and the Patterning of Class in the US* (University of Chicago Press, Chicago, 1981) p. 19.

9 See Thompson, E. P. *The Making of the English Working Class*, Penguin, Harmondsworth, 1963).

10 Cockburn, Cynthia, *The Local State* (Pluto Press, London, 1977) p. 163.

11 Mayhew, H. *London Labour and the London Poor* (1861); Booth, C., *Life and Labour of the People of London* (Penguin, London, 1971).

12 Pember Reeves, Maud, *Round About a Pound a Week* (1913); Spring Rice, Margery, *Working Class Wives: Their Health and Conditions* (London, 1939).

13 See, for example, Jamieson, Lynn, 'Growing up in Nineteenth Century Scotland' in Glasgow Women's Studies Group, *Uncharted Lives* (Glasgow Pressgang 1982); Melling, J. *Rent Strikes: People's Struggles for Housing in West Scotland 1890–1916* (Polygon, Edinburgh, 1983); Ross, E., 'Survival Networks: 'Women's Neighbourhood Sharing in London Before World War I' in History Workshop Journal no. 15 (1983); MacKenzie, S., 'Balancing our Space and Time: the Impact of Women's Organisation on the British City, 1920–1930' in Little, J. et al. (eds.), *Women in Cities* (Macmillan, London, 1988); Bondi, L., and Peake, L., 'Gender and the City: Urban Politics Revisited' in Little, J. et al., *Women in Cities*.

14 Booth, C., *Life and Labour of the People of London*; Mayhew, H. *London Labour and the London Poor*.

15 Quoted in Mitchell, J., *English Housing Policy in Scotland* Unpublished paper (University of Strathclyde, 1988).

16 Gauldie, Enid, *Cruel Habitations: A History of Working Class Housing 1730–1913* (Allen and Unwin, London, 1974) p. 116.

17 See Stedman Jones, G., *Outcast London: a Study in the Relationships Between Classes in Victorian Society* (Clarendon Press, Oxford, 1971).

18 See, for example, Himmelfarb, G., 'The Culture of Poverty' in Dyos, H. J., and Wolff, M., (eds.), *The Victorian City: Images and Realities* (Routledge and Kegan Paul, Oxford, 1973); Sutcliffe, A., 'Working Class Housing in Nineteenth Century Britain: A Review of Recent Research' in *Bulletin for the Society for the Study of Labour History* (1972); Lawrence, R. J., 'The Middle Class and British Towns and Cities of the Industrial Revolution 1730–1870' in Fraser, D., and Sutcliffe, A. (eds.), *The Pursuit of Urban History* (Edward Arnold, London, 1983); Englander, D., *Landlord and Tenant in Urban Britain 1838–1913* (Clarendon Press, Oxford, 1983).

19 Lawrence, R. J., 'Urban History, Housing and Politics in Britain' in *Environment and Planning*, vol. 3 (1985) pp. 323–36.

20 Simms, George, *How the Poor Live* (London, 1883).

21 Spring Rice, Margery, *Working Class Wives*.

22 Pember Reeves, Maud, *Round About a Pound a Week*, p. 168.

23 Ibid., p. 158.

24 Ibid., p. 93.

25 Roberts, Elizabeth, *A Woman's Place: an Oral History of Working*

Class Women, (Blackwell, Oxford, 1984).
26 Ibid., p. 11.
27 Ibid., p. 11.
28 For a more detailed analysis of the sample see Damer, Sean, and McGuckin, Ann, *The Good and the Bad: A Tale of Two Schemes*, ESRC Report (1989).
29 Handley, J. A., *The Irish in Scotland*, (University of Cork Press, 1947).
30 *Glasgow Herald*, November 14, 1933.
31 McGuckin, Ann, *Sectarianism – the Silent Battle*, Unpublished Paper, (Glasgow University 1990).
32 Morgan, N., '£8 Cottages for Glasgow Citizens – Innovations in Municipal Housebuilding in Glasgow in the Inter War Years', in Rodger, R. (ed.), *Scottish Housing in the Twentieth Century*, (Leicester University Press, Leicester, 1989).
33 See Butt, J., 'Working Class Housing in Glasgow, 1851–1914', in Chapman, S. (ed.), *The History of Working Class Housing* (David and Charles, Newton Abbott, 1971); Butt, J. 'Working Class Housing in the Scottish Cities, 1900–1950' in Gordon, G. and Dicks, D. (eds.), *Scottish Urban History* (Aberdeen University Press, 1983); Gibb, A., 'The Development of Public Sector Housing in Glasgow', Discussion Paper no. 6 (Centre for Urban and Regional Research, Glasgow University, 1982).
34 McGuckin, Ann, *Glasgow's Factors* Mimeo (Glasgow University, 1989).
35 McCrone, D., and Elliot, B., *Property and Power in the City* (Macmillan, London, 1989) p. 26.
36 See Melling, J., *Rent Strikes.*

SELECT BIBLIOGRAPHY

Bondi, L. and Peake, L., 'Gender and the City: Urban Politics Revisited,' in Little, J. Peake, L., and Richardson, P. (eds.), *Women in Cities* (Macmillan, London, 1988).
Butt, J., 'Working Class Housing in Glasgow, 1851–1914' in Chapman, S. (ed.), *The History of Working Class Housing* (David and Charles, Newton Abbott, 1971).
Butt, J., 'Working Class Housing in the Scottish Cities, 1900–1950', in Gordon, G., and Dicks, D. (eds.), *Scottish Urban History* (Aberdeen University Press, Aberdeen, 1983).
Gauldie, E., *Cruel Habitations: A History of Working Class Housing 1780–1913*, (Allen and Unwin, London, 1974).
Gibb, A., *The Development of Public Sector Housing in Glasgow*, Discussion paper no. 6, Centre for Urban and Regional Research (Glasgow University, 1982).
Jamieson, L., 'Growing Up in Nineteenth Century Scotland', in Glasgow Women's Studies Group, *Uncharted Lives* (Pressgang, Glasgow, 1982).
Melling, J., *Rent Strikes: People's Struggles for Housing in West Scotland 1890–1916* (Polygon, Edinburgh, 1983).
Pember Reeves, M., *Round About a Pound a Week* (1913).
Roberts, E. *A Woman's Place: an Oral History of Working class Women 1890–1940* (Blackwell, Oxford, 1984).
Ross, E., 'Survival Networks: Women's Neighbourhood Sharing in London before World War I', in *History Workshop Journal, no. 15*, (1983).

Siltanen, J., and Stanworth, M., 'The Politics of Private Woman and Public Man', in Siltanen, J. and Stanworth, M. (eds.), *Women and the Public Sphere*, (Hutchinson, London, 1984).

Spring Rice, M., *Working Class Wives: Their Health and Conditions*, (London, 1939).

INDEX